Coach Tommy Thompson and the
Boys of Sequoyah

Coach Tommy Thompson and the Boys of Sequoyah

PATTI DICKINSON

Foreword by Chadwick Smith

UNIVERSITY OF OKLAHOMA PRESS : NORMAN

Also by Patti Dickinson

Hollywood the Hard Way : A Cowboy's Journey (Lincoln, Nebr., 1999)

Library of Congress Cataloging-in-Publication Data

Dickinson, Patti, 1945–
 Coach Tommy Thompson and the boys of Sequoyah / Patti Dickinson ; foreword by Chadwick Smith.
   p.   cm.
 Includes bibliographical references and index.
 ISBN 978-0-8061-4070-4 (paperback)
   1. Thompson, Tommy, coach. 2. Football coaches—Oklahoma—Biography. 3. Teachers—Oklahoma—Biography. 4. Sequoyah High School (Tahlequah, Okla.)—Football—History. 5. Cherokee Indians—Oklahoma—Tahlequah—History. I. Title.
 GV939.T447D53 2009
 796.332092—dc22
 [B]

2009010157

The paper in this book meets the guidelines for permanence and durability of the Committee on Production Guidelines for Book Longevity of the Council on Library Resources, Inc. ∞

The manufacturer's authorized representative in the EU for product safety is Mare Nostrum Group B.V., Mauritskade 21D, 1091 GC Amsterdam, The Netherlands, email: gpsr@mare-nostrum.co.uk

Copyright © 2009 by the University of Oklahoma Press, Norman, Publishing Division of the University. Manufactured in the U.S.A.

All rights reserved. No part of this publication may be reproduced, stored in a retrieval system, or transmitted, in any form or by any means, electronic, mechanical, photocopying, recording, or otherwise—except as permitted under Section 107 or 108 of the United States Copyright Act—without the prior written permission of the University of Oklahoma Press.

*To my daughters, Kelly and Kerry,
with pride and admiration for simply being who you are*

The Boys of Sequoyah

We came to Sequoyah Orphan Training School
from every corner of Oklahoma,
knowing only our own pain and very little of the world outside.
We were Cherokee, Creek, Choctaw, and Seminole,
we were Seneca, Euchee, Kiowa, Osage, and Chickasaw,
but we were brothers, blood brothers.
When one of us hurt we all hurt;
when one laughed we all laughed.
We played together, pulled pranks on one another;
we fought, we studied, and did our chores together.
We all had our separate dreams,
but we shared an unwritten code of honor:
Treat elders with respect and do not snitch—not ever.
Brothers don't snitch.

Patti Dickinson

Contents

List of Illustrations	ix
Foreword, by Chadwick Smith	xi
Preface	xvii
Introduction	xxi
Prologue	3
1. We Only Have Each Other Now	5
2. The Three R's—Rules, Rules, and More Rules	10
3. Benevolence in a Bottle	18
4. Freedom—Everything It's Cracked Up to Be	30
5. The Perfect Match	36
6. Be Careful What You Wish For	42
7. Snagged by His Britches	52
8. Letting Go	63
9. Small, Medium, Large—Heroes Come in All Sizes	71
10. Front-Row Seats at the War	81
11. This Must Be What Hell Is Like	89
12. Four-Legged Ambassador	98
13. A Mourning Nation Is Reborn	105
14. We Came from Every Corner of Oklahoma	108
15. Halleluiah for the Third Time	119
16. Life Comes Full Circle	124

CONTENTS

17. Catch a Football or Milk a Cow	131
18. Cherokee Pied Piper	141
19. The Chameleon	146
20. Sacred Traditions	156
21. Ah-sky-uh—the Man	165
22. The Day Hell Froze Over	178
23. Sequoyah Dreamboats	188
24. Ambassador in Trouble	191
25. Goodbyes Don't Get Any Easier	201
26. The Board of Education	210
27. You're in the Army Now	216
28. Where's a Medicine Man When You Need One?	224
29. Fish-Eater, Blanket-Ass—Hut!	231
30. Make a Promise, Dance the Two-Step	241
31. Second Chances Are Hard to Come By	249
Epilogue	256
Postscript: Life after Sequoyah	265
Further Reading	273
Acknowledgments	275
Index	277

Illustrations

Tommy Thompson in Northeastern football uniform	33
Tommy, Dorothy, Jimmy, and Jean Thompson, 1935	49
Cecil and Rudell Shipp with their father, 1947	90
Fields Smith and Bill Baker, 1945	114
Coach Tommy Thompson, 1947	132
Sergeant Forman Ross	167
Danny and Dave Whitekiller in Sequoyah football uniforms, 1949	171
Milo Yellowhead, John Anderson, and Bill Cameron	179
Staff meeting in Tommy's Unit B office	195
Sequoyah boys at Lake Michigan, 1950	206
Cecil "Nip" Shipp, 1950	208
Tahlequah's 279th Army National Guard Infantry Division, 1950	217
Bill, George, and Dave Cameron, circa 1951	233
Bill Baker, 1952	242
The 1952 Sequoyah football team	253
Superintendent Jack Brown and Amon Baker	258

Foreword

This is a story about a unique relationship between a group of young Indian men and a dedicated Cherokee coach. The small part of the story is about how the boys at Sequoyah Vocational School and Tommy Thompson came together to achieve excellence in a sport.

It would be a sad commentary if winning championships in football were the highlight of a person's life. However, football championships at Sequoyah under Coach Thompson were lessons in the larger and more universal story of life. Sometimes the big lessons may not be recognized immediately, but over time they become evident and direct our decisions.

The Sequoyah football players not only learned those lessons for themselves but also demonstrated the success of those lessons for the Indian community. The Cherokee Nation was in a transitional period, moving from the aftermath of the federal forced assimilation period of allotment instituted in 1906, which brought abject poverty to the Cherokee people, to the post–World War II era, which shook Indian communities with change and uncertainty. Stories of success and perseverance were needed by the Cherokee community to deal with such traumatic economic and social change.

Sequoyah began after the American Civil War as the Cherokee Orphan Asylum. The United States abandoned the Cherokee Nation during the war by taking federal troops to other embattled fronts, leaving the Cherokee Nation vulnerable to the Confederacy. Two-thirds of the Cherokees fought for the North, and during the war, 1,500 Cherokees lost their lives, leaving behind 4,000 widows and orphans. The Cherokee Nation responded by building an orphanage in 1871. It was a time of great despair, misery, and destruction, with the Cherokee Nation suffering more loss of life and property per capita than the hardest-hit places of the Deep South. Forty years later, the United States instituted a policy of forced assimilation by liquidating the land and assets of the Cherokee Nation and distributed them pro rata to individual Cherokees. This allotment policy was designed to open the Cherokee Nation lands to outsiders, force the Cherokees into a cash economy, eradicate the Cherokee language and culture, and cripple the government of the Cherokee Nation. After Oklahoma achieved statehood in 1907, the Cherokee Nation's orphanage became an orphan training school following the model of a military academy. Children were dressed in military uniforms and followed a strict regimen. On its face, the federal policy achieved its goals to economically and culturally assimilate the Cherokees, whether or not they wanted to be assimilated.

By 1920, 90 percent of the Cherokees had lost title to their land because of theft, fraud, taxes, and economic crisis; in their former Indian republic they had become a small minority in a population of non-Indians, white and black people. When the Great Depression and the dust bowl hit Oklahoma in the 1930s, one-half of the Cherokee population left in hopes of finding work on the second Trail of Tears down U.S. 66 (along with others) during the *Grapes of Wrath* trek to California. The American Red Cross determined that among those who stayed in Oklahoma, many died literally from starvation.

During these times when Cherokee families could not afford to raise their children, parents would send their sons and daughters to Indian boarding schools so that they could have three meals a day. The story of Tommy Thompson evolved during these times of despair and misery. The comfort, strength, and fatherly love of another Cherokee, Jack Brown (long the superintendent of Sequoyah), converted Sequoyah from a military school to a home for hundreds of students. Jack Brown acknowledged that the federal effort of forced assimilation had failed and that the Cherokee spirit had prevailed despite adversity. Superintendent Brown and others created a homelike environment in which every child, in addition to receiving an academic education, also learned a trade, a skill, an occupation. Jack Brown became a father to hundreds of Indian children at Sequoyah. Tommy Thompson grew and thrived in this environment, and in turn, he helped Sequoyah students grow and thrive.

Sequoyah has a very special place in my heart. My dad graduated from Sequoyah in 1940 and spoke fondly of his huge, extended family among students and faculty. He told me of how he worked in the mechanics shop and learned to weld and repair machinery. He relayed stories of mischief with other students: taking fresh bread from the bakery, fresh-cooked beans from the kitchen, and cool milk from the springhouse and then hiking to the top of Bald Hill for a feast fit for a king. He went on to become a successful mechanical maintenance manager for a major corporation.

Leadership is often an ambiguous term. For me, it involves leading from point A, where we are today, to point B, where we want to go. Of course, many skills are needed for you to determine where you are personally today, what you want to be at some time in the future, and how to meet the challenges along the way. After the American Civil War, the Cherokee Nation demonstrated that leadership by going from the depths of despair and misery to building a great society and an admirable government that included 90 percent literacy, 150 day schools, two junior colleges, nine district courts, an insane asylum, the orphanage, the national capital building, and a supreme court building. U.S. Senator Henry Dawes, the architect of the forced assimilation and allotment policy, had previously reported that there was not a pauper in the whole nation; everyone owned his or her home, and the tribe owed not a dollar. He went on to say that the fallacy of the Cherokee system was that there was no selfishness, which is at the bottom of civilization: when the Cherokee Nation succeeds, the United States takes away.

The same spirit of leadership that Dawes wished to destroy was encouraged by Jack Brown and embraced by Tommy Thompson in the post–Great Depression and post–World War II period. The

FOREWORD

pair taught, exercised, and mentored leadership. The resulting leadership in students can be vividly seen in the sports teams that Tommy Thompson coached.

When I became principal chief in 1999, Sequoyah was over budget, enrolled only 206 students (despite having a capacity of 350 students), and was known as a school of last resort. I wanted it to become a leadership academy and a school of choice. Just recently, I learned of the Jack Brown and Tommy Thompson stories, which reflected in an informal way that Sequoyah had been a leadership academy more than fifty years ago.

My son attended Sequoyah a few years ago; he thrived and graduated. I have a daughter who now attends, finding herself in a warm, nurturing, and positive community and among a large family of tribesmen. The staff and students of Sequoyah shared with each of them the opportunity to learn leadership from a Cherokee perspective. Today, Sequoyah is designed to be a leadership school so that students can grow to their greatest potential and pass on the great Cherokee legacy to face adversity, survive, adapt, prosper, and excel.

Its enrollment of 402 today exceeds its enrollment capacity of 350, and we have waiting lists for additional students. It is now known as a school of choice. Academics, athletics, and leadership have all dramatically increased. The girls' basketball team has won three consecutive state championships, the boys' basketball team has won state and runner-up state championships in the past few years, and the cross-country teams are legendary for winning state championships over the past decade. The football team won its first district championship two years ago, which was the first time since the "boys of Sequoyah" played in 1952. The football team's record in 2007 was 11-1. Other sports thrive. Academics have dramatically improved, as evidenced by the presence of twenty-eight Gates Scholars and joint enrollment programs with Northeastern State University and the Oklahoma School for Science and Math.

Interestingly enough, the leadership of five decades ago has reemerged at Sequoyah. I have appointed alumni to sit on the

FOREWORD

advisory board, including Forman Ross, Amon Baker, Dewayne Marshal, and Roberta Gibson. Forman Ross is one of the Sequoyah students who played for Tommy Thompson; Amon Baker, a former superintendent at Sequoyah, married one of Tommy Thompson's daughters.

Although the story of Tommy Thompson and the boys of Sequoyah happened more than a half century ago, their story and lessons are still timely. These are lessons we have to remind ourselves of every day, lessons to remember. These are lessons that our children who are now at Sequoyah—and at every high school—need to learn. The lessons learned with the intensity shown by the boys of Sequoyah are hard to forget: they include sportsmanship, determination, teamwork, perseverance, understanding, learning from mistakes, and not fearing success.

In this book, we see those timeless and universal lessons. When we apply those lessons in sports, in academics, and especially in life's leadership roles, the end results of success, fullness of life, and happiness will not be the exception; they will be the norm.

Chadwick Smith
Principal Chief of the Cherokee Nation
Tahlequah, Oklahoma

Preface

The source of a true story can sometimes be almost as intriguing as the story itself. I have had two amazing true stories come to me in such a fashion that it makes me think I was meant to write them. Both involve heroes—not talented, overpaid athletes but ordinary men who either did something extraordinary or had a positive impact on other people's lives.

The first story, I heard when I stopped for lunch in a Montana tavern on my way to a nearby writers conference. Fast-forward five years to Tulsa and my book tour for *Hollywood the Hard Way: A Cowboy's Journey*. I did an NPR interview on the subject of heroes and what remarkable things they accomplish, and for some reason the Tulsa station continued to broadcast it.

Several months after I returned home, I received a call from Waleah Turner, who said she'd happened to be driving through Tulsa one evening and had heard my interview. She told me, "If you like heroes, I think you will want to know about Tommy Thompson, my grandfather."

I was living in Idaho at the time (April 2000), 135 miles south of the Canadian border. My initial thought was, *hero or not, how could I do justice to a story from fifteen hundred miles away?* Waleah and I kept in touch over the following months, though, and I learned enough about her grandfather to agree that his remarkable story should be told—just not by me. The distance between northern Idaho and Tahlequah seemed daunting enough that I tried to get an Oklahoma author friend of mine to write it. Thankfully, as it turned out, the project was not her cup of tea.

PREFACE

In October 2000, I flew to Oklahoma to meet Waleah and figure out whether there was any way I could write her grandfather's biography. She arranged for me to meet fifteen or twenty of Tommy Thompson's "boys" (now grandfathers), all of them former students at Sequoyah Vocational School. We met at an informal reunion in one of the gentlemen's homes. After spending an afternoon listening and talking with each one, I knew that I had a true hero to write about—except that Tommy Thompson was only half of the story. His boys were the other half. Each one spoke about him as a son would about his father and related the huge impact that Tommy had had on his life. It rapidly became obvious that a simple biography would not tell the whole story.

I returned to Idaho, and during the remainder of the year, I read a dozen or more books on government-run Indian boarding schools, on Cherokee history, on Oklahoma, and on the dust bowl and the Great Depression. All the while, I continued to interview by telephone the men I had met. I mailed questionnaires to many more boys who'd had Tommy as their coach and advisor. One puzzling aspect of my research was that the books I read on schools run by the Bureau of Indian Affairs (BIA) presented a negative theme that didn't at all match what I heard from the men I interviewed.

I flew to Tahlequah again the following spring and taped a dozen or more interviews with other former students, Tommy's daughters, his son and son-in-law (Waleah's father), and Marion Hagerstrand, the daughter of former superintendent Jack Brown. One former student I interviewed, Cecil Shipp, spent a day giving me a tour of the former orphanage, which is now Sequoyah High School. He plied me with tales of its history and offered anecdotes on what growing up in an Indian boarding school in Oklahoma had been like. Cecil told of nighttime raids on the kitchen, military tanks and half-tracks performing maneuvers behind the school, and boys playing checkers or penny-ante poker in the dorm library with Tommy after they finished their homework.

I came away from that day realizing that Cecil hadn't just showed me around a school he'd attended; he had shared with me his home and his memories. I suddenly had a more complicated

PREFACE

project but, for the first time, a glimpse of the entire story. It consisted of three parts: Tommy Thompson, a group of orphaned Indian boys, and an Indian boarding school that meant a lot to them.

I made two more trips to Tahlequah. Cecil Shipp lived there at the time and agreed to be my "go-to guy." He verified facts and stories, answered hundreds of my questions, and gathered information. My concern at being fifteen hundred miles from the heart of the story was resolved by accumulated frequent flyer miles, an unlimited long-distance calling plan, and Cecil Shipp.

I used fictional techniques, developing scenes and dialogue to give vibrancy to the adventures and tales that had caused me to laugh or brought tears to my eyes during my interviews, and to draw with words the people in the story as the boys had pictured them for me. The dialogue that I created accurately captures conversations that I had taped and later transcribed. More often than not, someone else who had taken part in the exchange would describe the conversation so closely and with such good recall that the dialogue was generally confirmed. Their stories were often accompanied by documents and pictures. The scenes and dialogue thus were not modified to enhance or alter the characters or events but instead reflect the story as it was told to me.

My primary sources include personal and telephone interviews with close to a hundred people, including former students who knew Tommy as a coach, advisor, and surrogate father; retired Sequoyah matrons and teachers; and Tommy's children and Jack Brown's daughter. Other primary sources include Tommy's official school records from Haskell and his employment record from the Bureau of Indian Affairs, obtained by Cecil with the help of Tommy's daughter Jody; these provided great insight and a timeline of his life.

Secondary sources include George Cameron's memoir of his twelve years at Sequoyah, which afforded an intimate look into daily life at the school. Sequoyah teacher Don Franklin's publication *Celebrating Sequoyah, 125 Years, 1872–1997* provided the history of Sequoyah and the Cherokee Nation. Franklin's extensive collection of newspaper articles gave me the names of Sequoyah players

PREFACE

and their opponents and details of Tommy's football and basketball games.

The 1949 football game in the rain, snow, and mud was told to me in excruciating detail by the boys who had played in it. The same is true of the other games. Nineteen men detailing the funny, the frightening, and the sad and happy moments and events at Sequoyah let me experience life in a large military-run institution. I wanted to offer the same experience to readers.

The boys' stories about Tommy were steadfastly similar: what made him laugh, his penchant for rules, and his belief that if he had done his job right, they would leave school ready to take their place in society. Tommy's dialogue with Superintendent Jack Brown I created from extensive interviews with Brown's daughter. Dialogue from Tommy's earlier life—for instance, when his father registered him and his sisters at the Cherokee Orphan Training School—is based on interviews with his three children. That day had a lasting impact on Tommy, and when he relayed it to his children, his tale left an indelible imprint on them.

I have not spent ten years solely on this story but worked on it as life and time allowed. This slice of history would tragically have remained undiscovered but for the efforts of a proud granddaughter who happened to hear an interview about heroes, and a group of gentlemen willing to share a pivotal period of their lives with a stranger.

Eight years later, we are no longer strangers but friends. Sadly, during the considerable time it's taken to interview, research, and write this story, I have lost several of these friends, including both of Tommy's daughters. The most recent loss (March 2009) is Jimmy Thompson, Tommy's only son. Much like his father, Jimmy was an upbeat, involved, and caring man. He not only provided dates, places, and facts; he shared memorable insights into the Thompson's close-knit family. An equally important contribution, Jimmy gave us an intimate glimpse of the man, the mentor, the surrogate father who realized his heartfelt dream to make a difference.

I feel honored indeed to be the one to tell this inspiring story.

Introduction

Libraries contain volumes on Indian boarding schools that were established and run by our government in the first half of the twentieth century. Decades of research by scholars in the field of American Indian history are responsible for the wealth of information on the subject, the sum perception of which is repressive institutions filled with children snatched from their homes, treated cruelly, and robbed of their Indian culture. Whether this image is ascribed as a tool of government colonialism, a blueprint for assimilation, a leftover remnant of nineteenth-century attitudes toward indigenous people, or (worst of all) the extinction of a culture, together the scholars paint a vivid mosaic of shameful treatment of American Indians of all ages.

In a recent essay by Clyde Ellis, professor of history at Elon University and noted scholar on the American Indians of the Great Plains, he acknowledges "low moments that characterized the life of every student." But Ellis proffers, "[L]ooking only at the (dark) side of the experience tells us what we have known for decades and tends to obscure the more complicated realities of school life." His *Boarding School Blues* essay on the Rainy Mountain school states, "It wasn't a perfect life and it wasn't what they deserved . . . but it was more than an exercise in resistance, oppression, and misery." Ellis's interviews with former students repeat the theme that Rainy Mountain failed to destroy their Kiowa culture and language.

Acknowledgment of assimilation's failure is shared by other scholars. For example, biographer and historian T. H. Watkins in his book *The Great Depression* writes, "[P]ossibly Collier's most

INTRODUCTION

enduring accomplishments [John Collier was appointed as commissioner of the BIA early in Roosevelt's New Deal] was reversing the fifty-year insistence on assimilation . . . one of the oldest and least successful impulses of American reform."

Assimilation was never at the core of Cherokee Nation institutions. Though established in the same era, they stand apart from repressive schools. In her essay in *Boarding House Blues*, Margaret Connell Szasz, senior professor of history at the University of New Mexico, describes the Cherokee Nation's "two-tiered school system in Indian Territory to educate its elite in the Cherokee Female or Male Seminary." Along with the Choctaw, Muskogee, and Chickasaw Nations, Szasz states, the Cherokees "used their educational institutions to enhance tribal sovereignty, self-determination, and Indian identity."

Their boarding schools, however, came about in response to a crisis. Cherokee men fought on both sides in the Civil War and suffered heavy casualties. At the end of the war in 1865, the Cherokees discovered that they had an alarming number of orphaned children. When their initial attempt to help these children fell short, the Cherokee National Council in November 1871 authorized construction of the Cherokee Orphan Asylum in Salina, Oklahoma. Its purpose was "the support and education of orphan children living in the Cherokee Nation Indian Territory."

The asylum operated first as an orphanage and then a boarding school for thirty-two years until 1903, when a fire destroyed it. The Cherokees replaced it with a new facility, this one located in Tahlequah. With Oklahoma statehood in 1907, the federal government dissolved the Cherokee Nation, closed the Cherokee Male and Female Seminaries, and transferred control of the Cherokee boarding schools to the Department of Interior.

What began as an orphan asylum changed names over the years as it grew in size and function. It exists today as Sequoyah High School, a sprawling state-of-the-art facility operated by the Cherokee Nation. Its 139-year history stands as testimony to the Cherokees' determination to care for and educate their own.

INTRODUCTION

The sheer quantity of written material and abundance of divergent focuses on Indian boarding schools demonstrate the depth and complexity of a subject that is not likely to be sorted out for many years, if ever. Given that interest in the subject is not likely to wane, additional clarity and perspective may lie with former students who up to now have remained silent. We can hope that even more will come forward and tell us their stories.

Such is the foundation of *Coach Tommy Thompson and the Boys of Sequoyah*. This true story is the result of more than five years of research and hundreds of hours interviewing former students. Its guiding force consisted of an outstanding Cherokee athlete named Tommy Thompson, nineteen down-and-out orphaned Indian boys with uncertain futures, and the Sequoyah Vocational Training School in Tahlequah, Oklahoma, where their lives came together. As boys' advisor, teacher, and coach, Tommy Thompson provided love and caring that turned his boys into a family, but it was through football that he helped them learn life's biggest lessons: how to win, how to lose, how to be a man.

In the twelve years (1947–58) during which Thompson coached at Sequoyah, the exact number of boys who passed through the school is unknown but is estimated to be over a thousand. Those whose lives are traced in this story I believe to be representative of all those whom he mentored. They came to Sequoyah because they had nowhere else to go. The similarities with other BIA-run boarding schools include a military-style format of operation, a coeducational student body with high school–age boys and girls required to take vocational training, and mandatory church services on Sunday. In the abundance of time I spent interviewing former students, whenever I raised the issue of physical or emotional abuse, all said it did not exist. Early in the school's history, however, two firsthand accounts told of youths getting their mouth washed out with soap for speaking Cherokee. When Cherokee scholar Jack Brown arrived in 1925 and began his thirty-two-year career as the superintendent of Sequoyah, he pledged that "no matter what school I'm in charge of it's going to be the happiest place I can make it."

INTRODUCTION

The "boys of Sequoyah," grandfathers now, are quick to say the heartbreak they suffered was not at the hands of the institution that took them in but their mother dying from cancer or a heart attack or tuberculosis before reaching thirty; or their father walking out and leaving seven or eight or ten children to fend for themselves, or being passed like hand-me-down clothes to relatives already struggling to survive. The Great Depression remained entrenched into the 1940s and resulted in Indian families in Oklahoma living on their allotment land and existing on what they could raise, hunt, or fish. Their houses had no running water, plumbing, or electricity. Children were not always able to attend school, whether because of distance, illness, or lack of proper clothing—circumstances dire enough to crush a child's spirit and foretell a miserable life.

That these circumstances did not have such an effect on the boys of Sequoyah can be attributed largely to their innate resiliency, to a boarding school that did it right, and to a coach who had a profoundly positive impact on their lives. Football to Coach Tommy *was* life: he excelled at it in his youth and devoted his later life to knowing and understanding the sport. Through football he believed that he could teach boys the skills and values they would need to succeed in life. His steadfast commitment brought out the very best in his boys. Through Tommy they gained a sense of pride, and from him the guidelines to become honorable men.

Every year, hundreds of graduates gather at Sequoyah to honor their school and in the process pay tribute to their mentor. It has been my privilege to attend three of these reunions; even though fifty years have passed since his death, the mention of Tommy Thompson's name sparks a profusion of funny stories, poignant memories, and always the feeling of brotherhood among the men whose lives he forever changed. Some still refer to him as Ah-sky-uh, which in Cherokee means "the man," a term of honor and respect.

INTRODUCTION

Coach Tommy Thompson and the Boys of Sequoyah may seem an anomaly in the context of the larger body of work on government-run Indian boarding schools because it does not fit the long-established picture that history has drawn for us. But this school, this ordinary man who made a difference in so many lives, and the boys who loved him represent a discovery in this field. Such a discovery is tiny, perhaps, when compared to the whole, but it is worthy of its place because of the men who lived it.

What follows is the story of the boys of Sequoyah, the school they still call home, and a coach they knew as Ah-sky-uh.

Coach Tommy Thompson and the Boys of Sequoyah

Prologue

All of us Cherokee boys called him Ah-sky-uh, "the man." Tommy taught us how to take orders and give orders, how to stand up to larger than normal tasks. He knew us inside and out, our feelings, our strengths, and our breaking point. Tommy was our coach, and the gridiron is where he taught us to be men.
—*Forman Ross*

ENID, OKLAHOMA, CLASS C FOOTBALL STATE CHAMPIONSHIP, DECEMBER 10, 1949

Coach Tommy Thompson could only watch as his boys fought for every yard, every down.

> No fans left in the stadium. Fourth quarter, a minute and a half to go in the game. My boys are half-frozen, dead-tired, rain-soaked, and wondering if they have it in them to get up off the ground one more time. But they do because they know we need one more pass, another run, some miracle play to give us a touchdown. So they keep trying, and I can tell by the look in their eyes they won't give up.
> A coach can't go on the field to pick them up, spur them on, or tell them what to do. I am standing on the sidelines, awestruck with pride at boys who will make it no matter what life throws at them. Courage, indomitable spirit, or whatever it is you call what I am witnessing can only come from the heart and the soul of a warrior.

PROLOGUE

Watching them, I have learned something about human nature. About life and this game I've dedicated my life to understanding. It inspires, it challenges. It reveals strength and flaunts weakness. Football IS life, with its darkest moments when we're not sure we can keep going and those glorious moments that make our spirits soar.

A spiraling ball brought down by eager hands, arms extended and body airborne, ignites the champion in all of us regardless of age. A player running full-out the length of the field into the end zone and thrusting his arms upward in victory sparks the pride in us that life has snuffed out. And for that brief glorious moment, his triumph is ours.

Football changes lives, this I know from personal experience. And whether a man is a coach or father, be it blood or surrogate, football is the best way I know to get a bunch of fun-loving mischievous boys to believe in discipline, teamwork, perseverance, and all the other values they'll need to succeed with whatever life brings their way.

I am convinced, through football, a boy can learn his biggest lessons—how to win, how to lose, how to be a man.

1

We Only Have Each Other Now
ᎨᎳ ᏃᏬ ᎯᏚᎶᏗ

APRIL 10, 1915

Eleven-year-old Tommy Thompson sat straight and stiff in a wooden chair in the superintendent's office, panic and a passel of unanswered questions filling his head: what had made his father show up out of the blue and haul him and his sisters to an orphanage? How long would they be here, and would they ever see their father or their aunt and uncle again?

Framed by the tall cathedral-style window, Mr. Griffith, who said he was the superintendent of the Cherokee Orphan Training School, looked and sounded important enough to be president of the United States. A fancy brocade vest showed beneath his black coat, and the stiff collar of his white shirt seemed to be holding up his double chin. Sitting ramrod straight, he peered at papers on his desk through gold-rimmed spectacles perched on the end of his nose. Tommy watched the superintendent jot down notes as Robert Thompson haltingly explained that he could no longer care for his son and two youngest daughters.

Care for us, Tommy thought. *You never cared for us, not for one minute.* His mother, Rose, had been the one Tommy and his four sisters counted on. He felt his sister's hand on his shoulder. Thirteen-year-old Susie stood behind his chair, her grip telegraphing that she wanted no part of this place. Dark-haired little Sammie, seven years old, leaned against his leg and reached for Tommy's hand, interlocking her fingers with his. Barely three when their mother died, she was about to be taken away from the aunt who loved her as her mother had done.

"My wife Rose died four years ago, and I . . . ah . . . I am away from Tahlequah a good deal of the time." Robert glanced at his sister-in-law sitting to his right, her round brown face impassive. "Nancy and her husband took my children in when Rose died, but I can't ask that of them anymore."

His aunt stiffened at the remark. She shot Tommy a glance that said, *Your father does not speak the truth.*

"I see," Mr. Griffith said. "Evidently Thomas did not attend school regularly. Eleven years old, he should be going into the fifth or sixth grade, but these records indicate he will enter grade three."

Robert shifted in his seat. "He got a late start because his birthday is in October, and he missed some school because of pneumonia." He glanced at Nancy as though expecting her to confirm what he said, but her expression told Tommy she wasn't going to help his father do this.

Just then, a movement through the large window behind Mr. Griffith caught Tommy's eye. A column of boys marched into view from the deep shade of a giant oak, its branches tipped with the new growth of spring. His father paused, distracted by the drumbeat.

Mr. Griffith turned and glanced out the window at a boy with a bass drum strapped in front of him and nearly as tall as he. "Ah, yes, the drum and bugle corps," Mr. Griffith said. "A fine group of young men, they're practicing for our graduation in June. Perhaps your son would like to join the corps."

His father shrugged but said nothing, which Tommy interpreted as not caring one way or the other. Tommy stared at the boys dressed in khaki uniforms, the bright midday sun dancing off the black shiny brims of their military caps. Each one wore black boots that reached almost to his knees. The group moved in perfect cadence, rifles angled against right shoulders, left arms held straight and swung smartly forward then back to the beat of the drum. As they marched out of sight, Tommy exchanged an anxious glance with Nancy, whose eyes glistened with unshed tears.

Mr. Griffith returned to his notes. "The children did well in public school?"

"Yes, but their mother was full-blood. I know she would want them to go to a Cherokee school." He spoke in a monotone, the same voice he used during the rare times Tommy accompanied him to the feed store in Tahlequah to buy a sack of chicken mash. To Tommy, it was a relief that he wasn't slurring his words this morning. "I have two older daughters, Eloise and Ida, at Haskell Boarding School in Kansas. I want Tommy and Susie and Sammie to get a good education, too."

How could you know what Momma would want? You were never around. Tommy felt helpless and abandoned, just as he had four years ago. One minute, it seemed, his mother had said she didn't feel good, and the next minute she was gone. Everything had fallen to pieces after that. Nancy had cried; his father had dabbed at his own eyes and told them, "Your mother has gone to heaven. She's in a better place."

Tommy remembered thinking that if anybody made it into heaven, it would surely be his mother. Hearing that she had gone to a better place, though, did nothing to ease his or his sisters' hurt. They had cried inconsolably. He had cried too, outside, by himself.

But not this time.

Tommy stared at his father's back as resentment gathered like storm clouds at this man whom they did not see for months at a time but had now, with a few words, turned their world upside down. Dressed in overalls, a faded shirt, and worn boots, he didn't look like someone who lived in a big house with servants to do all the work. From his rumpled clothes, you would think he'd just come from working in the fields—until you saw his hands. Anybody could see they'd never held a shovel or a hoe.

Tommy pictured his mother sitting at the kitchen table across from his father, whose hands cradled a bottle of moonshine that he would sip from until it was empty. Though he never heard his mother complain about the drinking, Tommy had seen the sad, silent glances she exchanged with his older sisters. He wanted to holler at his father and make him say out loud why he never remembered their birthdays or shared Christmas with them.

All questions vanished when his father reached for the pen and dipped it in the ink bottle. Mr. Griffith slid a paper across his desk.

"Sign at the bottom, if you will." Robert nodded and scrawled his name, then stood up and shook Mr. Griffith's outstretched hand. "I'm sure I don't need to tell you, Mr. Thompson, that your children are fortunate to be accepted at Cherokee Orphan Training School. There are far more Cherokee youngsters needing homes than spaces for them."

His father merely nodded and put on a faded felt hat.

Mr. Griffith glanced at the signed paper. "They will receive an education and, when old enough, be given appropriate vocational training."

Vocational training? Tommy's heart skipped a beat. He waited, hoping his father would ask what that meant, but Robert said nothing.

Mr. Griffith went on. "This release surrenders custody of your children to Cherokee Orphan Training School for five years. Thank you, sir, and good day."

Behind him, Susie gasped. Tommy dropped Sammie's hand and bolted to his feet in time to receive a passing embrace from his father, who was on his way to the door. Opening it, Robert stood waiting with his hand on the knob. Nancy came up to Tommy and touched his cheek. In Cherokee she whispered, "Be strong and make the best of this." She embraced Susie and mouthed something in his sister's ear, then opened her arms to Sammie. Tommy glanced at his father as Sammie buried her face in the folds of Nancy's dress. Robert Thompson's expression showed no emotion. Nancy untangled herself and, wiping tears away with the back of her hand, hurried out the door.

Tommy stared after her, his hand still raised in an aborted wave. *Five years:* the superintendent's words hung in the stillness. Stunned, Tommy jerked his hand down to his side and rushed to the front window in time to see his father climb into the wagon and wait as Nancy pulled herself up on the other side. Both looked straight ahead as he snapped the reins. The mules responded and the wagon pulled away.

And then they were gone.

She's never coming back. The finality sent a shock wave through Tommy as he stared after them. What little courage he'd mustered evaporated as the wagon disappeared from sight. *What would happen to Sammie and Susie without Aunt Nancy? And to me,* Tommy thought. *Five years. I'll be sixteen years old before I get out of here.* He glanced at his sisters; they were clinging to each other, crying. The superintendent indicated with a nod that Tommy should comfort them.

Dumbfounded, uncertain what to say, Tommy made his way to them on shaky legs. Mr. Griffith cleared his throat, a prompt for Tommy to say *something*. "We're . . . we're still a family," Tommy mumbled in Cherokee as he embraced them.

"English, Thomas. You must speak only English while you are here."

Sammie and Susie stiffened at the statement, and Tommy struggled for English words to comfort his sisters. "Aunt Nancy made us promise to make the best of things, so that's what we're going to do." Defiance crept into his voice as he whispered in Cherokee, "I don't care what he says, we'll speak Cherokee when we're together."

On the floor beside his chair were three flour sacks filled with clothes Nancy had washed and ironed. Tommy handed each sister her sack and then picked up his own, surprised at how heavy it felt. It held something more than clean clothes. Tommy peeked inside. On top of a folded shirt lay his mother's Bible, the one written in Cherokee that Aunt Nancy read to them each evening after supper. She had showed them the page at the front where, in their mother's writing, they read their name and the day they were born. But there was something else.

Cradled on top of the Bible in a handkerchief edged in lace embroidery lay a white Cherokee rose. Involuntary tears welled as Tommy breathed the fragrance captured inside the sack. The mother he had loved for too short a time was gone, and now so was Nancy. But he knew he had to be strong. Nancy was telling him to make the best of this; that was why she had sent the rose.

Tommy and the girls glanced at each other, exchanging an unspoken message: *We only have each other now.*

2

The Three R's—
Rules, Rules, and More Rules

KT ˙Ꭰ: ᎫᏬᏞᏣᏁᏬᎥᎫ, ᎫᏬᏞᏣᏁᏬᎥᎫ Ꭰᕷ ᎣᎪᕽ ᎫᏬᏞᏣᏁᏬᎥᎫ

1915–20

Like the boys who would come years after him, Tommy saw his world changed in the blink of an eye from a small log house filled with family to a huge military-run coeducational institution with 350 Cherokee students, their lives dictated by a steam whistle. "White man's time," the boys in his dorm room grumbled when they were sure the matron couldn't hear. The whistle blew at 6:00 A.M. to get everyone out of bed and then a dozen or more times during the day to signal breakfast, lunch, morning classes, afternoon classes, dinner, and study time. The last whistle sounded at 9:00 P.M. for lights out.

The Cherokee Orphan Training School, which began as the Cherokee Orphan Asylum in 1872, was operated by the Cherokee Nation until Oklahoma was admitted to the union in 1907. Statehood resulted in the federal government's dissolving the Cherokee Nation and its educational system. The orphan asylum remained open, but its management and operation came under the aegis of the Department of Interior through the Bureau of Indian Affairs.

In 1914, after growing in size and expanding its functions, the institution was renamed the Cherokee Orphan Training School (COTS). In the heart of Cherokee County, surrounding residents went about their quiet lives unaware that World War I was gathering steam. News of calamitous events taking place in Europe did not penetrate into the rolling hills of eastern Oklahoma. In July, Austria-Hungary declared war on Serbia. Early in August, Germany

RULES, RULES, AND MORE RULES

declared war on Russia, then quickly added France, Belgium, and Great Britain to its list of enemies. Great Britain reacted by declaring war on Germany. By November, more than twenty countries had issued declarations of war. With additional countries, colonies, protectorates, and commonwealths being insidiously drawn into the conflict, the nations involved numbered thirty-one by 1915.

In the spring of 1915, young Tommy was confronted with his own dilemma. Bitter over what his father had done and the callous way he had done it, Tommy's attitude toward COTS was anything but receptive. The three siblings talked secretly about running away, but they only talked. When it came time to execute their plan, Tommy couldn't follow through, for he remembered his promise to Aunt Nancy to make the best of their situation. By September and the start of the new school year, Tommy and his sisters had adjusted. Resignation gave way to new friendships and to a curiosity that caught them up into school life.

Located a few miles west of Tahlequah, the Cherokee Orphan Training School campus consisted of forty acres of rolling hills dotted with oak, maple, sycamore, and pecan trees. A lone three-story brick building sat at the foot of a knoll atop red dirt that sprouted wild grass in the spring from plentiful rain and turned brick-hard and dusty in the summer's fierce heat.

Personal interviews recorded and transcribed with two female former COTS students, conducted by a Sequoyah teacher and historian, speak of strict rules, unbending routine, and having to wear military-style uniforms. The girls wore middy dresses; the boys wore coats, pants, and military boots. The clothes were said to be better than the ragged hand-me-downs most students had on when they arrived. The two women mentioned having to line up and march to *everything*, but they emphasized having their own bed with clean sheets. They also remembered good food, including fresh-baked bread served with meals and turkey dinners at Thanksgiving and Christmas.

COTS graduate Sadie Parnell remarked about one Thanksgiving when the students found a pitcher in the middle of each table. Though the pitchers ordinarily held milk or gravy or syrup, on this particular Thanksgiving they held celery sticks, about which she said, "Nobody ate them, because we thought they were some sort of flowers." Sadie remembered Saturday supper as traditionally being chili, jerky, and corn bread: "Good chili and all the corn bread we could eat."

When asked about beatings or abuse, the interviewees said there had been none, though Sadie Parnell did recount getting her mouth washed out with soap when caught speaking Cherokee. "They should never have done that, but I guess that was their way of civilizing us," Sadie said. She added that "sometimes if a boy did something really bad they'd make him run a *hot line* between two rows of boys, each one holding his belt to whack the boy's backside as he went through."

Pictures during Tommy's years at COTS reveal normal school activities and functions of the time: proms with girls in long dresses and graduations with smiling seniors dressed in caps and gowns. Other photos show children at Christmas parties or May Day celebrations with them winding streamers around a Maypole. How much Tommy participated in these events is unknown. According to his children, Tommy and his sisters at first made a point of speaking Cherokee when they were alone but spoke English more and more as time went by. Tommy also expressed that he did try to make the best of things, something his children said seemed very important to him.

Tommy followed orders. He lined up for classes, for meals, and to take a shower on Saturdays. Every morning he lined up to brush his teeth and wash up in the boys' bathroom. Sometimes he even had to line up to use the boy's outhouse, which in 1915 may have been bigger and built better than a family outhouse but was still freezing cold in the winter and sweltering in the summer.

He took part in mandatory daily marching drills and morning exercises and, as time passed, began to enjoy the physical demand of calisthenics. Able to do more than the teacher asked, Tommy welcomed the good-natured competition that arose among the boys in his class. His greatest difficulty came from having a whistle dictate every moment of his day, from the time he woke up until

RULES, RULES, AND MORE RULES

lights out. Students were reminded not only of when a chore had to be done but also of exactly *how:* towels hung straight and even, dorm floors polished with no visible scuff marks, and each bed made with folded military corners and top blanket tucked tight enough to pass the student captain's bouncing a quarter off of it.

Sports offered Tommy welcome relief from the regimented rules and routine. He excelled in track, baseball, and basketball as in no other area of his life. Academically Tommy did average work, but he could outrun everyone in track, and it was rare for him not to score one or two runs in a baseball game or make baskets against COTS' best guards.

Tommy had found his niche.

Despite his success at sports, his simmering resentment toward his father remained. Robert showed up at COTS in 1918 for Susie's graduation—one of only two times Tommy saw him in five years at the orphanage. He recalled that after the ceremony Robert exchanged a few words with the three of them before disappearing into the crowd without a backward glance. The man remained an enigma, unapproachable and distant, though Tommy eventually learned that he had actually come from wealth.

Robert Thompson's grandparents were Georgia merchants who wagon-trained west on the Trail of Tears. They settled near the Oklahoma-Arkansas border, where they raised five sons and four daughters. Their fourth son, Johnson Thompson, married Eliza Christine Taylor. The couple (who would become Robert's parents) moved to Tahlequah, where they built a home befitting their social stature. They had five sons and two daughters of their own. Johnson and Eliza Thompson had high expectations for their boys. The youngest, Joseph, married well and became one of Tahlequah's leading physicians. An older son, Thomas Fox Thompson, married a girl his parents regarded as socially acceptable, but the marriage produced no children.

Tommy's father not only disappointed his parents but also disgraced the family name by marrying one of their maids. Rose Gritts, Tommy's full-blood Cherokee mother, planned to become a teacher. She enrolled in college at the Cherokee Female Seminary in Tahlequah and took a job in the Thompson household to pay her tuition. Upon learning that Robert had secretly married Rose, his furious parents vowed to have nothing to do with her or any children the young couple might have. Though he remained at home, Robert responded by taking solace in alcohol and indolence and paying only short obligatory visits to his lower-class family.

Tommy and his sisters never knew when their father might show up at Nancy and Charlie's house. Many years later, Tommy told his family that even after Robert's parents died, he remained in the mansion but chose not to invite his wife and children to join him. Though Tommy had been too young at the time to comprehend his father's decision, he did grasp its significance during his early teen years, and it became a defining moment. Tommy vowed that someday he would marry and have a family of his own but would *never* treat his family that way. And he would make damn sure to be a better father.

Comprehending the depth of his father's rejection created a reservoir of distrust that Tommy could still not reconcile even five years later. Those feelings and Susie's departure from COTS, however, were the only negative components in Tommy's life when classes began in September 1918. The war had gained his full attention the year before, on April 6, 1917, when America declared war on Germany. COTS teachers brought news into their classrooms, encouraging students to locate on wall maps the Meuse River, Cantigny, Soissons, St. Mihiel, and other French cities where major battles were fought. Great relief swept over the classrooms on November 11, 1918, when the superintendent dispatched student captains to break the news that an armistice had been signed and fighting had ceased. Four years of war had come to an end.

Wishes of peace and joy exchanged that Christmas had a great deal more meaning.

Tommy began his last year at COTS in September 1919 and turned sixteen on October 3. The school year ushered in a brand new sport, football, which sparked his interest and enthusiasm more than all the other sports combined. He had gotten his first taste of it on an outing into town when he saw a group of boys

RULES, RULES, AND MORE RULES

playing. Tommy asked to join in. The experience prompted him to join COTS's new football team. There were nineteen boys on the team; the names of the eleven starters were the only ones to survive. Tommy's name was not among them, but according to his family, he played his first season of football in 1919.

Entering football for Tommy could be compared to a duckling taking its first swim. It intrigued and delighted him, and he focused his time and energy on learning all he could. Team members became his friends; when they talked football, Tommy listened. He heard about famous Sooners making All-American and their 1915 undefeated season, the best in Oklahoma University's history. Attending COTS took on new meaning; he was lucky to be there.

Tall for his sixteen years, Tommy walked and stood with a military posture from four years of marching and training. He had well-developed chest and shoulder muscles from hours of calisthenics, sports, and vocational training, which included baling hay, planting, weeding, and harvesting a variety of crops. Whatever physical task was assigned, Tommy threw himself into it 110 percent. Thick black hair cut military style framed a boyishly handsome face. His easy smile and mischievous brown eyes caused girls to notice him. They would flirt with Tommy, and he found it easy to talk to them.

Years later Tommy would relate to his family that his last year at COTS was a "good year." He was excited at the prospect of graduating until the moment came when he had to say goodbye to Sammie. Twelve years old and no longer the frightened little girl who had buried her face in Nancy's dress, she also possessed a ready smile and mischievous eyes. After a tearful embrace, Tommy hurried away. After losing his mother and then having Charlie and Aunt Nancy exit his life, Tommy was beginning to hate goodbyes.

On June 7, 1920, Tommy emerged from COTS with a diploma from the seventh grade in his hand. Like a bad penny, his father was the first person he encountered. Robert announced that he had submitted an application for Tommy to attend Haskell Institute in Lawrence, Kansas, but because there were no openings at the moment, Tommy would have to attend public school. Tommy had heard about Haskell and knew it had become the leading school for Indian athletes after Carlisle Indian School in Pennsylvania closed two years earlier. Word was that after playing Oklahoma A and M, Kansas A and M, and Xavier in their 1919 season and ending with an 8-2-1 record, Haskell would be playing teams from the country's top universities.

Excitement ignited like a flame at hearing he might attend Haskell, but considering who said it, Tommy merely nodded. Two years had passed since he had last seen his father, and Robert's fragile and worn appearance came as a shock. Beneath a scraggly white beard, a network of spidery wrinkles revealed a sallow complexion. And at five foot ten, Tommy could now look straight into his father's eyes, still startlingly green and still devoid of feeling. Robert Thompson may have aged, but he hadn't changed.

Tommy moved in with his sisters in the house on Muskogee Avenue. He enrolled in public school and went to work as an usher and janitor for his cousin Jimmy Thompson, co-owner of Tahlequah's two theaters. Tommy's sisters Eloise and Ida, both graduates of Haskell, had jobs in Tahlequah. Eighteen-year-old Susie came home for the summer and would return to Haskell in the fall as a tenth grader. COTS allowed Sammie to spend summer vacation with her brother and sisters. Tommy recalled years later that the summer of 1920 was his happiest ever. On hot, humid weekends, the five of them swam in the Illinois River and had picnics with Aunt Nancy and Charlie at their place. Thanks to Tommy's job, they could see free movies anytime at their cousin's theaters. Located across the street from each other downtown, one theater showed B movies and served as a hangout for teenagers. The other, which was family oriented, played newly released silent films: *The Mark of Zorro* with Douglas Fairbanks, Charlie Chaplin in *The Kid*, and Jackie Coogan in *The Three Musketeers*.

Snubbed by Joe Thompson (his father's physician brother) and the rest of that family, Tommy treasured the relationship he had with his cousin Claude James (Jimmy) Thompson. They had traced their lineage and learned that Tommy's grandfather and Jimmy's

RULES, RULES, AND MORE RULES

great-grandfather were brothers, which meant that Jimmy's father, James Polk Thompson (mayor of Tahlequah and Jimmy's partner in the theaters), and Tommy were second cousins. Tommy soon learned why Claude James was also affectionately known as "Boozy" Thompson; Jimmy drank every day—and more than once. At the end of Tommy's workday, Jimmy would often ask his cousin to join him.

The year Tommy spent working at the theater cemented a close relationship with his cousin and offered Tommy a significant revelation: not all men who drank were cold and distant like his father.

3

Benevolence in a Bottle
ᏣᎳᎩ ᎠᏓᏛᎵᏗ ᏏᏏ ᎠᏆᎳᎩ

1921–23

Space opened up at Haskell in September 1921. Overjoyed at the opportunity, Tommy entered the eighth grade and turned eighteen the following month. Instructed to answer questions for an autobiography, he gave straightforward answers: "Percentage of Indian blood": *7/8 Cherokee.* "Religion": *Methodist.* "What trade have you learned so far in school?" *Engineering.* "Why do you think you are naturally adapted to this work?" *Because I have taken it before.*

He wrote that he belonged to the YMCA and Sacred Heart, a religious society. Asked whether he had ever held office in a school literary society, he answered *yes*; asked how he felt about it, he answered, *It was the first time I've held office and at first I was rather puzzled by the experience.* He wrote that he did not play a musical instrument, but if he could choose one it would be the violin. His favorite subject was arithmetic; his response to the follow-up question "Why?" was *Because it is my favorite subject.* Other favorites consisted of the following: sports, *football;* flower, *rose;* color, *white;* pet, *cat.* He listed the Bible as the most interesting book he'd ever read and *Tarzan of the Apes* as his favorite movie. Asked for suggestions to improve Haskell, Tommy wrote, *More work in religious societies.* Then, following the instruction "Do a sketch to demonstrate your natural artistic ability," at the bottom of the paper in a space about an inch and a half high, Tommy sketched what appears to be seven tiny fir trees. Recording the time it took him to fill out his autobiography, he printed 8:08 A.M. at the top of the paper and 8:30 A.M. at the bottom: twenty-two minutes to sum up the essence of his young life.

His first day on campus, Tommy went to the gym and waited in line to ask the new coach whether he could try out for the football team. Coach Marty Bell, a former star player at Central College in Kentucky, and his assistant, Frank McDonald, were interviewing new students. After being asked to sprint the length of the field, then throw and catch two or three passes, Tommy was thrilled when they issued him a uniform. He started at halfback position with the opportunity to compete, to hone his skills, and to learn all he could from Coach Bell.

Observing Bell in action, Tommy's wishful thinking about a coaching career became more entrenched. He made friends with the players, and when everyone on the team joined the Kansas National Guard, headquartered at Haskell, Tommy also joined. For attending training sessions two or three hours a week, he would receive about $10 a month, which provided him with spending money during the school year. Because he studied harder and longer than he had at COTS, Tommy's report cards reflected higher grades in algebra, English, arithmetic, civics, and history. His achievement card—which gauged such things as leadership, scholarship, initiative, and intelligence—showed either Excellent or Good assessments of his work. Tommy had come into his own.

The end of the school year arrived in June 1922 and with it the need to earn spending money. He applied to Haskell's summer program called Outings to help students learn and earn money at the same time. The written description of the program was "in order to secure the benefits of good home training pupils are sent out primarily to be taught." Tommy had to sign a lengthy contract outlining strict rules of behavior for students: "While working, boys and girls may not receive a letter unless it is first read by their employer. Girls may not go out without a chaperone and boys may not call on a girl unless he obtains written permission from a Haskell administrator."

After Tommy signed the contract agreeing to abide by the rules, it went to administrator H. R. Mote. Mote signed it, which cleared the way for Tommy to move in with a white patron family and do fieldwork on their farm. The pay was good; at $35 a month, it was slightly higher than a laborer's pay of a dollar a day. At the end of six weeks, Tommy had earned $53.85, of which he received $17.95 in cash from the farmer, the balance being sent to his individual Indian money account at Haskell.

As soon as he finished the job, Tommy left and spent the first two weeks of August 1922 in National Guard training camp with members of his football team. Getting up at the crack of dawn, marching and doing calisthenics, and enduring hours of rifle drills reminded him of COTS. One thing he had not done before was receive emergency training such as what to do if a tornado struck or a river flooded. Instructors reminded the boys that their main obligation was preparedness and congratulated them for their efforts, then ordered more marching and more calisthenics. Tommy collected twenty dollars for his two weeks.

Back at Haskell in September 1922, he again made the football team. Life was good; his grades on class assignments were higher than they'd ever been. He had spending money, and he and his sister found an hour or two each week to spend together. Tall and athletic, Susie liked for her brother to throw her the football, which she quickly learned to catch and bullet back to him. It delighted Tommy, though he took razzing from his teammates for playing ball with a *girl*. They received newsy letters from their sister Eloise. Ida had married a nice fellow, Virgil Clark, and they bought a place in the country.

Tommy and Susie did not go home for Christmas. Instead, they spent the holidays at Haskell. Classes resumed in January 1923. Not long afterward, their weekly visits became shorter. Susie then sent word that she didn't feel well and thought maybe she had the flu. Tommy sought permission to visit her, but Susie's dorm matron told him boys were not allowed in the girls' dorms. A few weeks went by with no word. He again sought permission to see his sister and this time was told that Susie could not have visitors.

Worried and frustrated, Tommy sought help from Mr. H. B. Peairs, chief supervisor of education, whom Tommy had chauffeured several times to and from Lawrence's train station. But before he had a chance to speak with Mr. Peairs, Tommy received word that Susie had left for Tahlequah. He had no alternative but to wait for word from his sister. Three weeks passed before he received a summons from Mr. Peairs.

Unlike most of the teachers and administrators at Haskell, who were retired military men, the supervisor had been a high school principal before coming to Haskell in 1887, three years after it opened. Gray haired and distinguished looking, Peairs reminded Tommy of the Cherokee Orphan Training School superintendent. Peairs sounded more like an English gentleman than an Indian school administrator. "I'm afraid I have some very bad news, Thomas," Peairs said. "This letter arrived today from your sister Eloise. She asked me to speak to you in person." Tommy's heart plummeted. "It seems that Susie has been diagnosed with tuberculosis." Before Tommy had time to digest the news, Peairs added, "Susie left school to see a doctor in Tahlequah." He shook his head. "Certainly understandable that she would be upset when he gave her the news of her illness."

Peairs slid the letter across the desk. "Eloise doesn't know why or how, but while she was in Tahlequah Susie became involved with a group of missionaries from Missouri. Perhaps they promised to cure her and she went willingly or they took her. The fact is Susie left with them."

Tommy gasped. "Missouri?" He scanned three paragraphs written in what looked like a shaky hand. "I have to go find her." He started to rise.

Peairs held up his hand. "No, Thomas. Eloise hasn't any idea where Susie is. She said we must wait for word from her. I realize this is a terrible shock, but be assured I will do whatever I can to help." Mr. Peairs rose, signaling the end of their meeting. "I will send for you the minute I hear anything." Tommy left, feeling powerless and abandoned.

Two months dragged by with only brief notes from Eloise saying she had no news. Finals week began in early May 1923. The day he finished his second final exam, Tommy received a summons from Mr. Peairs. All hope of good news vanished at the man's stricken look. "I just received a telephone call from Eloise. Evidently Susie's condition worsened in Missouri, serious enough that the missionaries put her on a train for home. Eloise said Susie arrived yesterday, on a stretcher and coughing up blood."

Tears stung as Tommy pictured her. Many of his friends had lost someone in their family to tuberculosis; coughing up blood was what happened near the end.

"Eloise took Susie straight to her doctor, who advised that Susie get to a TB sanitarium as soon as possible," Mr. Peairs said. "I know you want to help, Thomas. A sanitarium in the desert will require money. Perhaps that would be a way."

Tommy had fifty dollars, which he asked Mr. Peairs to send to Eloise. He left with one thing on his mind—to help Susie. He needed a job, and the Outings program had worked well the previous summer, so he quickly applied for the program again. On the bottom of the form, Tommy penned a question to Assistant Superintendent Mote, asking for the first two weeks in August off for National Guard camp. Both paychecks would go a long way to help his sister.

Tommy completed his exams and waited for Mote's okay. Of course he would approve the request; it was routine to grant time off to fulfill National Guard obligations. A few days later, the student captain in charge of Tommy's dorm delivered Mote's reply. He opened the folded letter, and the hand-printed REQUEST DENIED came as a slap in the face. It was no mistake, for H. R. Mote had signed underneath the denial. Tommy took no time to ask Mote's reason or to argue his case, but he thought Mr. Peairs might very well help. He ran as fast as he could to the supervisor's office, only to learn from the secretary that Peairs had left for an Indian Congress in Spokane, Washington.

Panicked, Tommy turned for help to the only person he could think of, his cousin in Tahlequah. Jimmy Thompson accepted a collect call, and Tommy blurted out the news about Susie and Mote's denying him a job. He told his cousin that he'd sent Eloise fifty dollars, all the money he had. Interrupting, Jimmy said he would gladly supply the money to get Susie to Arizona, but it was a loan and he expected to be paid back as soon as possible. His cousin's "as soon as possible" remark only slightly diminished Tommy's joy.

He telephoned the news to Eloise. "Thank God for that man," she said. "I will personally thank him when I pick up the money. I'm going straight to the depot to buy two tickets to Phoenix. Susie won't be riding by herself this trip." Tommy's gratitude and hope didn't hold up against his fury at being dismissed by the only man at Haskell with the authority to help him.

Well aware of the school's cardinal rule about leaving without written permission, Tommy nevertheless didn't intend to ask Mote for permission. Leaving his uniforms hanging in the closet, he packed the few clothes he had and sneaked out of his dorm. Nineteen years old, frightened yet bent on doing the right thing for his sister, Tommy took off on foot for the freight yards in Lawrence, Kansas. He caught a ride on the first freight train he found headed for Tulsa. From there, he would hop a train to Muskogee, then hitchhike the rest of the way home. The two-hundred-mile train ride from Lawrence to Tulsa took twelve hours, which was plenty of time for Tommy to silently rant and rave at Mote and agonize that he had likely destroyed all chances to finish his education. Disconsolate at the turn of events, he arrived at Tulsa's freight yard just as the sun broke above the horizon.

The noisy yard brimmed with the activity of a new day: dusty cars being loaded, trains arriving and departing, and hobos trying to be quick so as not to be caught by a railroad detective. Tommy did the same, keeping between trains as he trotted up and down, peering into open cars. If he found men inside, he asked whether they were headed to Muskogee. Some answered "no." Others said they didn't know but told him it didn't matter anyway: "It's goin' somewhere." After an hour of searching, Tommy found a car with three hobos inside who said they were headed for Muskogee. Exhausted, he climbed aboard and moved a respectable distance away.

Collapsing with his back against the car's rough walls, Tommy gulped in air that smelled of grain and oil and sweaty bodies. The three men sat in a tight circle a few feet away and spoke in hushed voices, occasionally glancing his way. Too exhausted and dispirited to care, Tommy closed his eyes and revisited his predicament. As always, someone else was in charge of his life, somebody who didn't give a damn, just like his father. He assumed that asking Mote for time off to go to training camp had prompted the denial, for why else would Mote have turned him down? Tommy tried to think of what else he could have done besides run away. Though it made him feel no better, he decided he had made the right choice.

"Hey, friend."

Tommy opened his eyes and squinted through a shaft of dust-filled light from the slightly opened door.

"You look like you could use a drink." A grubby hand held out a bottle toward him.

Tommy started to say no, then reconsidered. What he needed was money and hope, but they were offering kindness the only way they could. He accepted the almost-empty bottle.

"Go ahead, finish it," the hobo said. "Jake has a full one." Tommy nodded and drained it. "We're going to find fieldwork," the spokesman said. "What's in Muskogee for you?"

Friendly enough, Tommy thought. He dug in his pocket and found a dime and a nickel, then moved closer and handed the coins to the man who spoke to him. "It's a long story," he said, accepting a drink from the full bottle they passed around.

"Long's okay. We ain't got no place to go."

Tommy poured out his woes. He told them about his sister and Mote and that he had to borrow a lot of money from his cousin and needed to pay it back in a hurry. For the next few hours, Tommy and the hobos took turns swigging from the bottle. They told him their stories and sympathized with his; by the end of the bottle, when they let him have the last drink, Tommy's anger and hunger and exhaustion had melted away.

The dim, musty car swayed and clanked, and Tommy fell asleep, rousing only when he heard the screech of iron scraping iron as the train came to a halt. "Muskogee," the hobo spokesman said. He unfolded his lanky frame from the floor and pushed the heavy door open. Half asleep, Tommy watched the hobo's matter-of-fact movements that said he had done this many times before.

Tommy rose and picked up his suitcase, then hopped down from the car. Shading his eyes from the late afternoon sun, he waited as one by one his newfound friends jumped down. Each man shook his hand and wished Tommy and his sister good luck. In the dimness of the car he had pictured them as older, but the bright sun revealed that the men were about his age and all three white. Tommy thanked them and said goodbye. Deep in thought, he made his way to the Y at the highway, granting that he had just witnessed more kindness from three hobos than from the supposed gentleman in charge at Haskell Indian School.

Tommy hitchhiked the twenty miles to Tahlequah and walked toward his cousin's office. Sliding low on the horizon, the sun bounced prisms of orange light off store windows, a reminder he should be eating supper in Haskell's cafeteria. Instead, his dorm matron would have long since discovered his absence and reported it. There would be hell to pay, he decided. Tommy pictured proper Mr. Peairs hearing the news. Would he understand? *Likely not, unless his secretary told him I came to see him,* Tommy thought.

Fatigue slowed his steps as gut-wrenching fear overtook him. The gravity of Susie fighting for her life and his burning the only bridge he had to a coaching career produced an image of Tommy Thompson, hobo, endlessly riding freight trains in search of fieldwork.

He and his cousin talked over a good supper at Jimmy's favorite restaurant, with whisky before, during, and after the meal, and some of Tommy's fears subsided. He walked to the empty house on Muskogee Avenue and let himself in, a vase of dead flowers on the kitchen table a painful reminder of Susie and Eloise. Where were they? he wondered. Was his sister still alive?

Tommy began a new job for his cousin, operating the projector this time. Also serving as a janitor, he cleaned up and closed after the last show. During the day, he found work mowing lawns and weeding yards. When he could, he baled hay and picked fruit, which paid more than yard work. Three weeks passed before Tommy received a letter postmarked Phoenix. Eloise apologized for not writing sooner but promised to let him know about Susie's condition the minute she met with her doctors. At last in a permanent ward in the sanitarium, Susie was comfortable and resting. As for Eloise, she had taken a room in a nearby boarding house. Tommy read and reread the letter, taking small comfort in picturing Susie surrounded by nurses and doctors.

He continued doing yard work and fieldwork for as many hours a day as people were willing to pay him. Tommy grew leaner and more muscled. Exhausted as much from July's crushing heat and humidity as from the work, he welcomed sundown, when he could bathe and put on clean clothes and have supper. Operating the projector offered the opportunity to sit in a chair for a few hours. Most evenings after cleaning up, Tommy walked home and collapsed into bed. But sometimes, if Jimmy was still in his office, he invited Tommy to have a drink with him. His cousin never failed to ask about Susie and Eloise.

Tommy had few expenses except for food, and thanks to his cousin's generosity he did not have to pay interest on the loan. Disciplined with his hard-earned money, Tommy made payments faithfully each week and sent money to Eloise. Through what he earned doing fieldwork in the day and the theater job at night, Tommy hoped to pay Jimmy back by the end of summer.

Working twelve to fourteen hours a day left him no time to miss Haskell football or his friends. Tommy had followed Haskell's 1922 season with John Levi, who was the key to the team's success. An Arapaho, Levi was a triple-threat back, according to the newspaper. Levi's brother George was equally impressive. It stung to read about Haskell's last game of the season in San Antonio. In a 21–20 barnburner, they finished off Baylor, the Southwest Conference champions. *I would have played in that game,* Tommy told himself.

Knowing Haskell's strict policy about running away, Tommy was relieved that he'd had no word from the school. That changed in mid-July 1923. When he arrived at the theater, Jimmy told him that an agent from the Muskogee office of the BIA showed up with a letter on Haskell stationery signed by J. A. Canady, disciplinarian. The letter was asking for help to locate one Thomas Fox Thompson, AWOL, listed as a deserter. His cousin said he gave the agent no information. He did urge Tommy to "finish up with that damned school once and for all."

Alarmed at being on Haskell's wanted list, Tommy quickly penned a letter to Mr. Peairs on July 23, 1923. He broke the news about Susie and tried to explain his dilemma:

> While you were away I left Haskell Institute without the permission of my superiors for it was my wish to pay my debts. I inquired about going on an Outing but Mr. Mote refused to put me on the payroll or to let me out of the first half of August. It was very necessary that I earn some money so as to pay my debts. I am a member of the Kansas National Guard. I am coming to Haskell to go to camp with them. I'll have a chance to talk with you by the 15th of August. Will you please notify me at the earliest date whether or not I may reenter Haskell. Hoping I may have an early reply, I remain, Respectfully yours.

Peairs replied by return mail:

> Friend Thomas, I suggest that if you want to return to Haskell, you do so immediately and thus prove your good intentions. I think if you come without delay and put in the time faithfully until time to go to [National Guard] camp, Mr. Mote will be willing to give you another chance. But I doubt very much whether you could get in if you wait until time to go to camp. Furthermore, unless you come back and make good, I do not believe you will be permitted to go to camp.
> Very truly yours, H. B. Peairs

The letter confirmed Tommy's fear that he had destroyed his future. It also rekindled a long-buried loathing for Joe Thompson, his father's physician-brother. Tommy would never have had to borrow money to help Susie had he received the cash from an inheritance left to him by his uncle, Thomas Fox Thompson. The elder Thomas, who had no children of his own, left his nephew and namesake his house on Muskogee Avenue, several acres of land, and eight hundred dollars in cash. Because Tommy was a minor and his father "unavailable" at the time of his uncle's death, the court had appointed Dr. Joe as guardian. Rumors flew that the good doctor, known for his lavish lifestyle, had borrowed the eight hundred dollars. Tommy's rift with him became full blown when, a few years later, he asked Joe what had happened to his cash. Joe claimed not to know what had happened to it. That response brought Tommy's depression roaring back, matched by a fury he could not shake, as he agonized over what a difference a fortune like that would have made in his and his sisters' lives.

He also could not help but think how much easier it would be for Susie now. Only Jimmy Thompson's listening and offering understanding over drinks at their occasional late-night suppers brought calm. Jimmy obviously cared about Tommy, for at one of their meals, he suggested that Tommy see whether he could attend Northeastern Preparatory High School, on the campus of Northeastern State Teachers College. Tommy wasted no time and found out that he could attend but would need H. R. Mote's cooperation to get his grades and transcript.

Reluctantly, Tommy penned a letter to the Haskell administrator. Swallowing his pride, he apologized for leaving without permission. Then, unable to hide his resentment, he added, "But as you know why I left, I need not go further into detail." Tommy wrote that he intended to finish high school in Tahlequah and asked that his credits be forwarded to him before September. He signed the letter, "Yours respectfully, Thomas Fox Thompson," then impulsively scrawled "Deserter" in big, bold letters under his signature. The label stung, and he wanted nothing more to do with Mote or the school.

Mote complied, but because he granted only three credits for Tommy's entire ninth grade, Tommy sought help from Northeastern's registrar, R. K. McIntosh. After much correspondence between Mote and McIntosh, Mote eventually acquiesced. He forwarded Tommy's certificates of promotion for the eighth and ninth grades, paving the way for Tommy to begin classes in September. As soon as the certificates arrived, Tommy resigned from the Kansas National Guard and joined the unit in Tahlequah.

Tommy attended high school on the Northeastern campus and continued to work for his cousin, sending money from every paycheck to Eloise. The exact amount of money Jimmy loaned him is unknown, but Tommy repaid it in full, which Jimmy Thompson made known. Eloise wrote that she had taken a job at the sanitarium to help defray the expenses of Susie's treatments and closed by saying that Susie was doing as well as could be expected. Tommy interpreted that as meaning his sister was not getting any better.

Torn by the question of whether he should go to Phoenix or start classes, which were scheduled to begin in a week, Tommy once again sought the advice of the kindly registrar. Mr. McIntosh convinced Tommy that he should not throw away this opportunity and suggested instead that he save his earnings and visit his sisters in Phoenix during Christmas vacation. He took the registrar's advice and began classes in the tenth grade.

Tommy never saw Susie again. After spending her last months at a Phoenix tuberculosis sanitarium, she died before reaching her twenty-fifth birthday. Tommy completely broke down when Eloise called to say that she'd held their sister's hand as Susie passed on. Distraught, he turned to the one person who had consistently showed him kindness. On hearing his tearful news, Jimmy cried with Tommy, then offered his heartfelt condolences and a bottle of whiskey.

Tommy accepted both.

4

Freedom—Everything It's Cracked Up to Be

VᎦ ᎠᏏᎫ, hᏍⅰ ᎪᎳⱺᎫ ᎤᏢⱺᎴ ᏴᎢ

1925–26

Susie's death closed a sad, bitter chapter in Tommy's life. It deepened his resentment toward the father he could never count on, and it made stronger his longing to one day have a loving family of his own. Tommy completed the twelfth grade at Northeastern Preparatory High School in June 1925 and received his diploma, acknowledging that without his cousin's help and friendship he might very well have been riding freight trains in search of fieldwork.

With diploma in hand, the excited graduate received word that Mr. McIntosh wanted to see him. Another man who had been a caring friend, Mr. McIntosh presented him with what looked like another diploma. Tommy opened the cover and scanned the fancy printed words: "Thomas Fox Thompson is hereby awarded a four-year athletic scholarship to Northeastern State Teachers College." Tears clouded his vision as Tommy glanced at the beaming registrar, the scholarship obviously his doing. Too emotional to speak, he grabbed the registrar's hand and pumped it so long and hard that Mr. McIntosh laughed and joked that Tommy had wounded him.

Tommy fully recognized that the scholarship was much more than a gift that paid his tuition; it represented an opportunity to chart his own future. No longer would an unsympathetic school administrator or cold distant father have control of his life. He *would* have teaching credentials when he graduated and, God willing, a career of his own choosing.

FREEDOM—EVERYTHING IT'S CRACKED UP TO BE

Classes began September 2, 1925. Caught up by his unexpected good fortune, Tommy strolled across campus, its beauty bringing the awareness that his mother had once been a student here. How long ago had that been, he mused: 1891, 1892? She would have known it as the Cherokee National Female Seminary then. Had she walked these grounds, excited and happy about her future? Was his scholarship, his being here, an act of Providence? Was it his destiny to fulfill his mother's dream? He could still call up her memory; though it made him sad, it filled him with resolve to derive every bit of good from this opportunity.

As a pleasant afterthought, he realized that no longer would a whistle dictate every moment of his life. Despite ten years of vocational training designed to turn him into a farmer, he had other plans. Sports would be in Tommy Thompson's future.

The anger, frustration, and bitterness that had dominated much of Tommy's life to that point receded to the background, swept away by his newfound freedom. Classes were hardly under way when, like a harbinger of good things to come, on his twenty-second birthday—October 3, 1925—he received a notice from the commander of Tahlequah's National Guard stating that he had been promoted to first lieutenant. This meant more responsibility and more pay and served as confirmation that somebody viewed him as officer material.

Immersing himself in his studies, Tommy reasoned that as long as he maintained good grades in English, physics, zoology, and trigonometry, he could indulge in sports as much as he wanted in his off time. The new football coach at Northeastern, Ray Ballard, summoned Tommy to his office and asked Tommy to join the football team. The coach had a copy of the 1925 *Tsa-La-Gi Yearbook* on his desk, open to the page that showed Tommy's picture in a Redmen uniform. The photograph had been taken his first year of preparatory high school, and the caption read, "Freshman Tommy Thompson, 165-pound fullback halfback, always gets his man. The Redmen are sure of a gain when Thompson carries the ball." Ballard mentioned him playing for Haskell and congratulated him.

Tommy agreed to be on the team and showed up for practice along with forty other boys, one of them Doc Wadley, who had played with him the year before. The two took part in daily practice and predicted that they would have a good season, but the combination of a new coach, new plays, and new players proved too much to overcome. Their first game against Arkansas University turned into a 6–54 thrashing and an embarrassing lesson in just how much work lay ahead. The Redmen's ten-game season ended 2 and 8.

Tommy still followed Haskell football. Coach Dick Hanley, who had replaced Marty Bell three years earlier, was known as a tough disciplinarian and great coach. His first season was 8-2-0, but equally impressive was that Haskell outscored their opponents in total points 307–89. Hanley's success had drawn the attention of Glenn Pop Warner and Jim Thorpe, both of whom were quoted as extolling the Haskell program. After a three-year fund-raising effort, Haskell's administrators authorized construction of an 11,000-seat stadium as a means of bringing major universities to Lawrence. Tommy admitted that Northeastern football would never come close to Haskell's, but it had potential and he wanted to be a part of it.

The week after football season ended, Tommy started basketball and joined the boxing team. Then, like a kid in a candy store, as soon as those sports were over, he tried out for track. He ran his first race, the 220-yard dash, against Lee Derry, who the coach said would be trying out for the U.S. Olympic track team. Derry won by a two-second margin, but Tommy's teammates chose him as their leader. The *Tahlequah Citizen* ran his picture and a story under the headline "An Indian Leads 'Em, Tommy Thompson, Invincible Dash Man, Elected Captain of Northeastern Trackmen."

Tommy thrived on competition and viewed his participation in sports as striving for the highest level of play he could achieve. His taking part and excelling in every sport the school offered attracted the attention of sports writers from the *Muskogee Phoenix,* the *Tahlequah Daily Press,* and Northeastern's campus newspaper. They wrote stories accompanied by pictures of Tommy's every

Nineteen-year-old Tommy Thompson, Northeastern's star half back. Permission granted by Jimmy Thompson.

victory, and his continuous presence in their sports pages launched his reputation as "Tommy Thompson, Northeastern star athlete."

There was no sport he disliked, but Tommy loved football best. His friends were athletes; his closest buddies were football players as passionate about the game as he. They played touch football on weekends and held passing and running contests just for fun. The attention they attracted wherever they went could be embarrassing, but all of them, including Tommy, admitted they liked being the big men on campus. It garnered attention from the girls: pretty girls in stylish clothes with short, sassy hairdos. Made up with rouge and mascara and bright red lipstick, they looked like the models in *Vogue* and *Harper's Bazaar*. Though he remembered pretty girls from COTS and Haskell, Tommy viewed the stylish girls in knee-length dresses, rayon stockings, and fancy shoes as a pleasant reminder that he'd left the past, the years of uniforms and uniformity, behind.

And, indulging in a habit that would have been unthinkable at COTS and Haskell, nearly all the girls at Northeastern seemed to smoke. Tommy did as well, preferring Lucky Strikes, as did most of his buddies. The girls favored "Mild as May Marlboros," which were advertised heavily in their favorite magazines with a woman holding a cigarette along with the caption "Has smoking any more to do with a woman's morals than has the color of her hair?" During lunch and breaks between classes, girls and boys gathered in a shady spot on campus to visit and enjoy a cigarette.

Girls occasionally approached Tommy, falling in step beside him as he walked to class. They would ask whether he was going to Saturday night's dance or to the pep rally, in general letting him know they were available. Flattered, he sometimes made a date. He loved to dance and was good at it, as adept at the Charleston as he was the two-step. Most often, though, when done with his studies, Tommy could be found competing in some sport or palling around with football buddies Littlefield, McCullough, Riggs, Patterson, Rogers, and Doc Wadley.

The fact that they lost more games than they won did not stop Tommy and his teammate buddies from partying. They would share a bottle or two of whiskey that someone bought from one of Tahlequah's bootleggers. Still working part time at the theater, Tommy also enjoyed an occasional drink or two after work with his cousin. He reasoned that with his excellent grades and as involved as he was in sports, a few drinks on occasion posed no problem. He could see no resemblance to his alcoholic father.

No one recognized it, least of all Northeastern's star athlete Tommy Thompson, but at twenty-three years old, he had already crossed the line.

5

The Perfect Match
ᎤᏂᏠᏯ ᏗᎨᏴᎩ

1926–28

Seventeen-year-old Dorothy Jean Fudge stepped off the train at the Tahlequah station, and Mrs. Taylor, owner of the boardinghouse where Dorothy would be staying, stood waiting as promised in her letter. Lillian Fudge had picked Mrs. Taylor's house as the safest place for her daughter to live while in college; now Dorothy understood why. Mrs. Taylor looked as prim and proper as the strict mother she had just left behind in Briartown.

"Miss Fudge, nice to meet you. Your trunks arrived yesterday, but I'm expecting another boarder, a Miss Baker from Muskogee."

A commotion caught Dorothy's attention, and she and Mrs. Taylor turned to stare. A dark-haired girl alighted from the train and dropped several suitcases on the platform. Pretty enough to be a model, she looked stunning in a shift dress exactly like the one Dorothy had admired in *Vogue* magazine during the train ride. The girl waved at the porter and asked him to hand down the rest of her luggage.

Dorothy hurried toward her. "Here, let me help you." She took three suitcases from the porter and stacked them next to the others. Ruth Baker introduced herself and thanked Dorothy. *She didn't seem to notice my homemade dress,* Dorothy thought with relief.

Ruth chatted all the way to the boardinghouse with Dorothy taking in every word, mesmerized by the other girl's glamorous looks and fashionable dress. Ruth even wore perfume. She said her father used to be a jewelry broker in Muskogee but now he was a speculator—pronounced *speck-yew-laator* with a slight rise at the end. "Mama is a socialite. She just loves parties, going to them and giving them. I do too, don't you?" Ruth waited as though expecting Dorothy to agree. Hating to admit she had no idea what a speculator was and hadn't been to many parties, Dorothy managed to say she looked forward "to everything." She promised herself to find out what a speculator did, because whatever it was obviously made a lot of money.

When Mrs. Taylor suggested the two of them be roommates, Dorothy agreed immediately and waited, hopeful that Ruth would do the same; Ruth agreed without a moment's hesitation. Since they had so many trunks and suitcases, Mrs. Taylor assigned the two of them the biggest room in the boardinghouse. By the time Mrs. Taylor finished showing them the house and grounds, the rest of Ruth's luggage had arrived. The girls visited as they unpacked, with Ruth doing most of the talking. She paused when they heard a tap on the open door.

Four girls entered and introduced themselves. Smiling and friendly, Teresa, Jean, Mary, and Waleah said they had already unpacked and were settled in their rooms. Dorothy couldn't help but stare at Waleah, who was striking with her long black hair and expressive brown eyes. Beautifully dressed, she could have been a poster girl of the perfect college coed. Teresa, obviously impressed by all the clothes being unpacked, joked that they knew where to come if they needed to borrow something. Dorothy merely smiled. She had seen Ruth's wardrobe, all of it storebought and fashionable. Hers, in contrast, were the work of her mother and her White treadle sewing machine.

As Dorothy and Ruth put away the last of their things, Mary suggested that the other girls give them a tour of the campus. Dorothy couldn't believe her good fortune. The boardinghouse her mother had picked out was turning out to be wonderful, and these girls seemed as friendly to her as they did to Ruth. Dorothy's fear of being a lonely misfit drifted away like chimney smoke in a storm.

The six of them walked to town past streets named Magnolia, Hickory, Tanglewood, and Redbud and others named Choctaw,

Chickasaw, Delaware, Cherokee, and Shawnee. They arrived at Muskogee Avenue, which Dorothy decided had to be Tahlequah's main street. Both sides were lined with shiny roadsters, Model Ts, and touring cars, in front of shops busy with shoppers. How different from Briartown, with its dusty main street and parked wagons hitched to tired-looking horses or mules, she thought. An automobile caused a stir in Briartown.

Mary pointed out the Shack Café, described as a great place to meet boys and where everybody at Northeastern gathered. A Model T Ford sped around the corner onto a dirt side street, leaving a cloud of dust in its wake. The couple inside waved and shouted, "Sorreee!" The girls paused in front of Hinds Mercantile, known as Tahlequah's nicest clothing store. A stunning blue shift dress caught Dorothy's eye, and she mentally reckoned that $3.98 from her school money would not keep her from graduating.

College promised to be a whole new experience.

As they entered the campus, Dorothy noticed a crowd gathered in front of a building that looked like a castle. Jean commented, "Probably football players, the big men on campus. And what dreamboats, especially that Tommy Thompson."

Teresa wanted to know whether Dorothy and Ruth liked football.

Ruth said she loved football games. Dorothy had to admit she'd never been to one. "My Momma is Irish," she said. "She made it clear I was not at Northeastern to get mixed up with boys. And my brothers told me plain and simple to stay away from football players."

Mary reminded Dorothy that her Irish momma was a hundred miles away and there was no law that said she had to tell her mother *everything*. Even Dorothy laughed at that. Mary suggested they skip the rest of the tour and go to the Redmen Shoppe—"The place to be seen," she said.

Dorothy followed them inside. Three big ceiling fans stirred the air, swirling the sweet smell of ice cream tinged with cigarette smoke. A long ice cream counter ran along one wall. In front of it stood shelves filled with textbooks and supplies. Next to the shelves were booths jammed with students laughing and talking. Glancing around, Dorothy couldn't suppress a smile. Had she dreamed of a perfect first day at college, it would never have been this good. In town only a few hours, she had already made five friends, had a tour of downtown and campus, and found the best hangouts. She even knew about the big men on campus, not that she expected they would be of concern to her.

Academic performance had never been a worry, but whether a plain girl from a place like Briartown could fit in at a big college like Northeastern scared her to death. She came from a town so tiny that the post office was in the Fudge home. Lillian Fudge had been postmistress since long before Dorothy and her two brothers were born. Her postmistress mother not only knew all fifty residents of Briartown but also knew everything that went on in their lives.

Dorothy felt like pinching herself. *Briartown seems a million miles away,* she thought.

The girls took the lone empty booth. Each ordered a pineapple soda, which according to Waleah was the Redmen specialty. They talked of upcoming parties and dances. Conversation paused when the bell on the front door jingled and two boys walked in. "Oh, it's him!" Waleah said and jumped up. She motioned for the boys to come over, then breathlessly introduced Tommy Thompson and Will Riley.

Dorothy nodded, preferring to be an observer in this exchange. Mary, Theresa, and Jean said hello, their expressions clearly admiring. Ruth began talking to the boys, nonsensical silly talk about nothing. *She's babbling,* Dorothy thought, a bit embarrassed. She wished she had the corner seat instead of sitting in the middle. The boys asked whether they had picked their classes, and a discussion followed about professors they should avoid.

Curious, Dorothy ventured a glance up at Tommy Thompson and blushed. Whoever called him a dreamboat was right. He looked Indian, probably Cherokee, she decided, with pale brown skin, thick dark hair cut short, and an easy smile that made her heart beat faster. Her blush deepened because dreamboat Tommy Thompson seemed to be paying no attention to the other girls. He was staring back at her with a twinkle in his eyes that obliterated all of her thoughts but one: Why in heaven's name he would be looking at her like *that* when her new friends were far more glamorous?

Ruth and the other girls abruptly stopped talking and openly glanced at Tommy and then at Dorothy. She couldn't speak, nor would her throat allow her to swallow the cold pineapple drink in her mouth. He was the handsomest boy she had ever seen in all of her seventeen and a half years. And as crazy as it seemed, Tommy Thompson's smile seemed only for Dorothy Jean Fudge from tiny Briartown, Oklahoma.

Dorothy's status as the girlfriend of Northeastern's star athlete propelled her light-years ahead of the life she had led in Briartown. She loved college: studying different subjects, learning about far-away places and different cultures. Dorothy spent hours in the library, first following through on her promise to find out what Ruth's father did. Newspapers and magazines provided the answer and brought to her attention a world she'd never heard of: Wall Street, bull and bear markets, swollen stocks, declining stocks, buy low and sell high, millions of dollars and shares trading hands. *So that's what a speculator does,* she concluded. It sounded a bit like gambling, and Dorothy wondered whether Ruth really understood her father's occupation.

The plain girl who hadn't been to many parties went to lots of them now. She considered herself the luckiest girl at Northeastern, head-over-heels in love with Tommy Thompson, and even she could see that he felt the same about her. He made her laugh; he made her feel pretty. She was the envy of all her glamorous girlfriends.

When asked about her, Tommy described his girlfriend as "pretty, serious, smart as a whip, and damned independent." He admired the way she handled things, like the fallout from a prank he and a friend pulled: sneaking a mule into an administrator's second floor office in Seminary Hall. And she spirited him away from parties when he drank too much. They were a perfect match.

THE PERFECT MATCH

Tommy asked Dorothy to marry him in the spring of 1927. No records or pictures could be found of their June wedding, but it made headlines in the Tahlequah paper.

Miss Dorothy Fudge, Tommy Thompson Married June 27, 1927.
Mrs. Lillian Fudge of Briartown last week announced the marriage of her daughter Dorothy Jean, a student at Northeastern, on June 27th to Thomas Fox Thompson. The couple succeeded in keeping the wedding a secret for several weeks. Announcements went out last week after Thompson and his bride left Tahlequah for their honeymoon. The bridegroom is a picture machine operator in the employ of James Thompson, owner of Sequoyah Theater.

Their wedding proved to be the precursor of a banner final year for Tommy at Northeastern. He made Oklahoma's Collegiate Conference All-Star football team and was voted captain of the Redmen football team. Described in newspapers as "the flashy Indian halfback, Terrible Tommy, the Redmen flash who did enough by himself to beat the Durant Savages," Tommy added to his reputation every time he went on the field. He closed his college career only slightly more proud of his diploma than he was of his letterman's jacket. On June 20, 1928, Tommy graduated with a bachelor of sciences degree, Dorothy graduating alongside him.

Acknowledged as one of the most outstanding athletes to ever play for Northeastern, he had far and away surpassed the hopes and dreams of the struggling boy at the Cherokee Orphan Training School who had wanted sports to play some part in his future. By all measures, Tommy succeeded in his goal to derive every bit of good from his scholarship.

Years later, he told his family that his college years were the most carefree of his life. Traits emerged during those years that defined the man: the handsome jokester who made people laugh; the talented athlete who thrived on competition; the charismatic life of the party who couldn't see that he had a drinking problem. A long-established trait remained constant in the earnest student—to make the best of whatever life handed him.

6

Be Careful What You Wish For
GS⊖ᴅЅᴏL ꟼᴏᴑᴿ ⊖SWJᴏᴑET

1928–36

Tommy and Dorothy left Tahlequah in August 1928 for Tommy to begin his first job as athletic coach and industrial arts teacher at Claremore High School. Sixty miles northwest of Tahlequah, Claremore was close enough for them to stay in touch with friends and for Dorothy to visit her family in Briartown.

She waited until they arrived in Claremore and received confirmation from a doctor to break the news to Tommy that she was pregnant. At first he couldn't believe such good news, but when the reality sank in, it topped his job, his athletic career, and all the accolades he had received. Having a family of his own was far more important to Tommy than the college degree he had feared he might never achieve. He started his new job optimistic about the future, soon to be a father, and grateful for his life, which included a wonderful wife and a job that paid $1,600 a year, or $133 a month for doing what he loved.

Soaring spirits ruled the country as well; daily bull market stories could not be ignored. Tommy had no inclination to buy stocks, however, and told Dorothy as much when she suggested they might buy a few shares for their baby's college fund. Newspaper details of the market were indeed impressive. On the New York Stock Exchange, $577 million in shares were traded in 1927, $920 million the next year. Stock trading seemed to be a national frenzy. A conservative man, Tommy readily summed up his attitude: "That many people throwing that much money around scares me." Abundant oil and a lot of rich people buying automobiles contributed to Oklahoma's equally dynamic economy. Felt not only in Oklahoma City and Tulsa, the boom also touched small towns such as Seminole, Tahlequah, Cushing, and Okmulgee.

Tommy and Dorothy rented a two-bedroom house in Claremore, with the extra bedroom being for the baby. Dorothy seemed even more upbeat than usual as she put their household in order and found a job teaching at a Claremore elementary school. It seemed life couldn't get any better.

His first season as a football coach in 1928 brought success and more accolades in the Claremore and Tahlequah newspapers: "Tommy Thompson Wins Twin V Title First Year as Coach." Fired up, his Zebras came out of nowhere to win the Verdigris Valley Conference Football Championship. His notion that through football he could motivate and teach boys important values had worked. On top of his team's success, the birth of his daughter on January 2, 1929, seemed to validate that, finally in charge of his life, he had made some good choices. As their time in Claremore passed, he more than missed his whiskey, but coming home from work every day to an excited little girl waiting to hug him kept Tommy from acting on his desire to drink. Though Dorothy said nothing, he could tell his abstinence made her very happy.

Tommy remained a teacher and coach at Claremore High School for three years, until the fall of 1931.

The previous three years had delivered catastrophic change. How could an economy that had soared to unpredictable heights be brought to its knees in only thirty-six months? Confounding not just conventional people like the Thompsons, the calamitous events capsized the lives of nearly every American. The first real sign of trouble, stock prices beginning to slide, surfaced in September 1929. Early October produced more big losses, and by the end of the month the market had lost $50 million, 40 percent of the country's leading industrial stocks. News of men out of work, families forced out of their homes, and farms foreclosed on was devastating.

Adding to the misery, the Dust Bowl (as the newspapers named it) seemed to many people to be a sign that God must surely be angry about something. The downward spiral seemed steep and unending. During the next two years, Tommy taught and coached in three Oklahoma public schools: Henryetta, Schulter, and Webb City, the last a tiny town on the southeastern fringe of the massive dust storms. Ten miles from the Kansas border in Osage County, Tommy and Dorothy escaped the nightmarish storms that buried cattle alive, but they did experience choking winds that made even stepping outside dangerous.

Though grateful to have a job, Tommy nevertheless began to feel a vague but growing sense of discontentment. When he finally talked about how he felt to Dorothy, the reason became clear. "When I pictured teaching and coaching, I visualized Cherokees and Choctaws," he said. "Indian kids from any tribe. I don't belong in public schools." His wife's intuitive understanding showed on her face, her response that Indian children were the ones he connected with in his heart. But they decided that with times as bad as they were, he should stay with his job until things got better. Tommy sought relief with whiskey. He could stave off chaotic events and discontentment, but only for so long; then, as though his lapses were dictated by an unidentifiable internal clock, he would give in to the remedy that had yet to fail him.

A measure of hope for the country arrived in March 1933, when Franklin Roosevelt took office. Dorothy and Tommy listened to his inaugural radio address. Roosevelt said, "The only thing we have to fear is fear itself." Dorothy wept during the speech, and the president's words deeply touched Tommy. She declared the president "a saint" and told Tommy she would follow Roosevelt into hell because "that man would figure a way out." The new president moved quickly to rescue the nation, approving the Emergency Banking Act of 1933, which gave the federal government's backing to the banking industry. Next, the Emergency Farm Mortgage Act released $200 million to refinance farmers' mortgages that were about to be foreclosed. A third bill aided in establishing local banks and credit associations. Hope was reborn.

BE CAREFUL WHAT YOU WISH FOR

At the end of the school year, in June 1933, Tommy said that bad times or not, five years in the public school system was enough. Seeing how unhappy he was, Dorothy agreed and said her salary could sustain them for several months. When she gave him her blessing to quit his job, Tommy wasted no time in submitting his application to the Bureau of Indian Affairs (BIA), the agency in charge of all Indian boarding schools. Two months went by with no word from the BIA.

On August 26, their waiting ended. Tommy received his first assignment, as an advisor's assistant at the Pierre Indian School in Pierre, South Dakota. His annual salary of $1,500 was slightly less than at Claremore, but this was what he had wished for. The notice called for Tommy to report immediately and offered a description of his duties.

> 180 boys between the ages of 6 and 18, residing in two dormitories. . . . [You] will be responsible for their health, cleanliness, proper clothing, manners and general conduct, for a constructive program of recreational activities, the supervision and coaching of athletics, and the adjustment of social and personal problems. You must see that their study time is properly planned and advise and assist them in vocational and educational work, handle behavior problems, and assist in developing self-reliance and leadership, and organizing programs of self-government. This position has the help of one matron in the dormitories.

An accompanying letter from John Collier, commissioner of the Bureau of Indian Affairs, gave Tommy some advice and wished him success in his new job:

> My dear Mr. Thompson:
> The position of Boys' Advisor requires a high sense of responsibility, considerable initiative and resourcefulness, and a real interest in the boys' work, in addition to a liberal education and specific training. . . . Since you are familiar

with Indian boarding schools, you know this work is somewhat exacting, which will require residence in the boys' dormitory.
With my very good wishes for success,
John Collier, Commissioner

After Dorothy's initial shock, she handled the move with her usual efficiency. One saving grace was that when she enrolled Jean in kindergarten at Pierre's lone public school, the principal offered her a job. Reminding Tommy that he had gotten exactly what he wished for, Dorothy toured the school with him and acknowledged that he had a big job ahead of him.

A small town, Pierre occupied a site on the east bank of the Missouri River in the approximate center of South Dakota. It was in the middle of the state's Indian reservations: to the northwest was the Cheyenne reservation; downriver about fifty miles was the Crow reservation; the Sioux nation's reservations, home to Oglala, Rosebud, Flandreau, Standing Rock, and Lower Brule Rock tribes, were scattered around the state.

Pierre's Indian school had opened in 1891, and the sight of its weathered building inspired in Tommy a flashback to the Cherokee Orphan Training School—except that here, he could make a difference for Indian children. The 180 Sioux boys in his charge seemed excited to have a new teacher and advisor. They needed help in English and arithmetic—indeed, in most of their subjects. Tommy supervised their study time; he mentored and pushed and encouraged. The need for organized sports became all too obvious, so he formed basketball teams according to age and ability. He soon wished they would conquer their studies with as much enthusiasm as they brought to basketball. Sports accomplished what he hoped, however, for their outlook and participation in their studies immediately improved. His days were long and tiring, the challenge at times frustrating. Living in the boys' dormitory meant rarely being off duty. After a month, an exhausted Tommy sought escape with his reliable bottle of whiskey. It renewed him, at least for a while.

BE CAREFUL WHAT YOU WISH FOR

Dorothy brought home a copy of the *Capital Journal,* Pierre's newspaper, with news she said everyone at school was talking about. Her hero, President Roosevelt, had plans to help the country's Indians. The previous year, he had appointed John Collier as commissioner of the BIA. Collier announced sweeping changes under new legislation called the Indian Reorganization Act. It would repeal the hated Dawes Act, which had split reservation lands into individually owned parcels and ultimately set in motion the destruction of American Indian communal life and culture. Not merely an assault on native culture, the Dawes Act, over its fifty-year existence, also rendered ninety thousand Indians landless and reduced the amount of Indian treaty land by 90 million acres, most of which were eventually sold to non-Indians at bargain prices. The Reorganization Act would allow tribes to incorporate and elect their own leaders. Those that did would become eligible for a revolving credit fund for use by their tribal government. Perhaps Collier's most controversial move was his reversal of the government's policy of assimilation. Maintaining that it had failed miserably across the board, he replaced it with a system he claimed would allow Indians to be part of white society but retain their tribal identity. For Tommy, Collier's changes could not undo the damage that had already been done to Indians, but he credited the man for acknowledging the government's failures and trying to rectify them.

As the temperature dropped and winter's daylight grew shorter, the sun remained hidden for weeks at a time behind leaden skies. Dorothy seemed distant and withdrawn. When Tommy asked what was wrong, she confessed to feeling isolated and homesick. Dorothy rallied during the holidays, but the rally was short lived. At the end of February, Tommy submitted a request for transfer, "effective immediately upon my release from here." But of course no release came; who would want to transfer to South Dakota in the middle of the winter? Joyous news came two months later in April 1934, when they learned Dorothy was pregnant. Her demeanor brightened considerably, which cheered Tommy. And the prospect of a baby on the way restored a measure of his enthusiasm that fatigue and worry had diminished.

On November 22, 1934, five days before Thanksgiving, Tommy rushed Dorothy to St. Mary's Hospital in Pierre. Excited and nervous, he paced the hospital's hall like a coach on the sidelines until the doctor emerged from the delivery room with the news that they had a healthy baby boy. With a beautiful daughter and now a son, he could see his long-time dream of a family coming true. Tommy promised to submit a second request for transfer when school ended and told Dorothy that he had a favorite name if the baby turned out to be a boy; he asked what she thought about "James." They would call him Jimmy in honor of the cousin whose help and friendship had made such a critical difference in Tommy's life. Dorothy agreed but added that James Thomas would be even better.

The difficult school year ended, and Tommy received his transfer, but when the two of them discovered the location, Dorothy's tears broke his heart. They would be going to Wahpeton, North Dakota, in the southeast corner of the state, on the border with Minnesota. Tommy told his wife that the only thing he knew to do was try to make the best of it.

They arrived at Wahpeton in September 1935, finding another old school in a cold place far from home. At thirty-two years old, Tommy had to pass a physical and fill out a required update on his continuing education. Asked what books he had read in the last six months, Tommy listed *Efficiency in Education, The Wholesome Personality,* and *Men and Culture—Are We Civilized.*

After settling into their dormitory apartment, Tommy visited every dorm. Most of the boys, all of them poor and many orphaned, belonged to the Sisseton tribe. Their excitement at having a real coach touched Tommy. Their unbridled enthusiasm for basketball and the smiles it produced helped offset long hours and Tommy's scant time to spend with his wife and children. The grind made it difficult to go an entire month without whiskey, but he held out for a time.

Much as he did with his justification while attending Northeastern that maintaining excellent grades should allow him to indulge in as many sports as he wanted, Tommy began to expand

A loving family of his own. (*Left to right*) Jean, Jimmy, Dorothy, and Tommy Thompson, in Wahpeton, South Dakota, 1935. Permission granted by Jimmy Thompson.

that rationale. If he performed his difficult duties as teacher, coach, and mentor, as well as fulfilling all of the other responsibilities that came with his job, one bottle of whiskey a month seemed reasonable. Dorothy, caught in the era's social mores (which deemed human weaknesses to be private matters), may not have agreed with her husband's justification, but she felt she had no alternative but to accept it.

In September, Tommy received a letter with a June postmark, the envelope having been mistakenly mailed to Pierre Indian School. Tommy's sister Ida wrote that their father, Robert, had passed away on June 16, three months shy of his seventy-fifth birthday. The letter read, "Dad moved in with Virgil and me when his health got real bad a year ago. We buried him next to Momma. Their graves are a stone's throw from his parent's graves. I guess you could say Momma finally got her recognition as a Thompson."

"He's been gone three months and I didn't even know," Tommy told Dorothy. He tried to picture Robert, but his father's memory seemed as distant as the miles that separated them. Ever sensitive to her husband, Dorothy wanted to know how he felt about the news. He answered, "I don't know how I feel." Being responsible for two hundred boys' behavior and education left no time to dwell on Ida's news. His fifteen-hour days, 6:00 A.M. to 9:00 P.M., had few breaks.

With only one dorm matron to help him, Tommy felt overwhelmed but dared not share that feeling with Dorothy. The two of them had no time together, and she was already trying to make the best of a place she clearly did not like. Tommy thought back to their carefree days in Claremore; wished-for or not, this assignment seemed more a test of endurance than a fulfilling job. Only to himself could he admit how much he missed Oklahoma. On a map, the distance didn't look to be that great, but when he gazed out at the North Dakota landscape, the land and children of his vision seemed a million miles away. The bottle of whiskey that previously had never failed to banish sadness and difficult times no longer seemed to work.

BE CAREFUL WHAT YOU WISH FOR

He and Dorothy remained in North Dakota for a full year, until the fall of 1936. Then, like a gift from heaven, he received an assignment that would take them home, to Stilwell, Oklahoma, twenty miles from Tahlequah and a short drive from Briartown, Dorothy's hometown. For Tommy, her smile and tears of relief were as good as the news itself. They found a house to rent in Stilwell. Not waiting for their furniture to arrive, Dorothy left Tommy in charge and drove to Briartown with the children. Seven-year-old Jean saw the grandmother she hadn't seen in three years, and Grandma Fudge got to hold her twenty-month-old grandson for the first time.

Tommy reconnected with his cousin Charlie Scott, Jr., Charlie's wife, Diana, and their son and daughter, who lived in Stilwell. For the first time, Jean and Jimmy had cousins to play with. Once back in Oklahoma, Dorothy blossomed like a wilted flower that had been watered and returned to the sun.

Being field agent for the Five Civilized Tribes gave Tommy regular hours, evenings with his children, and a break from the crushing responsibility he had shouldered for the previous three years. Working out of the Stilwell BIA office, his jurisdiction included Adair, Mayes, and Delaware Counties. It was his job to provide financial assistance, counseling, or both to tribe members and their children. In short, he was to help them in any way he could.

A grateful, happy Tommy Thompson at last was doing what his heart told him to do.

7

Snagged by His Britches
ᎤᏣᏬᏗᏂᏋ ᎤᏎᏋ ᎬᏗ

1939–40

The eastern Oklahoma that Tommy returned to in 1936 was as beautiful as he had remembered. But caught in the grip of the lingering Great Depression, Indian families continued to be decimated by poverty, poor health, and death. Depending on their circumstances and proximity to help, many Indian youngsters languished in deplorable conditions; others got shuffled off to relatives. For Cherokees (indeed, for the majority of Oklahoma families), the difficult times would not end anytime soon.

Children who ended up in one of Oklahoma's Indian boarding schools were the fortunate ones. Some parents, no longer able to care for their children, enrolled them at school. In addition, many children were orphaned and simply had nowhere else to go. Good food, sound sleep in a clean bed, and medical care resulted in better health overall, though the schools did not cure loneliness. Time and friendships helped with that.

By 1939, the BIA's fourteen Indian boarding schools in Oklahoma had become home to 3,500–4,000 Indian children from more than forty different tribes. Well organized and staffed, the boarding schools maintained contact with each other through the *Oklahoma Indian School Magazine,* a statewide publication printed by student apprentices at Chilocco Indian School on the Oklahoma/Kansas border. Student editors from each school contributed news and articles to the monthly magazine.

Most Cherokee students received their education in Oklahoma's public schools, which the government helped support with funds made available by congressional appropriations. In 1933, the ten counties of the Cherokee Nation had a total of 14,224 students in public schools. Students in Indian boarding schools in eastern Oklahoma numbered about 3,000. Ten percent of those (about 300) were at the Sequoyah Orphan Training School in Tahlequah, capital of the Cherokee Nation.

It was at this institution, the largest BIA boarding school in Oklahoma, that the boys of Sequoyah would eventually gather. The winds of change would deliver them, like leaves scattered by a storm, to this unfamiliar place. Eleven-year-old Billy Cameron from Welling, Oklahoma, was the first to arrive; he was the only one whose future was determined by a pair of baggy overalls.

September 5, 1939. Billy Cameron raised his bamboo pole out of the swirling water, removed the wriggling crawdad, and deposited it in his bucket. He already had enough for tonight's supper, but that was hours away, and the water rippling over and around the rocks sang a pleasant song. He put his line in the water and leaned back against the cool concrete beneath the WPA bridge. At quiet times like this, memories of his mother returned.

How he missed her laugh, her mama hen–like energy while in charge of her brood of eight kids. She had assigned chores to the older ones and made sure they attended Hungry Mountain, their tiny one-room schoolhouse built by the Works Progress Administration, the WPA. Every so often, she would ask Nellie Maze, who taught all the grades, how her children were doing. Life had been hard, but he had felt secure then.

Emma Pack Cameron's life had surely been difficult, for their house had no electricity, no well, and no plumbing. Billy and Dave, the oldest boys, had hauled buckets of water for cooking and drinking from a nearby spring. They'd bathed in the creek in summer months but rarely in the winter.

Then his mother got sick—tuberculosis, the doctor said. She died not long after, and everything changed. Unable to work and care for eight children, one of them a six-month-old baby, their father (named Andy) moved himself and his young family in with his parents nearby. Thirteen people, three generations in all, lived in Grandma and Grandpa Cameron's house on his allotment land. Billy's aunt Susie (his mother's sister) and her husband also lived there. Susie's husband helped with the crops and the cattle and sheep they raised. Aunt Susie shared cooking duties with Grandma Cameron and took care of baby Fannie along with Willie, Billy's twin, who had been born crippled.

Grandpa Cameron was an interesting man. He could be found shearing sheep one minute and taking care of sick people the next. A full-blood Cherokee, John Cameron had been a medicine man for all of Billy's eleven years, and a long time before. Some evenings they would sit together on the porch after supper, listening to the whippoorwills' song. Mother earth's music, his grandfather called it. People would show up on a horse or mule or come by wagon to get treated for one ailment or another. His grandfather would take them to the sweat lodge out back and administer heat and herbs, sometimes tobacco, and always a Cherokee blessing. His patients swore that his medicine did the trick. John Cameron was well known in and around Welling.

Being all together was good, but Billy knew life would never be the same. He caught a few more crawdads and then decided he'd fished long enough. Bucket and pole in hand, he climbed the steep embankment and started toward the house, the hot sun stinging his bare shoulders. He followed the worn path toward the house, stepping lively with bare feet on baked-hot dirt. The loud hum of cicadas followed as he crawled under the barbed wire fence and walked alongside the pasture. Their milk cow raised her head and eyed him but kept on chewing. At the end of the day, his father would return with the mules, Kit and Jack, and turn them in with the cow to graze.

Straight ahead, Grandpa's house stood silhouetted against a thick stand of green and gold elms, sycamores, and oak trees. Off to his right Billy spotted bright red tomatoes and long pole beans ready to be picked. Everybody except baby Fannie and Willie had helped plant the garden. Billy paused and cocked his ear at an unfamiliar sound—a car engine. He set down his bucket and pole and stepped off the hot dirt onto dry weeds. People around Welling walked or went by wagon or rode a horse or mule where they needed to go. Nobody owned an automobile. Squinting into the late afternoon sun, he saw a shiny black car pull up in front of the house and stop in a cloud of red dust. Caution raised the hair on the back of his neck. That wasn't somebody needing a Cherokee medicine man, he realized. *Something must be wrong.*

A man got out of the car and, glancing Billy's way, motioned for him to come. *Sure as hell something's wrong.* Billy spun around and took off running back along the path toward the creek. "Billyeee, wait," the man hollered, but Billy didn't slow. The sound of hard-soled shoes pounding on baked earth told him the man was coming after him. Heart hammering, he didn't look back. He figured that as soon as he made it under the barbed wire fence, the man would never catch him. Reaching the fence, he dived under the bottom wire and wiggled forward on his belly in the hollowed-out ground as he'd done a hundred times before. Certain he had made it, Billy started to rise, but he moved too soon: the back of his britches caught on a barb. He pulled and tugged, trying to rip loose, but the barb held firm. Stuck flat on his belly, Billy looked back. Not far behind, the man had slowed to a walk. Two dusty black shoes approached and, at his eye level, stopped next to him.

The man reached down. Billy felt his britches freed from the barb. Holding onto the back straps of his overalls, the man helped him to his feet. "Come on, son. Let's go back to the house. No reason to be afraid." They walked in silence. The man paused once for Billy to pick up his fishing pole and bucket. Billy considered swinging the bucket at the man's knees, but the grip on his overalls felt too tight; the stranger might not let go.

The man guided him up the steps and across the wood porch. He knocked on the door frame with his free hand and nodded for Billy to put down his bucket and pole. Through the screen, Billy watched his aunt approach, with baby Fannie balanced on her hip. Susie told them to come in. The man gave his name, Floyd something-or-other, and said he was a field agent from the Tahlequah office of the BIA. Billy's heart sunk as his aunt nodded. *She knew he was coming to get me. Why? What did I do?* Billy stared hard at her, beseeching with his eyes what he could not say aloud. *Don't let this stranger take me away.*

Billy's twin, Willie, glanced up from his spot at a table in the corner where he was playing solitaire. He stared open-mouthed, looking as shocked as Billy felt. Susie asked the agent whether Willie could also go to school. He shook his head and told her, "We don't have provisions for crippled children." She then mentioned Dave, the oldest, but said he wasn't home.

"I'll talk to the school about him and the other children." The agent placed a paper on the table and handed Susie a pencil.

She shifted the baby to her other hip, marked her X at the bottom of the paper, then straightened and turned to Billy. In Cherokee, she said, "You must learn English, Billy, and get an education. Education is important." Her expression betrayed little emotion, but the catch in her voice asked him to understand. Aunt Susie embraced him. Caught between them, baby Fannie protested. Billy breathed in her baby scent as Susie pulled away.

The agent took hold of the back of his overalls and led him outside. Tucked into the front seat of the big black car, Billy watched as the agent pushed down the lock before closing the door and starting the car. *I'm done for,* he thought, as he stared at his aunt through the screen. She raised Fannie's hand in a wave as the agent drove away. Billy craned his neck and caught a final glance of his grandfather's house. Fear and dread the size of a baseball were solidly planted in his stomach.

Afraid to move, he saw the familiar landscape race past and wished he knew where they were going and whether he would ever come back to Welling. Autumn's tinge on the trees reminded him how much he looked forward to the cooler evenings that October would bring. His grumbling stomach made him think of the corn and pole beans and okra his aunt would cook and he wouldn't get to eat. Billy wondered whether he would ever see his brothers and sisters again, but that and all his other questions went unspoken. He could feel the agent staring at him.

At last the man said, "Sequoyah is really nice, Billy, so don't be afraid. It's a big school, but you'll get used to it. The food is really good. Actually, those cooks make the best fried chicken and corn bread I ever had. And the pumpkin pie they make for Thanksgiving and Christmas is as good as my mother's." The agent smiled as though tasting it.

They didn't drive very long, but distracted by the thought of a big piece of pumpkin pie, Billy was surprised when they turned into the school grounds. Alongside the entrance road were white-painted boulders arranged to spell SOTS. "Sequoyah Orphan Training School," the agent explained. Billy gaped at all the buildings—so many that he couldn't count them all at one glance. The agent pointed to a three-story brick building surrounded by towering trees casting elongated fingers of shade over the grass.

"That's Cherokee Hall, the big girls' dorm. And see that one?" He pointed to a two-story white building. "Next month when you turn twelve you'll move in there, but for now you'll be in Home One, the little boys' dorm."

Billy knew why the agent knew his birthday and exactly how old he was. Aunt Susie had told the stranger everything he needed to know.

"Do I need to hold onto you?" the agent asked as he unlocked the door. Billy shook his head and followed him into a brick building and up a flight of stairs. "Registration office," the agent said. He answered the clerk's questions, signed several papers, then stepped back and offered Billy his hand. "It's going to be okay, Billy. Your aunt wanted you to get an education. You'll get a good one here." Billy shook the agent's outstretched hand and watched as the last link to his family disappeared down the stairs.

More painful than his fear and grumbling stomach was Billy's growing sense of betrayal. Why had no one—not Aunt Susie, not his father or grandfather—told him about someone coming to take him to boarding school? And except for his aunt's brief hug, none of his family even said goodbye. The more he thought about it, the madder he became. This morning his father had hitched Kit and Jack to the wagon and left to work on the WPA road near Welling. He had driven off with a wave, no sign that he wouldn't see his son until . . . until when?

Maybe never, Billy thought, fighting back angry tears.

A boy in uniform walked up and motioned for Billy to follow. He led Billy to a big room with a line of tall stalls along one wall. The next thing Billy knew, he was standing naked in a stall with water raining down over him. The boy handed him a bar of soap and, in Cherokee, told him to scrub up, including his hair. As soon as he finished, the same boy handed him a towel. Billy wrapped it around his waist and followed the uniformed boy into another room with bins filled with clothes lining one wall.

A lady looked him up and down. "Mister Cameron?" It sounded like a question, so he nodded. "All right, then." She gathered clothes from the bins. "These look like they should fit," she said and handed him a pair of trousers, a shirt, a belt, shoes and socks, and some thin white short pants. Billy held them up, not sure what they were. His Cherokee guide pulled down the waistband of his trousers and in Cherokee said, "They go on first."

He led Billy to a dressing room. The trousers were too big around the waist. He tucked the tail of his shirt inside the pants and hitched the belt as tight as it would go. The stiff black high-top shoes chafed feet that hadn't worn shoes all summer.

Returning to the room, Billy was directed to a table covered with white paper. The clothes lady, standing behind it, said, "This won't take a minute. We're going to check for lice. Please bend forward and place your cheek on the paper." Billy silently complied and felt a comb against his scalp, then gentle tugs as she slowly combed through his shoulder-length hair. "Three," she said. Billy heard the rasp of pencil against paper. "You may straighten up now." The lady motioned to a tall chair a few feet away.

A second uniformed boy draped a cloth around him and, with silent concentration, cut his hair. When the boy finished, Billy glanced down at the floor, now covered with clumps of black hair. He felt his head; the boy had cut off his hair all the way to his scalp! Tears stung. He wanted to jump down and run away, wanted to hear his family tell him they were sorry for what they had done. But there was no place to run.

"The worst is over, Billy," the lady said.

The barber removed the drape, and Billy slipped down from the chair.

"Now you get to see your new home. I'm sure you're going to like it here." Speaking English as she walked, the lady mentioned the names of boys he would soon meet. He understood most of what she said, but he was so hungry that all he could think about was his bucket of crawdads. About now, Susie would be frying his catch in bacon grease and would serve it with plenty of taters and greens from the garden. The image of his family gathered around the long supper table brought tears, but he gritted his teeth and fought them back. *Do they wonder how I'm doing? Do they care?* Too proud to say anything, Billy did not tell the white lady he hadn't eaten since morning.

She would not see Billy Cameron cry.

Tears came later after lights out, when Billy lay in his bed in the third-floor room that the agent and white lady had kept calling his new home. The agent had described it right: there were a dozen or more beds with a boy about his age in each one. A few acknowledged him, but the lady had turned off the lights and said there was to be no talking. Billy lay on his bed, loneliness gripping his chest, making it hard to breathe. Hearing a noise, he raised up on his elbows. It wasn't whippoorwills singing mother earth's music. Billy lay back down, too hungry and exhausted to figure out why—but the sound of somebody else crying made him feel not nearly so alone.

January 1940, Claremore, Oklahoma. Seven-year-old Everett Nave took one last look at their log cabin out the back window of his uncle's car. Snow dusted the cabin's low roof, and smoke curled out the chimney from a fire meant to make sure the place would be warm when his mother and little brother returned.

Beside Everett in the back seat, his younger half-brother, Jimmy Ollis, sat uncharacteristically still and quiet. In the front passenger seat, his mother and her brother were talking softly in Cherokee; his uncle was agreeing that this was the best thing for Everett. Straining to hear, Everett was quite sure that leaving his mother and Jimmy and getting shipped off to boarding school wasn't at all the best thing.

After breakfast, his mother had sat him down and haltingly explained that she would be taking him to a nice boarding school. "I've tried but times are so hard I can't take care of you the way I want to. You need clothes and shoes and I want you to have a better life than this." She gestured at the tiny cabin. "You're seven now. You need an education."

Everett only half listened, for he was trying to think how he could convince her that he didn't need or want an education if he had to go away to get it. But his mother was already crying, so all he asked was where she was taking him. "Sequoyah Orphan Training School," she said.

Everett wanted to remind her that he was not an orphan, so he didn't belong in a school for orphans. He had a father; his father just wasn't around anymore. But he didn't tell her this, because the few times he'd asked about his father, his mother had become very sad. She told Everett that when they'd divorced, his father had taken his older brother and sister but had left him because he was a baby. Until she mentioned a brother and sister, Everett had forgotten them. His mother had married again and had given birth to Jimmy, but that marriage hadn't lasted either. Everett couldn't picture either of her husbands.

His mother and uncle didn't say much during the rest of the ride. When his uncle stopped the car in front of a big brick building, little Jimmy started to get out. "No, son, you have to stay here," his mother said in Cherokee. "Tell your brother goodbye." Jimmy began to cry. Everett hugged him and his uncle, then got out of the car. Several boys were trying to play kick ball on snow-covered ground, but mostly they were slipping and falling and laughing.

On the other side of the walk, boys and girls his age were building a snowman. *They look like they're having fun,* Everett thought, and for a moment curiosity replaced his fear.

His mother registered Everett, then kissed him goodbye. Following instructions, he took a shower, got dressed in the new clothes and shoes they gave him, and had a lice check and haircut. When they told him he was all finished, he followed his dorm matron to the second floor of Home One, which she called the little boys' dorm. Long and wide, the room was twice the size of his cabin home. A dozen beds lined each wall, and a central aisle ran the full length of the room. Two beds over, a boy who looked about his age glanced up and silently watched as the matron showed Everett how the bed had to be made. After she told Everett that the boys' washroom was "just down the hall," she left, promising to be back in a few minutes.

The boy who had been watching approached. "*Osiyo*" (hello), he said in Cherokee. He said his name was George Cameron. "I got here two or three weeks ago. Did the agent bring you in a big black car?"

"My uncle and momma brought me," Everett answered in Cherokee. "She said she couldn't take care of me anymore."

"Well, at least she told you. Me n' my sister found out when the agent showed up. Same thing happened to my brother, Billy."

For having been there such a short time, George knew how things worked. He said the dorm matron did a bed check at 9:00 P.M., and every Sunday the cooks served fried chicken with gravy and biscuits—"All you can eat." George told Everett he might as well get used to lining up for everything. As they spoke in Cherokee, George kept glancing at the door. "Don't talk Cherokee in front of a teacher or matron. We're supposed to learn English for when we graduate. If you be respectful to the matron and say 'yes, ma'am, no ma'am,' she's real nice." George suddenly looked very serious. "But, no matter what, don't go snitchin' on anybody. For anything." His raised eyebrows showed he meant business. George said he was full blood and either six or seven years old. "That'll make me seven or eight on July nineteenth. That's my birthday."

"I'm full blood, too, and I know I'm gonna be eight on May thirteenth, so I'm older n' you," Everett said.

George grinned. "That don't make you any smarter."

"We'll see about that." Everett's fear edged aside.

8

Letting Go

ᏛᎬᏋᏗᎴ

1941

Dorothy stood, hands clasped, as Tommy slit open the envelope from the Department of Interior. He dreaded getting a new assignment. They had been in Stilwell for five years, long enough to put down roots and time enough to appreciate being close to family. He read the letter aloud. "Thomas F. Thompson, effective April 1, 1941 you have been recommended for classified service under Section 3, Executive Order No. 7916, Grade 10, annual salary $2,300, as Education Field Agent at the Tahlequah agency of the Five Civilized Tribes."

"Tahlequah?" Dorothy exclaimed, palms flying to her face.

"I can't believe it, either," Tommy said. "Do you realize we've been gone thirteen years? Just the thought of Tahlequah brings back a lot of memories." He did not elaborate, because not all of them were good memories: Cherokee Orphan Training School, an uncaring father as elusive as smoke, and a sister who had died far too young, to name a few.

Tommy glanced at his wife as she took the letter from his hand. She said, "You don't have to say a word. I know what you're thinking, and the only way you're going to get rid of bad feelings is to face them. First of all, Ida said Sequoyah is nothing like COTS. That place is gone and you need to let it go. Your father, too—we'll go to the cemetery so you can say goodbye. And your sister Susie, you did everything possible you could for her. I'm sure she knew how much you loved her." Dorothy stared at him with complete understanding as she verbalized feelings he hesitated to express. Amazed, he had no idea what to say. Her intuition, her strength, and all the other qualities he'd seen in the college girl who didn't think she was pretty still humbled him. She was excited enough for both of them, which dispelled some of Tommy's doubts.

They found a six-room house on State Street to rent; it had a big backyard and giant sycamores out front that shaded the porch. The BIA shipped their furniture, and Tommy went to work while Dorothy put the house in order. She enrolled twelve-year-old Jean in Bagley Junior High and seven-year-old Jimmy in Bagley Elementary. Before April ended, she secured a teaching job to start in the fall at a country school not far from town.

Tommy's second assignment as educational field agent called for him to work out of the BIA's basement office in downtown Tahlequah. He spent his days driving the back roads of Cherokee County, his job being "to aid and assist any and all Indians within your jurisdiction that belong to a Federally-recognized tribe." As he'd done in Stilwell, he lugged around a horsehide briefcase, the equivalent of a walking bureau office, loaded with government forms, a checkbook, and a ton of responsibility.

During his first week on the job, Tommy wrote a check to cover food and medicine for a Choctaw family with five children under six years of age. They had oil money due them but no idea how to apply for it. He spread the application papers on the hood of his car, filled them out and had the couple sign them, then took the forms back to his office to mail. The husband could not find a job. A handshake sealed the man's promise that he would take vocational classes to learn a trade. The agency would help him with the cost, and Tommy promised to help him with the enrollment process.

The job meant close contact with families, many of them isolated and poor and caught in a changing world they were ill prepared to handle. They lacked the basics of food, medicine, and clothes that would allow their children to attend school. Others needed financial advice or family counseling—often both. Need never failed to outstrip the resources he could offer. Sometimes on a weekend when he found it impossible to block out the image of a young mother devoid of hope or a father stripped of dignity because he could not find work, Tommy would find a quiet place away from home, away from everybody. Parked in his car, he would drink one bottle and then sleep. The next morning he would return home, ready once again to make the best of whatever life handed him. Dorothy did not complain about his drinking. She never mentioned it at all.

During their five years in Stilwell, Tommy and Dorothy had driven to Tahlequah several times for short visits to friends or to attend a BIA function, and the changes in the town had gone all but unnoticed. When they moved back in 1941, the changes came as a shock. The town had more than three thousand people. Streets that used to be dirt were paved. Homes outside the city had electricity and telephones, consisting of eight party lines that connected families to each other and the outside world. Hinds Grocery got one of the first and shortest phone numbers, *3;* the hardware store number was *183.*

A new National Guard armory and U.S. post office graced downtown. The W. W. Hastings Indian Hospital was only three years old. The biggest shock was that Tahlequah had turned into a tourist town, full of fishermen and whole families of vacationers crowding the streets and campgrounds. The Flood Control Act passed by Congress in 1938 had created a system of reservoirs on the Illinois River and opened access to beautiful Lake Tenkiller. Downtown bustled with shoppers.

Tommy's hometown now sported a big-city-style Safeway with big-city prices. Two pounds of Folger's coffee cost 22 cents; a pound of bacon, 17 cents; ten pounds of sugar, 49 cents; and a family-size box of Oxydol laundry soap, 19 cents. Long-time McCollum's Grocery prices were cheaper. At Hinds Mercantile, where everyone in Tahlequah shopped, a lady's pretty spring coat cost anywhere from $1.98 to $10.75.

But progress had also taken its toll. Landmarks that Tommy thought would always be there had either been abandoned or disappeared altogether. After the railroad discontinued its service to Tahlequah, the company abandoned the brick depot. Though it was currently forlorn and deserted, the depot had once served as an important connection to the outside world. World War I soldiers had departed from and returned to the depot. People had gathered there to hear politicians deliver speeches from the back of a train. Tahlequah's citizens, city and country folk alike, had bade hello and goodbye to loved ones—such as his sister. Susie Thompson had arrived at the depot from Missouri and a few days later had left with Eloise for Phoenix. Tommy could not pass the empty building without thinking of her.

Something else he missed was the old oak tree that had dominated Courthouse Square in the center of town for a hundred years. There were lots of new smaller trees, but Courthouse Square looked barren without the ancient towering oak. Tommy learned that it had died and was removed in 1938, exactly one hundred years after the Trail of Tears began. Cherokee chiefs had given speeches in the shade of that oak. Chief John Ross was known to have sat and talked with tribe members under its branches.

Alden Dryer of the *Tahlequah Daily Press* reported that in the days when Tahlequah was Indian Territory, cowboys riding into town thought it sport to put a slug in the tree, no doubt hastening its demise. When city fathers had the oak cut down, they found nearly twenty pounds of lead and thousands of tacks. Businessman M. E. Franklin later turned the lead into gavels and sold them as souvenirs.

On his days off, Tommy sought out fishing spots he remembered. He knew himself to be a restless man with seemingly endless energy, so the fact that he could enjoy sitting alongside a lake or riverbank long enough for a fish to bite seemed a contradiction even to him. He encouraged his family to join him, but (always a coach) he stressed "the fundamentals of fishing correctly." When he caught Dorothy and Jean baiting their hooks with watermelon rind, Tommy declared it the equivalent of fouling out. He drove them home and returned to fish with Jimmy, who Tommy said at least understood and honored the ground rules of the sport.

Tommy and his family could see free movies anytime at his cousin's theaters. Young Jimmy begged to see every new western that came to town; his second love was riding the pinto mare that belonged to his Aunt Ida and Uncle Virgil. Jimmy inherited his father's love of sports, and Tommy was generous with his time, causing Jimmy to say that he had "the best baseball coach in Oklahoma." Tommy taught his son how to hit, bunt, and catch, essentials that even at the tender age of seven Jimmy had no trouble incorporating.

Sports often brought the Thompson family together around the radio. A special event such as a Joe Louis boxing match or a football game involving Nebraska, Kentucky, or Oklahoma meant that Tommy would insist that they gather around their large Philco. In June 1941, the "Brown Bomber," Joe Louis, defended his heavyweight title against an Irish fighter named Billy Conn. For twelve rounds Tommy listened, totally absorbed, shushing questions and observations as the announcer's running commentary had Conn ahead in points. When, in the thirteenth round, Louis ended the fight with a stunning knockout, Tommy was on the edge of his chair feigning imaginary punches and hollering for his idol.

Joe DiMaggio was another of his heroes. Tommy admired athletic achievement, and no one had come close to DiMaggio's record fifty-six-game hitting streak. In July 1941, when DiMaggio and the Yanks played in Cleveland, Tommy told Dorothy to get out the popcorn and gather the kids because they just might hear history made. Jimmy remembers his father's disappointment that the streak ended that night, but it didn't lessen his admiration for DiMaggio.

Late in August 1941, Dorothy reminded Tommy that he had put off visiting his parents' gravesites long enough. She bought flowers and insisted that they go on Sunday afternoon. An unmerciful midday sun beat down as Tommy, with Dorothy by his side, laid the flowers at the foot of granite headstones. One was etched with the words "Rose Gritts Thompson, July 18, 1867–March 23, 1911" and beside it "Robert J. Thompson, October 29,

1860–June 16, 1935." Two dates carved in granite appeared under each name: the day they entered the world and the day they left it. In between was a line so tiny that it was hardly noticeable, yet it represented the sum of their life.

His mother was thirty years old when her first child was born and forty-four when she died. She left behind five children, the youngest not quite four. Tommy lamented that his mother had never realized a happy marriage such as the one he had. Nor had she ever had the respect of the husband whom, at some time in her life, she must have loved. What kind of life, Tommy wondered, would the family have shared had Robert Thompson treasured his wife and children?

Tommy would never know the answer, but he realized Dorothy was right. It was time he let go.

Dorothy knelt beside him, her arm tight around him as he released tears held too long. He expressed aloud his love for his mother, then told his father goodbye and rest in peace. Tommy wiped his eyes and gripped Dorothy's hand as he got to his feet. She praised him for letting go of memories that had haunted him far too long.

Dorothy and Tommy's children speak of their parents' unwavering devotion to each other. He was the love of her life, and she of his. She was his anchor, supportive of whatever he undertook and so attuned to him that she could verbalize what he was thinking before it came out of his mouth. Even his drinking she seemed to understand. Tommy readily admitted that her acceptance and unwavering faith in him were the stabilizing forces in his life. "I would be devastated without Dorothy," he told family and friends.

Tommy had also put off visiting Sequoyah since their arrival in April, but Dorothy kept reminding him that it needed to be done. On Labor Day in 1941, she told him that this would be her last opportunity to go with him before she started her teaching job. Tommy, recognizing that his wife would not let him ignore her, agreed to go.

He was surprised at what he found.

LETTING GO

The campus he saw was unrecognizable from the one he remembered. There were thirty or forty buildings instead of one, and towering trees everywhere cast inviting shade from the hot September sun. Formerly weed-covered grounds were green; the grass was mowed and neatly trimmed around each tree and along the walks. As the two of them strolled the campus, somewhere out of sight a tractor could be heard. And from another direction came the sounds of children laughing and playing.

They came across a gymnasium that looked new. "This, I've got to see," Tommy said. He led Dorothy inside. They sat down on sideline bleachers so he could watch a group of boys playing basketball. Laughing and teasing each other, the boys missed more shots than they made.

Dorothy nudged him. "What are you thinking?"

"That they're having fun and that tallest kid isn't setting his feet before he shoots."

She laughed. "We came for a tour, not for you to coach."

They exited the building through a different door, and Tommy had another surprise. Dirt paths that had traversed the campus were now concrete sidewalks that outlined flowerbeds full of blossoming plants. Dorothy remarked that she didn't see any weeds. Everywhere Tommy looked, the grounds and the buildings had the appearance that somebody really cared; the sight made his spirits soar. COTS no longer existed.

They toured Home One (the little boys' dorm) and Unit B (home to tenth- and eleventh-grade boys). Tommy introduced himself to four teenagers and visited with them about classes and sports. They liked being at Sequoyah, and all of them played on the Indians' basketball and football teams. Studying each face, Tommy found no sign of the pain he remembered feeling as a student. They asked whether he had played basketball or football when he was young. Tommy answered that he had and that he still had his letterman's jacket from Northeastern.

Tommy and Dorothy peeked into an empty classroom that smelled of new paint, the walls' bright colors covered with students' art, writing, and poetry. "Sequoyah is nothing like the school I went to," Tommy said.

Exiting the building, he recognized Superintendent Jack Brown walking toward them. Mr. Brown's picture appeared regularly in the newspaper. He smiled as he approached. "My goodness, Tommy Thompson. I am glad to finally meet you." Mr. Brown offered his hand.

Surprised at being recognized, Tommy shook his hand. "I'm sorry, Mr. Brown. I should have come to the office and introduced myself."

"Only so we could have visited," Brown said. He greeted Dorothy, then asked, "Well, Tommy, what do you think of your old school?"

Doubly surprised that Brown knew he had attended COTS, Tommy answered honestly. "It may occupy the same ground, but it bears no resemblance to the school I went to. What you've done must have taken years. Everything is better—the buildings, the grounds, the classrooms. It's easy to see what caring accomplishes."

Mr. Brown smiled. "Well, thank you. Coming from a former student, that is doubly nice to hear. You know, I am also a product of Indian schools. I remember the old days all too well. You're right, it's been a long road to get this far, but I would like you to come for a personal tour. We'll have lunch in the cafeteria. I believe you'll even find the food has improved."

Tommy chuckled. "I appreciate the invitation, sir, and you can bet I will." Jack Brown bade them goodbye and continued on toward Cherokee Hall. Tommy squeezed Dorothy's hand as they watched him walk away. "I am so glad you made me do this. You saw those boys. They looked and sounded as happy as our own kids."

Seeing firsthand the transformation that Jack Brown had accomplished deeply touched Tommy. The harsh school he remembered had disappeared, and with it his memories of five difficult years. Awed by the vision and leadership of one determined man, Tommy added Jack Brown to his list of heroes, the only person on it not involved in sports.

9

Small, Medium, Large—
Heroes Come in All Sizes

ᎤᏍᏗ, ᎠᏰᏟ ᎡᏆ, ᎤᏪᎾ, ᏂᎦᏛᎴ ᏧᎾᎴᎤᏞ ᏂᎵᏗᏢᎢ

1941

In 1941 when Tommy and Jack Brown met for the first time, Brown had been superintendent of Sequoyah for seventeen years, having arrived four years after Tommy graduated. Intelligent, scholarly, and pragmatic, the half-Cherokee Brown prudently waited until he graduated from the Cherokee Male Seminary (a college in Tahlequah) and secured a teaching job before he asked schoolteacher Nola LeFlore to marry him.

Nola came from a prestigious Indian family. She was the great-granddaughter of Chief Greenwood LeFlore, the half-Choctaw/half-French statesman and diplomat who negotiated the 1830 Dancing Rabbit Treaty with representatives of President Andrew Jackson. The treaty ceded 11 million acres belonging to the Choctaws to the government in exchange for 15 million acres in Indian Territory and paved the way for the removal of the Choctaws from their traditional homeland.

Even as a youngster, Jack Brown knew that English held the key for him to succeed in the world. At six years of age on his first day of school, he stormed out of the one-room log cabin schoolhouse in a huff and walked barefoot the mile and a half home. When his mother asked why he had done such a thing, young Jack replied that the teacher taught in Cherokee and not one other child spoke English. So determined was he to become expert in English that the following year, at seven years old, Jack went to live with an aunt to attend a school of his liking.

Thirty years later—fifteen of them spent as a teacher and a principal at rural Oklahoma schools—Brown took over leadership of COTS in 1924. He made it known from that moment that any school under his direction would be as happy and homelike a place as he could make it. Visionary and sensitive, Brown launched into his plan to make COTS the institution he believed it should be. Bringing about change to the system he had inherited required just such a man as Brown, who had foresight, energy, and unwavering determination.

Establishing the Cherokee Orphan Asylum in 1872, the Cherokee Nation welcomed 150 students. An addition two years later brought 200 more, many of them orphaned during the Civil War. The school's goal was not only to educate Cherokee children but also to be their home, with faculty and administration supplying a parent's guidance to help and encourage students to make wise choices about their future.

The school went by several names and experienced various temporary locations before a permanent building was built in Salina, Oklahoma. When a fire destroyed that structure in 1903, the Cherokee Nation built a new facility in Tahlequah, on forty acres that had formerly been owned by Dr. Lewis Ross, nephew of former chief John Ross. More than one hundred years later, after several more name changes that marked an expanded focus and mission, the institution still occupies the same property:

1872–1914	Cherokee Orphan Asylum (COA): operated by the tribe
1914–1925	Cherokee Orphan Training School (COTS): operated by the Department of the Interior
1925–1945	Sequoyah Orphan Training School (SOTS)
1945–1964	Sequoyah Vocational School (SVS)
1964–1985	Sequoyah High School (SHS): operated by the BIA
1985–present	Sequoyah High School (SHS): operated by the Cherokee Nation

In 1924, the same year that Brown became the superintendent of COTS, Congress passed a law that officially made all Indians in the country citizens of the United States. The hubbub created by this congressional act brought national attention to the issue of Indian education and a public outcry that government was shirking its duty. Though the Department of the Interior had built fourteen Indian boarding schools in Oklahoma in the late 1800s, the public perceived the goal of these schools more as supplying shelter and food and making sure children became self-sufficient; education seemed to take a back seat.

Historical records reveal that the first superintendent, W. A. Duncan, served twelve years and "was revered as a father figure," as was Reverend J. F. Thompson, who held the position for the next sixteen years. The earliest records suggest that the school was innocent of the kind of abuses attributed to many boarding schools of the era. An individual well versed in Sequoyah history is Cecil Shipp, holder of a master's degree in education. He has a twenty-one-year connection with Sequoyah, having spent eleven years there as a student and another ten as teacher, coach, counselor, and principal. When asked about abuse, Shipp said, "There's never been any evidence of abuse at Sequoyah, but if there were, it would probably have been a paddling for some sort of infraction. Cherokee parents were strict—they wanted their kids to behave, and if they didn't they wanted us [teachers or administrators] to 'whupp 'em good.'" Shipp maintains that teachers received constant reminders to use appropriate language and avoid any unsuitable contact with their students. Jack Brown's arrival in 1924 brought strong leadership and reemphasized the rules of conduct for teachers and employees.

In 1925, one year after Brown arrived, Cherokee Orphan Training School became Sequoyah Orphan Training School, named in honor of the famous half-Cherokee who had invented the Cherokee syllabary. To the lone campus building of Tommy's time, a new dining hall had been added, as well as Cherokee Hall, the big girls' dorm. In 1930, Congress allocated even more funds to add new buildings and replace old ones.

With a decision that would forever label Jack Brown as frugal, he personally presided over ten years of construction of the multitude of new buildings to ensure that not one dime of the funds was squandered. He made daily checks on classrooms under construction, on the auto and industrial shops, on the home economics building, the gymnasium, the steam plant, the pottery house, and the laundry building. He kept close tabs on construction of a new dormitory for on-duty employees and of cottages for teachers and advisors and their families. He oversaw the completion of a campus hospital and hired a full-time nurse and assistant. He hired Dr. Allison, a local physician, to work two or three days a week administering to sick and injured children.

The Cherokees originally patterned their school on a military academy curriculum, which included the three Rs and practical training. This meant that elementary-age children attended class six hours a day and the rest of the day was devoted to study, play, and assigned chores. Brown's certainty that responsibility and pride in accomplishment could be taught, regardless of age, led to all students having some kind of job: cleaning their room, sweeping the stairs or the sidewalk in front of their building, gathering eggs, or picking vegetables from the garden.

High school–age boys and girls attended classes three hours a day, which was scant class time to absorb the complexities of algebra, geometry, biology, and general science. Homework assignments were meant to offset brief class time in those subjects. Believing that English should be the top priority, Jack Brown made sure his teachers drove home the basics of composition, grammar, spelling, and punctuation. He also emphasized literature, and students studied the likes of Shakespeare and Edgar Allen Poe. They read and recited classics in poetry. Sequoyah offered chemistry to seniors as an elective, but with minimal class time, only a few could achieve more than a basic introduction to the subject. In music, however—through the efforts of an outstanding dedicated teacher who chose to spend her entire career at Sequoyah, Miss Portia Vaughn—students had an abundance of choices of study in all types of music.

High school–age youngsters spent their other three hours a day doing vocational training. They interned in a variety of jobs on campus; each internship lasted nine weeks, then the student moved on to a new one. Boys learned farming, from planting to harvest, animal husbandry, and the fundamentals of mechanics. Girls interned in all aspects of homemaking, working alongside school cooks in preparing meals as well as canning and preserving fruits and vegetables from the school's enormous garden. General health education included basic hygiene instruction from the nurse in charge of the campus hospital. Home economics classes taught girls to sew, embroider, crochet, and knit. They made dresses, skirts, and blouses for themselves as well as tablecloths and curtains needed by the school.

Readily admitting that he became a scholar "in spite of the system rather than as a result of it," Brown set out to expand the institution's original goal of "preparing Indian children to survive the vicissitudes of life." He wanted them to thrive, not merely survive, in the world outside the Cherokee Nation. In his vision, successful children needed exposure to and the opportunity to use social skills in the outside world that awaited them after graduation. He encouraged attendance in academic, social, and religious organizations already in existence and promoted the formation of new ones. He endorsed the expansion and improvement of Sequoyah's participation in a full range of sports.

On a personal level, he had great empathy for students trying to adjust to institutional living while still grieving over the death of a parent. Aware of the limitations of a large school to deal with a loss of that magnitude, Brown reemphasized the Cherokees' original model of hiring teachers, staff, and employees who not only were qualified to do their job but also would give a parent's advice. He wanted good teachers, but he wanted them to be interested, caring men and women who would help children make wise decisions about their future.

While accomplishing his job to house, feed, educate, socialize, and care for the needs of 350–75 students, Brown also had to adhere to the BIA's requirement that his school be entirely self-sufficient. Sequoyah's vocational program held the key, with student internships supplying the labor that made it possible. Boys, under the supervision of a teacher, helped raise and slaughter the school's cattle and hogs. They froze enough meat with ice from the school's ice plant to supply beef and pork through the winter. They made soap from rendered hog fat; they planted and harvested sugarcane and sweet corn for eating and canning. Boys took part in growing grain and preparing silage, stored in campus silos to provide winter feed for the school's herds.

Boys and girls planted and weeded a huge garden that supplied fresh vegetables in season plus enough to preserve for the winter. What summer fruits the school did not grow in sufficient quantity to serve and preserve were bought from local farmers, with Sequoyah boys doing the picking. A school bus transported them to and from the orchards around Tahlequah. In the fall, they picked apples for the cooks to make applesauce and cobblers from, with the remainder stored in the school's large root cellar.

Processing crops grown on campus supplied the kitchen with canned sweet corn, sorghum syrup, and a host of other basic staples. With supervised student help, the bakery turned out hundreds of loaves of bread every other day and also made corn bread, an Oklahoma favorite. In addition to the other livestock, the school had sufficient chickens to supply meat and eggs year round. The dairy produced milk, cream, butter, and even ice cream.

Sequoyah's pump house and extensive water system supplied drinking water to campus buildings and watered landscaped grounds. Sheets and pillowcases for more than 400 beds, plus towels and the children's clothes, were washed in the school's laundry building. The steam plant, which generated heat from coal the school purchased, heated thousands of square feet of classrooms, dorms, and offices. In short, Sequoyah produced within its own borders (with much of the labor being supplied by students) almost everything that was grown, processed, consumed, or necessary in the operation of a school with a student body of 350 and a staff of 50 employees.

Surprisingly, amid this intricate and constantly shifting system of supply and demand, Sequoyah's administrators, staff, teachers, and other employees took time to counsel and mentor students and to act as sponsors for classes and clubs. They helped plan and chaperone proms, Friday night dances, and weekly movies. The school had a choir, an orchestra, and a swing band. There was a Christmas party—complete with Santa Claus, presents, and treats—for the student body, administrators, teachers, staff, and other employees.

Students in the upper grades were privy to the full high school experience. They published a yearbook and staged an elaborate all-school pageant. They had class rings, debating contests, 4-H projects, and Boy Scout and Girl Scout troop activities, not to mention a full schedule of football, baseball, basketball, and track events. Graduations were elaborate, as were proms, in which the girls donned formal gowns and the boys wore their government-issued suits and ties. Every year they elected a queen and king for the prom and homecoming game. Romances blossomed; students paired off to go to dances, movies, and football games. Other girls and boys met and dated students from Tahlequah High.

The abundant information written about Jack Brown makes clear that Sequoyah was his life. A devout Christian, he considered church mandatory and made it so for his students. He invited pastors from churches in Tahlequah to conduct the service, and he would use the last fifteen minutes to deliver his own sermon, which was more often about right and wrong and the importance of being a good person than about God.

A stickler for order and routine, he delegated with authority and left no room for misunderstanding. He expected jobs and assignments to be completed properly and efficiently. Though only 5' 8" tall and slender, Jack Brown was not above rolling up his shirtsleeves and taking part in a project, whether painting or digging a trench.

Yet in the midst of the whirlwind that defined his job, Brown somehow found time to visit classrooms every day to observe his teachers in action and check how the children were doing. He was famous for his daily walks around campus, in which he would stop to greet and talk with boys and girls. They felt comfortable approaching him, and many called him "Dad Brown."

Brown promoted industriousness by being industrious; he inspired loyalty and confidence through the way he treated others. He personally set the example of how he expected his students to conduct themselves by the way he lived his life. More than fifty years after he retired, Jack Brown's ethics and influence still linger at Sequoyah.

Though students had to complete homework assignments on time and fulfill their various internships, they nevertheless found time to participate in sports and social activities. They invented games to play in their free time, took part in the give and take of relationships in a large coed institution, and formed lasting friendships.

Tahlequah's hot, humid September gave way to October's cooler nights and occasional blustery winds that scattered leaves across the landscape. Tommy welcomed the change. Fall meant the onset of basketball season. He notified surrounding high school basketball coaches that he was available to referee their games and tournaments. Because he was still remembered as one of the best athletes Northeastern had ever produced, coaches quickly responded and began calling for him to officiate.

Tommy invited Jimmy to go with him on Friday night referee jobs; busy with his players during halftime, he encouraged his son to shoot baskets. A captivated audience applauded and cheered on a pint-sized seven-year-old who could sink baskets through a regulation-height hoop. Some even threw coins onto the court. At the end of halftime, Tommy would sweep up his son and, smiling and laughing with the crowd, raise Jimmy's arms in victory. On the way home one evening, Tommy asked Jimmy, "How much money did you make, son?" Jimmy promptly answered, "I didn't *make* any money, Dad. After all, I'm *not* a professional."

For Tommy, October also meant the advent of quail season, a chance to hike beautiful country and to relish solitude—a rarity. Having had no time to hunt during his years in the Dakotas, he began the annual tradition on returning to Oklahoma in 1936. How many quail he bagged came secondary to the day itself. Tommy took off the first Saturday in October 1941 and left early in the morning for the country. He took along the lunch Dorothy packed for him and, quails or not, planned to spend his day away from work and responsibility.

A pleasant breeze carried woodsy smells, damp earth, pungent grass, and occasional smoke. Some families had their woodstove going. After hiking for an hour without seeing a bird, Tommy crossed the road and headed toward a distant thicket of trees. Twenty yards ahead he spotted a barbed wire fence. As he approached, Tommy shifted the shotgun from his left hand to his right and used his left hand to push down the top wire.

He had one leg over the top wire, when *snap!* the wire gave way, causing Tommy to pitch forward and let go of the shotgun. He heard it discharge as searing pain ripped through his left foot. Tommy collapsed on the bottom wires, entangled and unable to move. Blood streamed out a gaping hole in his boot, and he could do nothing to stop it. The thought crossed his mind that if he didn't get out of this predicament quickly, the newspaper would soon be printing his obituary.

He would later attribute what happened next to the Big Guy looking after him: an Oklahoma Highway Patrol car happened to drive by on the road. Tommy hollered to gain their attention, but they had already spotted him. Two officers leaped out of the car and bounded toward him. Together they gingerly untangled him from the wires. With sirens blazing, they rushed Tommy to Hastings Hospital in Tahlequah. He spent the next four days being cared for by doctors and nurses, getting stitches and shots and attracting a lot of attention.

The accident made headlines in the *Tahlequah Citizen* on October 2, 1941: "Tommy Thompson Shoots Self in Foot in Hunting Accident." The accompanying story, which detailed how the patrolmen "found him hanging on the fence," garnered Tommy a lot of razzing from his friends and BIA coworkers. Dorothy handled the incident with her usual composure, but upon learning that he could not referee for at least six weeks, she told him he would be spending his evenings at home with the family. The doctor backed her up by warning Tommy not to drive for at least two weeks.

For two weeks, he had no choice but to hobble around the house on crutches or sit in his chair listening to the radio with his throbbing foot propped up on the ottoman. Unaccustomed to being immobile, Tommy complained enough that Dorothy admonished him for being a terrible patient. She did her best to make him comfortable; she brought him sports magazines and never left for work without putting a bowl of popcorn by his chair.

After a week of hearing her husband complain about being housebound, Dorothy drove the family to his cousin's theater to see a movie. Bob Hope, Bing Crosby, and Dorothy Lamour in *Road to Zanzibar* helped Tommy forget his foot for a short while, and it gave the family something to laugh about. But the MovieTone newsreel afterward shattered all sense of fun and make-believe. Ominous black-and-white scenes showed Nazi and Finnish soldiers fighting in Russia. Another pictured the president of Finland defiantly rejecting U.S. and British requests to stop its war against the U.S.S.R. President Franklin Roosevelt, looking somber and drawn, pronounced the war "a failure of diplomacy."

Uncharacteristically quiet as they left the theater, seven-year-old Jimmy asked his father whether the Germans were going to invade Tahlequah. Assuring his son that they would not, Tommy shared a silent glance with Dorothy, acknowledging that the United States appeared to be headed for war.

10

Front-Row Seats at the War
DEᏬJP SSᏜᎩꟻ DLᏖℂᎢ

December 7, 1941

Nine-year-old George Cameron awoke to the six A.M. whistle, which instantly transformed the large dorm room into chaos. Thirty yawning and grumbling boys scrambled out of their bunks and with automatic movements made their beds military style. Their CQ, Wadie Miller, clapped his hands to get their attention. "It's Sunday, so suits and ties. And make sure your shoes are shined. Mr. Brown is already in the kitchen making his special flapjacks. It snowed last night so soon as church is over you can go sledding."

Excited at the prospect, George dressed in his blue government-issue suit, white shirt, and tie. He'd already shined his shoes. He joined his friend Everett and the other boys as they lined up two-by-two and walked to the cafeteria. Going through the food line, George and Everett held their trays and received scrambled eggs and ham and a stack of flapjacks served up by Dad Brown at the end of the line. Smiling and greeting everyone, he was clearly enjoying himself.

The two friends polished off their ham and eggs, saving for last the flapjacks that they had drowned in sorghum syrup. Church was next, and then they could play outside for the rest of the day. Wadie lined them up again outside the cafeteria and led the group toward the gymnasium. Thick, fat snowflakes swirled about, settling on bare tree branches and crisp brown grass. They followed the CQ into the gym, took their seats, and waited for Mr. Brown to arrive to start the service.

But ten minutes went by, and neither the superintendent nor the minister appeared.

"Wonder what's going on?" George asked his friend.

Everett shrugged. "Maybe something happened to Mr. Brown. He's pretty old, you know. Wadie told me he's *fifty-threeeee*." With the word "three," Everett's brows spiked upward.

Something had to be wrong, George knew; Mr. Brown was as punctual as a school clock. George glanced over his shoulder. Almost everyone had taken a seat on one of the folding chairs set up on the basketball court. Girls sat on one side of a central aisle, boys on the other. Ten more minutes went by and still there was no sign of Mr. Brown or a minister.

Though the students were scarily quiet at first, an expectant buzz began to circle the gym. It grew louder until a side door opened and the buzz stopped. Principal Maude Parker entered and walked to the podium, her posture even more stick-straight than usual. "May I have your attention, please." She didn't sound like the friendly Mrs. Parker who usually called their assemblies to order. Instead, her knitted brow and the stern set of her mouth confirmed George's fear that they were about to hear bad news. "Today's church services have been cancelled. Superintendent Brown asks that students return to your rooms in an orderly fashion and wait for further instructions."

Frightened, George glanced at Everett, who also looked scared. Wadie hurriedly led them back to their dorm and went to get his radio. Soon after, the boys gathered around him in a circle and sat silently, waiting as he tuned in a station.

Loud static erupted and then, finally, the solemn voice of an announcer gave them the news. "Japanese war planes attacked our base in Pearl Harbor, Hawaii, this morning. Damage to our fleet is heavy. The number of casualties is unknown." George Cameron later recalled, "Some of us cried right there. Some covered their face with their hands. A few sat looking dumbfounded. Nobody had said much to say. We were too shocked to say anything."

FRONT-ROW SEATS AT THE WAR

No one went outside to sled or play. George and Everett and the other boys changed clothes and stayed close to the radio the rest of the day. They listened to Mrs. Roosevelt's address to the women of the United States. Her reassurance included a personal message as well as a call for strength: "I have a boy at sea on a destroyer—for all I know he may be on his way to the Pacific. Two of my children are in coast cities on the Pacific. Many of you have boys in the service [who] will now be called upon to go into action. You cannot escape anxiety . . . the clutch of fear at our hearts and yet I hope that the certainty of what we have to meet will make you rise above those fears. I feel as though I am standing upon a rock and that rock is my faith in my fellow citizens."

The boys ate dinner, then returned to their room and gathered again around the radio. Anticipating more news, they couldn't believe it when the Jack Benny show came on at its regular time and, right after that, the Edgar Bergen and Charlie McCarthy show.

Distracted and only half listening to the shows, the boys released their fears. The "Japs" right now might be headed for the United States, intent on more bombing. One of the boys said his cousin lived in California, "pretty close to the Pacific Ocean." That brought another round of speculation that ended only when Wadie announced lights out.

George lay wide-eyed in his bed, with his heart racing and sleep unthinkable.

Classes resumed the following morning amid the news that ten hours after the Pearl Harbor strike, 196 Japanese Navy bombers and fighters had destroyed the radar station at Iba, an airfield located on the Philippine island of Luzon, then bombed Clark Airfield on the island of Manila, destroying almost half of the United States' aircraft in the Pacific. George recalled that they didn't accomplish much on their lessons in class that day. Instead, they talked about the attack and located the Hawaiian Islands, Japan, and the islands of the Philippines on big wall maps. On December 8, the United States declared war on Japan, as did Great Britain. Two days later, on December 10, Germany and Italy declared war on the United States.

Christmas Day 1941 began with the announcement that the British forces in Hong Kong had surrendered to the Japanese. Wadie left, telling the boys he would find out what they were supposed to do about Christmas. When he came back a few minutes later, he said that the word direct from Superintendent Brown was that he wanted classes to celebrate like they always did.

"We tried," George remembered, "but we couldn't. It wasn't the same."

Prior to December 7, the war in Europe had seemed distant and impersonal, but Pearl Harbor brought it into Sequoyah, which responded as a microcosm of the nation, with shock, fear, and then outrage. Dozens of senior boys and girls left to join the army or navy.

Talk of the war quickly enveloped Tahlequah. When students went into town, they overheard people talking about air raids and casualties or discussing someone's son or brother who had joined up or was already on his way to fight. Within a week, signs sprang up at gas stations announcing that tires and gas would soon be rationed and could be purchased only with coupons. Grocery stores put up similar notices about meat, butter, and a host of other food staples that would no longer be available.

As the war's impact deepened, Tahlequah's city fathers set up a USO to entertain servicemen and women. Not only did the town's residents save fat drippings, scrap metal, rubber, and aluminum foil, but so did the students at Sequoyah. Patriotism ran high, as everyone proved willing to embrace sacrifice for "our troops overseas."

People openly expressed their hatred of Nazis and "the Japs."

WAR ENGULFS MUSKOGEE AND CHEROKEE COUNTY, 1942–43

The *Tahlequah Citizen* and *Muskogee Phoenix* reported that Congress had released designated War Aid funds to beef up coastal defenses, build arms and munitions plants, and construct new military training camps. Next came the bold headlines that a pilot and infantry training base would be built in Cherokee and Muskogee counties.

A decade earlier, the government had laid claim to 27,000 acres in both counties by declaring the land submarginal and placing it under federal stewardship as a parks and recreation project. Now the Resettlement Administration used War Aid funds to buy up the land outright and relocate every farmer whose property fell within the boundaries of the proposed camp. Once this was accomplished, the U.S. War Department owned 109 square miles of prime eastern Oklahoma property.

In January 1942, one month after the attack on Pearl Harbor, workers from the Manhattan-Long Company arrived and began construction on the 260-acre Cookson Hills Project. The company had constructed other military camps, the most recent being Fort Riley in Kansas. Working at breakneck speed was nothing new to them. Using a force of 12,000 men working around the clock, the company built 479 barracks, 1,252 frame buildings, 100 hospital buildings, 210 mess halls, 55 administration buildings, a bakery, 12 chapels, a laundry, 221 recreation buildings, 258 storage warehouses, 5 theaters, 19 guard houses, 59 motor repair shops, 50 officer quarters, 261 miscellaneous buildings, and a water system that included a three-million-gallon concrete storage reservoir.

Four months and $30 million later, in May 1942, Camp Gruber stood ready to occupy. Named in honor of Brigadier General Edmund L. Gruber, a Fort Sill artillery officer and composer of the "Caisson Song," this instant city located twenty-five miles from Sequoyah brought the sights, sounds, and smell of war up close and personal for the institution's students. It didn't take long for Camp Gruber to in some way affect every resident in Cherokee and Muskogee County.

At the end of 1942, 4,000 civilian workers, the 88th Infantry Cloverleaf Division, the 202nd Field Artillery Division, and the 42nd and 86th Infantry Divisions called Camp Gruber home. When all four divisions' artillery units began an exercise with their big guns booming and shells exploding, the students at Sequoyah thought for sure the war was in their backyard.

George Cameron remembered those days: "Tanks and half-tracks performed maneuvers on the land in back of the school.

Sometimes the explosions went on all night long and rattled our windows so hard we thought sure our building would get hit. From our dorm we watched the tanks and when they fired we could see flame come out of their guns. It was like having a front row seat at the war."

Camp Gruber proved important enough to the U.S. war effort to warrant a personal visit by President Franklin Roosevelt in 1943. On the afternoon of April 18, under heavy security, FDR's massive Pan Am 314 Dixie Clipper landed at Davis Army Air Force base in Muskogee. From there, the president was driven by motorcade to Camp Gruber, officially to view a dress parade by the 88th Division on the camp's two-mile-long parade field. The men of the division had trained for a year and were shipping out to Fort Sam Houston in Texas, then on to Europe. Roosevelt declared the parade a wonderful show and then, in the real reason for his visit, honored the men of the 88th by dining with them in the mess tent, where he wished them safety and Godspeed

Half a world away in Africa, U.S. forces either ran off or captured nearly all the German soldiers from Field Marshal Erwin Rommel's Afrika Korps. That victory brought Tahlequah and Muskogee even more into the war: the U.S. military shipped the prisoners from Rommel's campaign to Camp Gruber's POW camp.

Because so many of the area's workers were away in the service, German prisoners were bussed out to orchards in Cherokee County to plant, weed, and pick fruit. Dressed in olive drab uniforms with "POW" stenciled in big white letters on their backs, they often ended up in the same orchard as boys from Sequoyah.

Everett Nave said later, "It was the first time any of us had ever seen a German, let alone talked to one. We were surprised how many of them spoke English and how friendly they seemed. They weren't at all how we pictured Nazis."

Guarded by U.S. Military Police, the POWs may have worked in the fields on weekdays, but on weekends they were confined to camp. Friday evening through Sunday night, Camp Gruber soldiers and a hefty contingent of military police and camp personnel invaded Muskogee and Tahlequah in search of fun. A round trip from the camp to Muskogee on the Victory Bus Line cost a soldier sixty-one cents; a ride into Tahlequah was even less. For forty-eight hours, both towns' normally quiet streets took on the atmosphere of a county fair. In Tahlequah, soldiers crowded Jimmy Thompson's two movie theaters; they filled the USO and every restaurant and beer bar. Oklahoma state law forbade the sale of hard liquor, but the soldiers provided Tahlequah's four bootleggers with a lively business.

1943–44

As 1943 dawned, fighting escalated in Europe and the Pacific. On top of the grief Tommy felt over young men and women dying, the war also presented a personal dilemma for him. His BIA visits to Indian families brought home to him the fact that it didn't matter whether a boy was Cherokee, Choctaw, Seneca, or Seminole: the minute he turned seventeen, he dropped out of school and enlisted in the military. Even sixteen-year-olds signed up after somehow convincing their parents to sign a release form. Tommy likened it to war fever—boys who had only recently started to shave wanting to go fight.

He talked to them about college scholarships. He tried persuasion, encouragement, and everything short of out-and-out bribery to convince a boy to remain in school and focus on education and the future. Each boy listened respectfully and would smile when Tommy talked about how much fun he would have playing football or basketball. Tommy made it a point to shake the boy's hand and believed at first that he had perhaps saved this one from making a terrible mistake. But then on his next visit, the boy would be gone, and the parents would show Tommy a picture of their fresh-faced boy in uniform. He had no choice but to hide his fear and disappointment and acknowledge their pride.

The first few times it happened, he shared his distress with Dorothy, but when he saw how much it upset her, too, he stopped. In his mind, sixteen-year-olds should be thinking about girlfriends and football and college. These boys would soon be trying to stay alive, which was not an easy accomplishment, according to the newspaper stories Tommy found impossible to ignore. They would be lucky to return at all or, if they did, to come back in one piece. Radio reports and newsreels of fierce battles with the count of American casualties dominated every waking hour. Reporters had tallied the June '42 victory on Midway Island and the Solomon Islands in November. For every victory, though, there seemed to be a defeat: 22,000 Americans killed in the July 1943 Allied invasion and battle for Italy alone. The very air seemed saturated with war and death. Tommy tried to turn off the pictures in his mind of bandaged young men smiling at the camera from their hospital beds, but keeping his imagination in check grew more difficult each month.

When sleep evaded him and the images overwhelmed, Tommy sought escape with the relief he had learned to count on: the bottle.

11

This Must Be What Hell Is Like
ᎦᎳ ᏆᎳ ᏓᏱᏃᎦ

SEPTEMBER 1943

"Lucinda Brown Shipp has gone home to be with her Lord," the Baptist minister intoned. Eight-year-old Cecil Shipp tried to block out the minister's solemn voice but found it impossible. A circle of relatives stood gathered at the Brown family cemetery, a stone's throw from his empty house. An open grave lay exposed between the cross that marked Grandpa Simon Brown's grave and two small ones belonging to brothers who had died so many years ago that Cecil couldn't remember them.

His brother, Rudell, and his sisters Gay Don and Sandra stood beside Cecil. No breeze tempered September's staggering heat and humidity; the air was so hot and sticky that it was hard to breathe. Feeling dizzy, Cecil edged himself into a patch of shade cast by his relatives standing shoulder to shoulder in front of him. His mother's half-sister, full-blood Seminole Fannie Brown Woolridge, stood beside her husband, Marshall. Next to them were their son and daughter, Noah and Bessie. Another lady, a full-blood Seminole cousin, held Cecil's baby sister, Mary Louise, who was fussing. *Probably hungry and hot,* Cecil thought. The minister's words intruded, and Cecil heard something about walking through the valley of death and not being afraid. That made no sense to him: a valley of death sounded like a scary place.

He and Rudell had learned that they would live with their mother's brother, George. Cecil didn't know about Gay Don and Sandra; he hoped they would get to stay together. The Seminole cousin said she would take nine-month-old Mary Louise home

(*Left to right*) Cecil "Nip" Shipp, father Jimmy Shipp, and brother Rudell Shipp in 1947, before the boys' mother became ill. Permission granted by Cecil Shipp.

with her to raise. Cecil had no tears left to cry. It was inconceivable that their happy mother was gone. "Thirty-nine years old. Death due to a heart attack," the doctor had told them. Cecil pictured her—not the tired, hollow-eyed woman in bed at Fannie's house but the short, round mother with her shiny black hair pulled back in a bun. She had made bad times seem good and good times even better.

Their house sat vacant and silent now, looking as sad and abandoned as he felt. Would he ever see his father again? Cecil nudged his brother, their eyes sharing the unspoken question why their father hadn't come. Though Cecil hadn't really expected him to show up, Jimmy Shipp's absence heaped more sorrow on top of the mountain already pressing on the boy's shoulders.

Bitterness edged its way into his thoughts at the few determined relatives of his mother's who hated his father and made sure he knew it. Cecil thought back as many years as he could remember, but he couldn't pinpoint when the hatred had started or why. Was it because his father was white? Or that he was such a good baseball player that he could have been in the pros if times hadn't been so hard? Cecil decided it was probably because his father had been so friendly, inviting everybody to play baseball on the diamond he'd built near the house. Adults or kids, white or Indian, it didn't matter; Jimmy Shipp had welcomed whoever wanted to take part in his weekend baseball games. Lots of people from the town of Maud came with their kids. Those were happy times, at least for a while.

Cecil cast a sidelong glance at the diamond his father had taken such pride in. The manicured grass was dead, the infield and outfield taken over by weeds. All that remained of Jimmy Shipp's perfect diamond was a narrow strip of red dirt that snaked its way between the three grain sacks that had served as bases. Cecil looked away, unable to quell the feeling that if those few hateful relatives hadn't threatened his father, Jimmy Shipp would have moved heaven and earth to be here. As hard as it was to endure the church service in town and then watch his mother's casket being lowered into the open grave, Cecil dreaded what was still to come.

Aunt Fannie had moved his mother into her own house, taking care of her half-sister after Lucinda became really sick. Following Seminole custom, before they left for the funeral, Fannie's family had removed his mother's bed and mattress and piled them on the ground in the front yard. They proceeded to carry out her clothes, her Bible and pictures, and even her hairbrush and comb, adding them to the pile. Cecil stood watching, helpless to stop them. There would be nothing of his mother's to remember her by.

Graveside services ended, Cecil dutifully shook the minister's hand as Fannie Woolridge instructed. A few neighbors and people from town approached to say how sorry they were; then they said their goodbyes. As soon as everyone else left, the family followed Fannie the short distance to her house, where they gathered in a large circle. Marshall Woolridge, Fannie's husband, knelt and put a match to the mattress and pyramid of personal belongings.

Cecil watched the flame take hold and spread: blue-tipped orange tendrils growing, leaping skyward, snapping and popping as they devoured his mother's earthly belongings. Twenty feet away, Cecil felt the heat envelop him. *This must be what hell is like.*

The minister's final words replayed over and over in his head as the fire reduced the pile to ashes. "Almighty God, we commend the soul of Lucinda Brown Shipp and commit her body to the ground in sure and certain hope of her Resurrection unto eternal life through our Lord Jesus Christ."

Ten-year-old Fields Smith sat in the back seat of his mother's car on the way from their home in Vian to Tahlequah. His hand gripping the door handle, Fields wondered how bad he would get hurt if he jumped out when she slowed to turn or stopped at a stop sign. His sister, Edith Marie, sat in the front beside his mother. Glancing at him in the rear-view mirror, his mother assured them in Cherokee that once they got used to Sequoyah they would like it. Edith Marie didn't respond. Nor did he, because he was still thinking how he might get away. By the time Fields made up his mind to jump, his mother had entered the school grounds and pulled up in front of a big brick building.

Mary Smith turned around and asked Fields whether he was okay. She looked about ready to cry. Crestfallen, Fields said yes, because that's what she needed to believe. The truth was, after just one glance at all the buildings, he was sorry he hadn't jumped.

His sister opened the back door. "Come on, Fields, let's get this over with." Brother and sister followed their mother to the registrar's office on the second floor and stood aside as she signed all the papers to enroll them. "I'll see you after the check-in process," she told them. "You know my cousin, Lizzie. I'm going to stay in her room tonight and drive home tomorrow."

Fields remembered hearing that his aunt, Lizzie Welsh, was a dorm matron in the big boys' dorm. He watched Edith Marie and their mother embrace, and then his sister hugged him. She didn't look scared, but then, she was fifteen years old, practically grown.

It didn't matter; he was scared enough for both of them. Before the ink had dried on his registration, he was homesick.

After his shower, lice check, and haircut, Fields dressed in the new clothes and shoes they gave him. Then a lady who said her name was Miss Goodman showed him his dorm room and bunk. Like Hansel and Gretel walking through the woods, Fields tried to remember every hallway, every turn and doorway they traveled to reach his room. At five o'clock, a big boy that everybody called the CQ had them line up two by two and walk to the cafeteria for supper.

Fields looked around but didn't see his mother or his aunt Lizzie. Later that evening after Miss Goodman turned the lights out, Fields waited until the room quieted. He slipped out of bed and retraced his steps to the ground floor, where he let himself out. Fields waited for his eyes to adjust to the dark, then turned right, toward the closest building with lights in a window. There were only a few lights on in his building; outside, there was only moonlight.

Fields stopped. Straight ahead, he made out the silhouette of somebody sitting on a bench at the edge of the sidewalk. Thinking it might be a guard, he sneaked toward the back of the bench, but as he drew closer he recognized the lone figure: it was his mother. He wondered why she would be out here in the dark when she said she'd be with Aunt Lizzie. Barefooted, he walked up to her and found out why—she didn't want her cousin to see her crying. Startled, his mother glanced his way. "My gracious, son, you scared me. What in the world are you doing out here?"

He sat down beside her and scooted as close as he could. "I don't like it here. I want to go home with you."

She pulled him close. "I'm sorry, Fields, you can't. Remember our talk? This is the best place for you and Edith Marie now. I've tried to take care of you since your daddy died, but I don't make enough money." His mother couldn't seem to stop crying. Even her voice sounded full of tears. Fields sat, feeling helpless and at a loss for how to comfort her. He thought maybe she was sad because she was remembering when her mother and father had died and she'd had to come here. She had never talked much about it, except she called it the Cherokee Orphan Training School.

His mother took his face in her hands and pressed her lips to his forehead. "I want you to go back to your room. Be a good boy, and I promise I will see you tomorrow before I leave."

Fields stared up at her. "Cross your heart and hope to die?"

She smiled. "Cross my heart and hope to die."

Not wanting to upset her more, Fields relented. She took his hand, and they walked back to the front of his building. "I love you, son. Now go inside."

Fields sneaked back to his room and crawled into bed, his mind full of questions. Would he get used to Sequoyah like his mother said? Why did the registrar call him and Edith Marie orphans? They had a mother, and even after his father died, their eight uncles and aunts and a bunch of cousins all lived nearby. Fields had never thought of himself as an orphan. *I guess I am or I wouldn't be here,* he decided.

For all of Fields's ten years, his father—Samuel Smith, full-blood Cherokee medicine man and chief of the Keetoowah Society—had *made* people well. Samuel wasn't supposed to get sick and die, but even with his three medicine-man brothers using heat and herbs and seeking God's permission to heal him, he had died anyway. The white doctor had said it was pneumonia; his uncles said it was his father's time to die.

Fields lay awake thinking about his mother. He hoped that in knowing he and Edith Marie would be taken good care of at Sequoyah, she wouldn't be sad anymore. But when he closed his eyes and pictured her tearful face, he knew deep down that giving up her son and daughter must hurt as much as it had when his father had died.

Fields rolled over and cried himself to sleep.

NOVEMBER 1943

Cecil Shipp stared wide-eyed at the big buildings as Mrs. Galeena Walkingstick drove through the gates of Sequoyah. During the two-hundred-mile drive from Maud, she had talked about what a wonderful school it was and how nice the teachers were. She had assured him and his siblings that they would like it. Cecil got out of the car and shivered, his thin sweater no match for the cold November breeze. Holding onto Gay Don's hand, Cecil followed Rudell and the Wewoka BIA social worker up the steps.

"Gay Don, this is Home Three, where you will live. Your room is on the third floor. There are lots of nice girls your age," Mrs. Walkingstick said. "Let's get you registered so you can meet them." She sounded excited and happy for them.

Maybe this is going to be okay, Cecil thought.

An earth-shattering explosion went off just as Mrs. Walkingstick pulled open the big door of the building. A bomb? Cecil froze until in rapid succession he heard a second and third blast. Rudell raced through the open door, Cecil and Gay Don sprinting right behind him. "Oh, dear," Mrs. Walkingstick said and followed them inside as though nothing had happened. "I forgot to warn you about the artillery units," she said. "The army performs maneuvers in back of the school. The war, you know. You'll get used to it."

She led them up a wide staircase to the registrar's desk on the second floor. Light filtered in through tall windows as she handed over papers to the clerk, who asked her to sign some documents. Turning toward him, Mrs. Walkingstick told Cecil, "I don't want you to worry about Sandra and Mary Louise. I will check on them just like I did you and as soon as they're old enough, I will bring them to Sequoyah. I promise you will be a family again."

Cecil decided that, besides his mother, Mrs. Walkingstick was about the nicest lady he'd ever met. She registered Rudell into the third grade, Cecil into the second, and Gay Don into kindergarten, then stood aside as a lady appeared and took his sister's hand and told her, "Let's go and see your room." The lady sounded friendly, but at seeing his sister led away, all the excitement Cecil felt about coming to Sequoyah melted away like ice on an August afternoon. When Gay Don glanced back, her brown eyes glistening with tears, Cecil panicked. "No, wait!" His words slipped out.

Mrs. Walkingstick touched his shoulder. "Cecil, I give you my word everything is going to be all right." She promised to check on them during her next visit. Then she said goodbye and disappeared down the stairs. She had paid weekly visits to them in Maud ever since their mother's death, and for a moment, Cecil wanted to chase after her, but then a tall, brown-haired lady walked up.

"Cecil and Rudell Shipp? I'm Miss Goodman, Home One dorm matron." She asked them to follow her. Though wishing that Mrs. Walkingstick would have stayed with them a while longer, Cecil had no choice but to follow. Miss Goodman explained as they walked that the check-in procedure included a shower, a lice check and haircut, and getting new clothes and shoes. She made it sound very matter-of-fact, and it went exactly as she said.

Afterward, she led them to Home One and gave each boy a cardboard box measuring twelve inches by fifteen inches, with "Home One" and a number written on the outside. She said the boxes were for their personal belongings and added that the number would remain the same until they moved to one of the big boys' dormitories. She seemed businesslike, Cecil thought as she led them into her office. The room looked bigger than their entire Maud house, at least thirty feet long and nearly as wide. Miss Goodman's desk occupied the wall nearest the door. One wall held cardboard boxes stacked floor to ceiling in rows according to the number marked on the front. A treadle sewing machine and ironing board, which Miss Goodman said she used to mend and press her boys' clothes, sat against the opposite wall.

The way she said *"my* boys" made Cecil feel a little better.

As another series of explosions rattled the windows, Cecil flinched, then walked over and peered out at camouflaged army tanks and half-tracks. They looked as if they were racing each other. Thick clouds of red dust followed in their wake. "They use dummy shells," Miss Goodman told them. Cecil wasn't totally convinced, for with each boom, fire spewed out the end of a long gun, looking very much like the real thing.

THIS MUST BE WHAT HELL IS LIKE

After the boys slid their boxes in with the others, Miss Goodman told Rudell that he could take a look at his dorm room across the hall and asked Cecil to follow her upstairs. She pointed out the washroom he would use, then showed him his room and bunk. "You'll meet the CQ in charge of your quarters later." Miss Goodman explained that a CQ was usually a senior who looked after the boys in his assigned room. Rudell joined them upstairs, and Miss Goodman said she would give them a few minutes. "When you come downstairs, I'll take you to the cafeteria. It's almost lunchtime."

Cecil waited until she left. "You scared?" he asked his brother.

Rudell nodded. "A little, but so far everybody seems nice enough."

Cecil nodded, running his hand over his bed. "Mrs. Walkingstick said this is a wonderful school with nice teachers. She said she was sure we'd like it here. I believe her. Mrs. Walkingstick wouldn't say that if she didn't mean it."

12

Four-Legged Ambassador

ᏅᏳ ᎫᏪᏅᎰᏍ ᏪᏅᏏᏝ

1943–44

Weighing eighty pounds and with long hair the color of honey and his four paws perfectly tipped with white, Boots showed up at Sequoyah at the exact time he was most needed. George Cameron first spotted him in the spring of 1943 trotting happily alongside his master, Austin Pritchett, a farmhand who worked at Sequoyah and lived in a house on school grounds. George figured Pritchett and the dog had to be new to Sequoyah, otherwise he and his friends would surely have noticed them. They may not have noticed Pritchett, but they sure would have paid attention to the dog.

For the next three days, minutes after the five o'clock whistle blew, Pritchett and the dog walked past where the boys gathered to get in their last few minutes of play before the 5:30 dinner bell. The fact that they took the same route made it easy for the boys. Hearing the five o'clock whistle, they would stop their play and wait, anticipating the chance to catch sight of the happy-looking dog. A month went by of admiring from a distance. Then one day, unable to ignore the boys' stares, Pritchett stopped and introduced himself. The dog sat obediently at his feet as Pritchett told them his dog's name was Boots; Boots was part Collie and about two years old.

George asked if he could pet Boots, and Pritchett gave his okay. "Boots came up to me wagging his tail so hard it made me laugh," George later recalled. He petted Boots, and so did the other boys; the dog seemed to love the attention. Every day after that, they waited for Pritchett and Boots, who would bound up, barking and wagging his tail, a clear invitation to be petted. Pritchett would wait for each boy to have his turn and then whistle. Boots would immediately run back to him, and off they would go home.

Every one of the boys longed to have a dog of his own. Instead of satisfying them, the brief visits became a painful reminder that Boots belonged to someone else. George and Everett and their friends looked forward to their daily meeting so much that they dreaded Fridays because three days would pass before they could see Boots again.

After two months of the five o'clock encounters, Boots evidently decided that he liked playing with the boys rather than watching Pritchett work. He began to seek out the boys during the day, finding them during recess or after class. They welcomed him like a gift from heaven. They played ball with him. They threw sticks for him to retrieve, and he never tired of returning with stick in mouth. They chased him, and he chased after them. Boots got hugs and pets and the unbridled affection of dozens of boys.

Still, when the five o'clock whistle blew and Pritchett appeared and called, "Come on, Boots, let's go home," the dog obediently trotted off beside his master. He did so until one Friday in the fall of 1943.

New student Fields Smith had joined Everett, George, and the other boys. They were playing leapfrog with Boots and having so much fun that they didn't hear the five o'clock whistle or see Pritchett approach. When they became aware of him, they stopped their play. Pritchett called his dog. "Come on, boy, let's go home," but Boots didn't respond. Instead, he stood with ears perked, panting, and wagging his tail. After a second command produced no response, Pritchett grabbed his collar and whacked him on the rump. "Get home!"

George and Everett and the other boys watched in horror as Boots took off running, tail between his legs. Seeing Boots get punished brought them close to tears. But they had come to count on their time with him so much that the thought of never seeing him again was unthinkable. They continued to play with him every day. For the next few weeks, all too often the same scene happened. It made the boys feel terrible to cause Boots to be punished when he had done nothing wrong. They talked among themselves but could find no solution. Then one Friday evening, everything changed. George remembers that the weather had turned very hot and humid. Pritchett showed up looking tired, dirty, and in a hurry. The minute he walked up, the boys stopped playing with Boots. Pritchett issued his customary command: "C'mon, Boots, let's go home."

The boys stood motionless, almost hoping Boots would obey so Pritchett wouldn't get mad and swat him. But Boots didn't obey; he just stood there wagging his tail. Pritchett whistled and called again. This time Boots gave his master a clear response. He lay down at the feet of one of the boys. The boys took a collective breath. Would their four-legged friend get a whipping for his insubordination? None of them anticipated what happened next. His eyes on Boots, Pritchett merely shook his head in disgust and said, "Go ahead and stay here, then. You'll come home when you get hungry."

Boots never again went home with Pritchett, nor did he ever go hungry. Given the opportunity, he opted for Sequoyah as his home and the boys as his masters. After that, every day at five o'clock when Pritchett finished work he stopped wherever Boots and the boys were playing. He would pet the dog, then walk on home alone. George Cameron later said, "I guess he could see how much we loved him and that Boots felt the same way about us. I believe Pritchett stopping like that was his way of saying what happened wasn't our fault. Or Boots' either."

Not long after, Pritchett left Sequoyah and joined the army.

Boots had the run of the campus. The boys took him rabbit hunting around the three ponds behind the dorms and on Bald Hill, a favorite hangout. If they went swimming, he swam with them. Boots slept in whatever dorm room he chose; he trotted alongside big kids and little kids, accompanying them to and from their classes. He didn't hesitate to visit the gym or a classroom when he found a door left open. His food bowl, which sat by the back entrance to the kitchen, was filled each day with leftovers from every meal. Ready to play anytime with anybody, the dog seemed to understand that he filled a huge void.

Eighty pounds of pure love, he belonged to no one. Boots belonged to everyone.

Despite the war and the chaos it created in Tahlequah and his school, Jack Brown saw to it that life at Sequoyah remained steady and on schedule. Cows got milked twice a day, every day. Students fed the hogs and chickens on time; they collected eggs every morning. They helped keep the grounds "spit-spot clean," the way Mr. Brown expected. He never missed his daily walk to each classroom to personally wind the wall clock, which actually gave him a chance to observe the teacher and students in action.

Nothing—not the tiniest addition or change—escaped Jack Brown's attention, and certainly the dog was no exception, though his tacit acceptance of Boots ran counter to everything he stood for. The school's cardinal rule dictated that dogs belonging to employees living on campus had to be kept leashed or in an enclosure. A stickler for rules, Brown chose to ignore Boots's free run of the campus. Perhaps this was because merely by his presence and personality, the dog had become an ambassador of goodwill, unifying 350 children regardless of tribe, gender, or age; first graders adored the lovable canine, as did twelfth graders. By the spring of 1944, even Mr. Brown had to admit that Boots owned the place.

1944. Sixteen-year-old Bill Cameron arrived at a decision: he would not be left behind when all of his buddies were dropping out of Sequoyah to enlist in the navy. He would need his father's signed consent, though, because seventeen was the minimum age to join any branch of the military. Having spent six years at Sequoyah and completed the tenth grade, Bill decided that he'd had enough school—for now, anyway. The truth be known, studying and chores had gotten old a long time ago.

Nobody except his brother, George, called him Billy anymore. When George heard about his brother trying to enlist, George begged Billy to change his mind. It gave Bill pause, but he still went to see his father. If Andy Cameron gave his consent, he would go; if not, George would be happy. His father signed the consent with no objections and told Bill he was proud of him for enlisting. The visit was short and to the point. Bill thanked him with a handshake. Six years had passed, and this was the first time he'd seen his father since the agent had brought him to Sequoyah. Bill said goodbye to his brother and sisters and left for basic training in San Diego.

Seven months later, he and a shipload of other new recruits boarded Landing Ship Tanker #611, bound for Hawaii. They arrived ten days later and were sickened at the sight of Pearl Harbor littered with the burnt shells of ships destroyed on December 7. The commander of LST #611 skirted the buoys cordoning off where the USS *Arizona* had been anchored. Bill and the 150-man crew of the #611 stood silent and at attention as they passed the watery grave. The USS *Oklahoma* resembled a dead whale floating on its belly.

The crew went to work refueling their ship, loading needed equipment, and restocking their food and supplies. Between shifts, they intermittently made excursions ashore to see up close the damage inflicted by Japanese warplanes. Bombed-out buildings, damaged hangars, and a list of names on a bulletin of "missing in action" served as visual reminders why they had enlisted. Two weeks later, LST #611 steamed out of Pearl Harbor, ready for duty.

Back at Sequoyah, George Cameron and the other classmates with siblings in the service listened to radio broadcasts and sat fixated, anxious to know about their loved ones, through horrific MovieTone newsreels. "I was sad and proud of my brother at the same time," George later recalled. "And scared, except I figured he had a better chance on a ship than in the infantry."

June 1944. Tommy Thompson recognized the familiar Department of Interior envelope that arrived in the mail. Home at last after more than a dozen years away, they'd only had three short years in Tahlequah, but that was not enough. Thankfully, this assignment took them only sixty miles away, to Okmulgee; according to Jean and Jimmy, though, it might as well be Alaska. Jean had just completed her sophomore year at Tahlequah High and wanted to graduate with her friends. Nine-year-old Jimmy was equally upset, for he would no longer get to see free movies or ride his aunt and uncle's pinto mare on weekends. Even Dorothy expressed her disappointment at having to leave home, but she did her best to smooth over her children's feelings.

Tommy advised his children, "If you tell yourself you're going to make the best of this, you will. And I give you my word you will make new friends." Neither of them seemed convinced.

Okmulgee, the Creek word for "bubbling water," sprang from a settlement around the governing house of the Creek Nation. County seat of Okmulgee County, the city had experienced an oil boom in the early 1920s; twenty years later, it was still a boomtown. Mansions built by oil tycoons lined the residential section of Main Street, and each house seemed to sport an architectural feature more flamboyant than the one next door. Citizens had a varied choice of ornate churches to attend. Indeed, Okmulgee was one of the few cities outside Tulsa and Oklahoma City that could boast of a seven-story office building.

Because of the war, Tommy and Dorothy could find no house to rent. By pure luck, they stumbled across a three-bedroom house on a shady tree-lined street with a For Sale sign in the front yard. For the first time in their fourteen years of marriage, the Thompsons became homeowners. Having a home with a big backyard helped Dorothy adapt. Jean chose spending her afternoons window-shopping along the commercial section of Main Street as her way of making the best of things. She soon came across several other girls who liked to do the same thing. And after Tommy found enough boys to form a junior-size basketball team, Jimmy began to like Okmulgee better.

Tommy's location had changed, but his duties as an education field agent remained the same. In the black 1941 Chevy issued to him by the BIA, he spent hours each day driving to Creek families in rural Okmulgee County. Upon discovering what families most needed, he made every effort to help them. A few short weeks into his job brought him face to face, though, with the same disturbing problem as he had found in Tahlequah: young Creek boys dropping out of school to enlist in the military. Tommy did his best to talk them out of it, extolling the difference that education would make later in their lives. But promises of a better future proved no match for overwhelming poverty.

Near the end of August, Dorothy registered nine-year-old Jimmy and fifteen-year-old Jean into Saint Anthony's school, a few blocks from their house. That done, Dorothy applied for a job at Preston Elementary, whereupon the principal hired her on the spot. Life settled into a routine, and Jean's smile returned when she discovered that nearly all the girls she'd met during the summer were students at St. Anthony's.

Tommy spoke to Creek parents desperate for news of their sons and daughters in the service. Most families had no telephone or radio, and he could only relay what news he'd heard: the situation in Europe had greatly improved, but fighting continued in the Pacific. And though he could give no specific word about their children, he could offer hope with some degree of assurance that the war might be ending soon.

To combat the problem of crushing poverty, Tommy used every resource allowed, but it was never enough. Little of the oil money had filtered down to the Creeks, and daily he confronted sickness and hunger—and all too often, death and sorrow. Though he tried to keep his feelings in check, when frustration and grief piled too high, Tommy turned for relief to his favorite remedy.

13

A Mourning Nation Is Reborn

1945

The spring of 1945 brought the shocking news that less than four months into his fourth term, President Franklin Delano Roosevelt suffered a cerebral hemorrhage at his estate in Warm Springs, Georgia. The somber radio announcement of his death on April 12 plunged the school and the nation into mourning.

Revered by their parents and grandparents, Roosevelt was the first and only president most of the students had ever known. His was the eloquent voice on the radio that brought the country together when catastrophe struck and that rallied people and resources against the enemy. Having FDR at the nation's helm was an assurance that whatever problem America might encounter, there was no doubt that the country would triumph. Roosevelt was the man who said of the office, "The presidency is not merely an administrative office. It is preeminently a place of moral leadership."

According to her family, upon hearing of his death, Dorothy Thompson became inconsolable. Harry S. Truman was quickly sworn in as the thirty-third president. Only after hearing his remark the following day to the White House press corps, "Boys, if you ever pray, pray for me now," did Dorothy gain a measure of control. Her sorrow was tempered by sympathy for the little man from Missouri who she said had the impossible task of filling Roosevelt's shoes.

Less than a month after being sworn in, Truman and the country received word that Adolph Hitler was dead and Germany's military had collapsed. A week later, the new U.S. president and Britain's prime minister, Winston Churchill, jointly declared May 8, 1945, to be V-E Day, the end of the war in Europe. Relief and elation displaced much of the nation's melancholy. Cities all over the country celebrated with speeches and parades.

There was no formal celebration at Sequoyah, but there was joy over Truman's announcement that troops would soon be on their way home. Nearly one hundred students had enlisted in some branch of the military. No one could be certain who or how many would return, but anticipation ran high about brothers and sisters for whom Sequoyah was the only home they'd ever known.

Through the ups and downs of the news, Jack Brown handled the daily business of running Sequoyah with a steady hand. Graduation was imminent, and following on its heels came summer, which presented a unique set of issues to deal with: housing students who stayed at school, finding them jobs by which to earn spending money, and making sure that summer crops got harvested to ensure that the school would have sufficient food during the winter.

While the nation rejoiced, life at Sequoyah remained routine. For many boys, that meant getting paid for helping employees harvest the school's hay and wheat crops, or weeding, watering, and harvesting vegetables from the school's huge garden. Students who stayed at school in the summer received pay for doing the same chores they did as vocational training during the school year. The cows still had to be milked twice a day, seven days a week. School garbage had to be picked up every day and processed, kitchen refuse fed to the pigs, trash taken to the school's incinerator and burned.

With the spending money they earned, boys could buy snacks at the school store. They could walk or hitchhike into Tahlequah and, for a dime, see a double feature at the movies or buy a milkshake at the drugstore. Though they wore uniforms while at school, the boys liked to look in the windows of Hinds Mercantile. The mannequins were dressed a lot differently than before the war. Female mannequins no longer wore dresses; instead, they had on slacks, sloppy joe sweaters, and military-style jackets with epaulets.

A MOURNING NATION IS REBORN

Male mannequins could have been in the military. Dressed in khaki pants and short peacoats or bomber jackets, they looked like ace pilot Pappy Boyington and the flyboys in his squadron. There wasn't a boy among them who didn't wish to have an outfit like that, but it would take a lot more than the spending money they had.

Signs of the war were everywhere, including posters of Uncle Sam, big movie advertisements showing *G.I. Joe* (about war correspondent Ernie Pyle) or the biggest war movie, *They Were Expendable*. Set in the Pacific and starring John Wayne, Donna Reed, and Robert Montgomery, the movie showed a different war than the one practiced in back of the school. It was scary enough but not nearly as bad as the MovieTone newsreels they saw between features. Sometimes the boys opted to see something funny and paid their dime to laugh at Disney's new wise-guy cat, Sylvester. Still, with Uncle Sam posters, big splashy pictures in the theater windows, and the uniformed men and women on the streets coming and going from the USO, the war remained close and ever present.

On August 6, 1945, when news that the U.S. crew of the B-29 *Enola Gay* had dropped an atomic bomb on Hiroshima, everything at Sequoyah came to a standstill, if only temporarily. Three days later, on August 9, a second U.S. aircraft dropped an atomic bomb on Nagasaki. Uncertainty filled Tahlequah and Sequoyah, then turned to euphoria at the news of the Japanese response. The August 10, 1945, *Tahlequah Citizen* headline read, "Japan Surrenders Unconditionally, Ending History's Most Destructive War."

Far from forgotten, Franklin Roosevelt's legacy remained strong in the hearts of America's citizens. He was still revered by Tahlequah citizens, but like the rest of the country, they were ready to put four years of death, sacrifice, and mourning behind. For many, defeat of the hated enemy responsible for Pearl Harbor symbolized the triumph of good over evil. In this igniting of hope and anticipation, a mourning nation was reborn.

14

We Came from Every Corner of Oklahoma
ᎻᏍᏗ ᎻᏚᎳᏏᏆ ᎻᏙᏞᎱᏯᏟ ᏬᏎᏈᎭ

SEPTEMBER 1945

A new school year brought its own excitement. This year the prospect of Sequoyah veterans returning soon added to the anticipation of reconnecting with students who had gone home for the summer. On the first day of registration, students who remained at school in the summer traditionally gathered in front of the registration building to greet friends and get a look at new arrivals, who were easy to spot because they were not in a Sequoyah uniform; some had expectant smiles, while others appeared curious and uncertain. A few—almost always boys—put on a show of bravado. From as far away as Anadarko, Pawhuska, Hugo, and Miami, Oklahoma, newcomers from the Caddo, Osage, Seneca, and Choctaw tribes added to the already diverse mix of students at Sequoyah.

Cecil and Rudell Shipp and their sister Gay Don were among the group gathered out front. Mrs. Walkingstick made good on her long-ago promise; Cecil couldn't believe his eyes when he saw her approach holding his sister's hand. The reunion was joyous, though in the two years since he'd seen her, Sandra had changed and no longer resembled the little girl he remembered. Mrs. Walkingstick bent down and whispered something. Sandra's smile grew bigger when she spotted her siblings. George and Ann Marie Cameron also welcomed their little sister, Fannie. Everett Nave's half-brother, Jimmy Ollis, had already arrived—delivered by their upset mother when she found out he had played hooky from public school for months.

Fifteen-year-old Danny Whitekiller and his younger brother, Dave, were two of the new arrivals. Neither one had wanted to transfer from Seneca Indian Boarding School, but they had been given no choice. Dave made sure Danny knew it was his fault. Earlier in the week, the two boys had accompanied their parents to Seneca to register, only to have the principal inform them that Dave was welcome but not Danny; his running away at the end of school had caused too much worry for everyone at Seneca, so Danny would have to go someplace else. Dave had pleaded to stay at Seneca with his friends, but the Whitekillers had said they wanted the brothers at the same school.

Danny had no choice but to acknowledge that, thanks to his running away, he and Dave were at this new school, with no friends, unfamiliar teachers, and the two of them in separate dorms. He had already felt an inch tall after the scene with the principal of Seneca, and every glance from his father had reminded him of their initial encounter upon his return from his misadventure.

He had tentatively walked into the clearing around their house, and there was Walter Whitekiller with an axe in his hand. Danny remembered desperately trying to think of some defense he could offer for his actions, but since none had come to mind, he had stood silent.

Walter Whitekiller stopped chopping wood. He placed the axe head flat on the stump and stared at Danny. "Well, you're finally home," he said in Cherokee. "What did you do?"

Danny figured he'd better stick to the truth. In Cherokee, he said, "Me and two buddies walked to Westville."

"You *walked* a hundred miles? Why would you do that?"

"To visit a buddy. School was almost out anyway, so we figured it'd be okay to leave."

His father shook his head. "You think you did good by running away?"

Danny knew better than to answer yes. "No, sir, but I've been thinking. I have a seventh-grade education, a lot more than most of the Cherokees around here. Maybe I'll quit school and get a job. I figure I can make it on my own."

His father raised the axe and brought it crashing down, sending two split pieces of wood flying. Danny stood frozen, afraid to move or speak. His father stared at him so intensely, he could feel it. "Son, I am going to give you two choices. You can go back to Seneca this fall on your own or I am going to kick your butt all the way back." Big black pupils bored into him. Despite the afternoon heat, a chill streaked across Danny's shoulders. Those years of hearing his mother and father say how important it was to get an education hadn't been idle talk. They meant it. And because he was the oldest, they counted on him to set an example.

Up to that point, every time they had said that, Danny had rationalized that for living deep in the woods on the wrong side of a creek with no bridge, he had done darned well to make it to the seventh grade. He and his brothers and sisters had gone to the nearby school regularly, except when Fourteen Mile Creek was too dangerous to cross or they were sick. After some of them had fallen behind and had been required to repeat a grade, though, his parents had enrolled them in Seneca Indian Boarding School, a hundred miles away in Wyandotte.

And though his father had never owned a car, the man staring at him so intensely had every year found a way to bring them home for summers and Christmas. Only in that moment, while standing in disgrace in the clearing, did Danny grasp the significance of his parents enrolling them in the Seneca school: they had sacrificed having their children close in order to give Danny and his siblings the education they never had. Ashamed and humbled, Danny could see on his father's face how much his foolishness had disappointed and hurt the older man.

Knowing that his father would not want to hear an excuse or an apology, Danny took a deep breath before he spoke. In Cherokee he said, "Dad, I never really understood just how important education is to you and Momma. I do now, and I give you my word I will graduate from high school. And I won't stop there. I will get a college degree."

The intense stare softened, but his father merely nodded and returned to chopping wood.

Two months after making that vow, while sitting on his bunk alone in his new dorm room at Sequoyah, Danny heard the sound of approaching laughter. Six or seven boys entered through the open door. Their conversations halted at the sight of him. "Osiyo," Danny said automatically, in greeting. "Osiyo" echoed back at him in several voices. The boys approached, wanting to know what grade he was in and what sports he played. When they told him how lucky he was to get into Sequoyah, the best Indian school in Oklahoma, Danny breathed his first breath of relief.

Good thing, he reasoned, *because I intend to graduate from here.*

Five Speaks brothers—Maynard, Stanley, Sterling, Boyd, and Theron Dee—arrived at Sequoyah in 1945, along with their sister, Jennie Lee Speaks. Their full-blood Chickasaw mother had passed away two and a half years earlier. Minnie Cubison Speaks had been ill with pneumonia when she gave birth to Benjamin; three weeks later, she had died. An uncle of the children, Clarence Speaks, and his wife had taken Baby Benny to live with them, but the children had rarely seen their baby brother after that, because Clarence lived twenty miles away in Durant, too far for a family with no car to travel.

With the death of his wife, their father, James Dee "J.D." Speaks, inherited the responsibility of caring for five sons and a daughter on what he earned as a sharecropper. There was little else to do around the tiny town of Milburn, Oklahoma. Paying jobs were hard to come by, but J.D. occasionally found work for the railroad. Unfortunately, that meant he had to travel to other counties and be gone for weeks at a time.

Though their Grandma Cubison lived across the road, Jennie Lee (the second oldest, and the only girl) filled in for her mother. They all had chores, but Jennie Lee did the cooking and made sure the boys went to school. On weekends, they would hunt and fish. They invented games to play, but mostly the Speaks children waited for their father to come home.

Two and a half years of this fractured existence led their father to conclude that his children would be better off in an Indian boarding school. Upon receiving word of their acceptance at Sequoyah, J.D. asked his neighbor who owned a car to drive him and his six children the two hundred miles to Tahlequah. Stanley and Sterling later remembered that it seemed like a thousand miles. While the neighbor waited outside in his car, J.D. registered them and then bade a hasty goodbye.

"Watching that car drive away was one of the darkest moments of my life," recalled Stanley later. The oldest brother, Maynard, stayed only one month, then ran away. Though his sister and brothers tried to convince him to stay, their pleading failed to persuade him.

Five Speaks siblings settled into classes, ranging from the first to the sixth grade. Sterling later remembered that they saw each other almost every day. "We were still a family."

Ten-year-old Bill Baker and his brother, Leon, arrived in 1945. Bill entered the fifth grade. Shortly after he had completed four years at Euchee Indian School in Sapulpa, a small town near Tulsa, Mary Ella Hammond Baker heard about Sequoyah's excellent reputation and changed her mind about her sons' schooling. In later years, Bill recalled, "All our life our mother made sure we knew she valued education, so the transfer to Sequoyah came as no surprise."

In 1945, a good education and college degrees for her five children was a bold dream for a single full-blood Cherokee woman. Despite the fact that their white father had abandoned the family when Bill was six months old, Mary Ella made clear all along what she expected of her children. The absence of any child support from their father had not deterred her. Mary Ella Baker had rented out her allotment land to sharecroppers and worked at a string of jobs, first as a seamstress and later repairing books at a bookbindery. When the war had broken out, she had taken a job at Dupont, a Tulsa factory that produced gunpowder for the military.

Their mother drove Bill and Leon to Sequoyah.

"We followed Mom into the administration building," Bill recalled later. "On both sides of the road as we walked up were hundreds of kids greeting friends coming back to school. It seemed like all the girls had the same haircut, a Dutch boy bob. And they all had on uniforms: blue denim coveralls. Leon and I went through the check-in procedure and got our GI clothes and shoes. He went to the big boys' dorm, and I went to Home One, the little boys' dorm." Bill woke up in a huge room with red and blue stars pasted all over the ceiling. He sat up and looked around. "There were maybe forty beds in the room with a boy in each one. Even though I had spent four years at an Indian boarding school, that was an intimidating sight."

DECEMBER 1945:
THE FIRST MERRY CHRISTMAS IN FIVE YEARS

In early December, George Cameron received a letter from his brother. Bill wrote that his ship had been headed toward Tokyo Bay as part of a possible U.S. invasion force when news came of Japan's surrender. The letter read, "Every one of us on board felt grateful to President Truman. We figured a lot of men wouldn't have survived that invasion, maybe none of us." Bill described life aboard ship and talked about some of the cities he'd visited. He closed, asking George to give his sisters a hug and ended with "see you soon."

George later recalled hoping that the postscript meant Bill would be home in time to celebrate Christmas with them. Following a Cameron tradition, George made peanut brittle the way his parents had taught him. He had access to the ingredients because in October every year, he and a large group of boys harvested ten acres of sugarcane that, as part of their vocational training, they had planted in early summer. Come November, George and the same crew processed the cane into sorghum syrup, a staple no kitchen in Oklahoma could be without.

Two weeks before Christmas, George asked the cooks for permission to use the kitchen and some of the sorghum syrup to make holiday treats. Given the go-ahead, he and Everett Nave and Fields Smith boiled the syrup in a big pot. When it became thick, they

New friends, big school. Fields Smith (*left*), and new arrival Bill Baker (*right*) in 1945. Smith quarterbacked the Sequoyah Indians in the 1952 championship game against Tonkawa. Permission granted by Bill Baker.

added roasted peanuts, then spread the mixture on large baking sheets. While it cooled, the boys popped corn, poured a small amount of sorghum syrup over it in the pot, and mixed the combination well. As soon as the sticky concoction was warm, no longer hot, they formed it into popcorn balls. On Christmas day, the three boys shared their treats with friends.

Though Bill hadn't arrived, George remembers Christmas 1945 being the first merry holiday in five years. Just the promise of troops returning made class parties festive and fun again. They drew names and exchanged Christmas cards that they made. George Cameron, Everett Nave, and Fields Smith remember making theirs with construction paper and a lot of imagination. A similar celebration went on in every classroom, with the teacher reading a Christmas story, the students singing Christmas carols, and then treat time: Kool-Aid and oatmeal cookies fresh from the kitchen.

The day before Sequoyah's official Christmas vacation began, tradition called for the staff to prepare and serve Christmas dinner to the entire student body. Staff even did the cleanup. That evening, the music teacher, Miss Portia Vaughn, and her students produced an elaborate Christmas cantata, a musical event attended by everyone at Sequoyah, their families, and lots of folks from Tahlequah.

The following day marked the official beginning of Christmas vacation, when parents could come pick up their children. Walter Whitekiller arrived in a friend's pickup to get Danny and Dave and any kids who lived near their home. Students who had been sent a bus ticket caught the Transcontinental Trailways in front of the school.

But a good number of students stayed behind. George later recalled hearing his friend Kenny Vann being asked whether he was going home for Christmas. Kenny answered, "Hell, no, I am home."

"That was true for a lot of us," George said in reminiscing about those days.

Every year, though, a few students did not return after the Christmas break. Some enrolled in other Indian schools; others simply dropped out of sight and were never heard from again. Cecil Shipp remembered the sadness they felt when that happened:

"We didn't get to say goodbye. A good friend of mine, Jo Ann Hogshooter, didn't return and I've often wondered what happened to her."

Though the five Shipp children could have visited their Seminole relatives in Maud, they preferred to spend Christmas at school. "It was home, and we liked Christmas at Sequoyah," Cecil recalled. "Superintendent Brown visited with us. The teachers and dorm matrons tried to make it nice. We got to stay up later and the atmosphere was more relaxed. Brothers and sisters had more time to visit and play, and if a couple stayed at school, it was a good chance for boyfriend/girlfriend relationships to blossom."

The same held true for George Cameron and his sisters. "We looked forward to Christmas like all kids do, and to us Sequoyah was our home."

The music teacher remained at school and just by her presence made the holidays special. A statement around campus was often repeated about her: "If there is any music in a piano or a child, Miss Vaughn will find it and bring it out." She held a master's degree in music from the University of Kansas and used her summer vacations to take graduate courses, including one from the Juilliard conservatory in New York City. As dedicated to the students and the school as her boss, Superintendent Brown, Miss Vaughn had a love of music that transcended race and cultural differences. She devoted her thirty-one-year teaching career to those she called "my Indian children at Sequoyah."

The finale of the Christmas season came with the Christmas Eve party in the gymnasium. Students gathered around a decorated Christmas tree. Miss Vaughn played Christmas songs on the piano and led everyone in singing carols. Her rendition of "Here Comes Santa Claus" signaled a waiting red-suited Santa to enter and make his way around the floor while handing out candy, ho-ho-ing, and wishing every little girl and boy a Merry Christmas. Santa's helpers dragged in big cardboard boxes filled with gifts. Every student received a paper sack with an apple, an orange, some candy, pecans, and peanut brittle. This was the time when students who had earned enough money to buy a gift could give it to their brother or sister. Superintendent Brown handed out presents that had been mailed to students in care of the school. At the end of the evening, everyone joined together and sang "Silent Night."

Nine days of vacation remained, which meant no classes, extra movies, and more time for fun. The one negative aspect was that students who stayed at school had their own vocational jobs to do and also had to take up the slack for those who went home. Boys did extra duty in the dairy barn, power plant, and kitchen. Girls worked extra hours in the cafeteria and campus hospital.

Cecil Shipp later estimated that sixty to seventy-five students stayed at school every year for the holidays. "We'd divide up use of the gym; girls got it in the mornings, boys in the afternoons. We mostly played basketball, except when it snowed, and then we'd have snowball fights or bring out sleds we'd made and go sledding on campus. Though we were told not to play in the hay barns, boys especially would slip out there and play tag or hide and seek," Cecil recalled. "We'd build tunnels and forts with hay bales and play king-of-the-hill. Those were fun times."

The ground floor of the little boys' dorm as well as Unit A for senior boys had reading/entertainment rooms. The boys spent their evenings playing dominoes and checkers, listening to records, or reading comic books and magazines. Cecil Shipp remembers that very few kids had a radio, but "if you did you were in tall cotton." They would gather around it to listen to *Fibber McGee and Molly, The Green Hornet, Inner Sanctum,* and *The Lone Ranger.*

The holidays ended with the traditional New Year's Eve dance. Though Friday night dances were held throughout the school year, New Year's was the grand event. The dance was held in the gym, which had been decorated by a committee. The girls wore formals and boys were dressed in suits and ties. Boys could walk to the girls' dorm and escort their dates to the gym, though according to George, they were always under the watchful eye of two matrons.

For ninth through twelfth graders only, the dance consisted of boys and girls dancing to records or to live music performed by the school's swing band. George later recalled that the senior class sponsored a stand where the attendees could buy pop, candy, ice cream, and popcorn. Students danced and had refreshments until five minutes before midnight, when everybody stopped and formed one large circle. Everyone held hands and together counted down to twelve o'clock and sang "Auld Lang Syne," officially ending the party and the year.

Two matrons escorted the girls back to their dorms in one large group: one matron walked in front, the other in back. Boys and girls on a date could hold hands, but they had to walk with the group. Girls not old enough to attend the dance would peek from upstairs windows to watch boys kiss their girlfriends goodnight.

So rarely did a school romance land a boy and girl in trouble that when one did, it warranted a story in the local newspaper. A December 1945 edition of the *Tahlequah Citizen* included an appeal by a Sequoyah English teacher for information on the whereabouts of his sophomore daughter. She had run away with a former Sequoyah boy who had gone on to become a freshman at Northeastern. Because the boy had taken his parent's car, the newspaper printed a description: "light blue Ford two-door sedan with Oklahoma plates 43-33." The article instructed anyone spotting the vehicle to call the boy's father at telephone number 1617.

Bill Baker later recalled his time at Sequoyah and how important it was to his mother. "Mom had such dreams for her kids and it rubbed off on us. She never said, 'If you go to college'; she said, '*When* you go to college.' And at Sequoyah I found out I wasn't the only one with a parent like my mother, or the only one who wanted to make something of himself. We were fortunate to end up at Sequoyah."

15

Halleluiah for the Third Time
?WMꬶ KTꞰ TGCAJ

1946

Tommy Thompson paced the length of the waiting-area floor at the Okmulgee County hospital, back and forth in front of Jean, who kept glancing up from her magazine. "Daddy, why don't you sit down and read the paper or something? Momma's in good hands," she said.

He shrugged, not missing a step as he strode past his seventeen-year-old daughter. "I admit I'm a little superstitious, but I'm not changing things now. I paced while I was waiting for you and when Jimmy was born. You two came out fine and so did your mother."

An hour later, the doctor appeared. "Mr. Thompson, you have a healthy baby girl. Your wife and baby are doing fine. The nurse will let you know when you can see them."

As soon as the doctor left, Tommy plopped down on the couch next to Jean. "Halleluiah for the third time," he said. Jean tossed her magazine on top of the *Life* and *Saturday Evening Post* on the coffee table and remarked that she thought he might have wanted another boy.

"A healthy baby is what I want." Tommy leaned over and kissed her cheek. "I couldn't be happier with another girl. Seems like yesterday you were born. Now you're so busy with school and friends, your mother and I hardly see you. Jimmy either. I loved those first years. This baby means I get to live them over again."

Years later, Dorothy told the story of Tommy teasing her: "If we ever separate, I'll get the kids because I will swear in court you're their stepmother. They look just like me, so all the judge has to do is look at us to know I'm telling the truth." Not long after that, Dorothy and the children were at the Five and Dime in Okmulgee. The clerk remarked on how well she treated her stepchildren. "What makes you think they're my stepchildren?" Dorothy asked. The clerk then told her that the last time Tommy had come in with his children, he'd said that their mother was his first wife.

Dorothy could hardly stop laughing long enough to tell the clerk, "I *am* his first wife."

For the first time in their nineteen-year marriage, Tommy and Dorothy owned a home of their own. He had a good-paying job doing what he wanted to do, and he had the loving wife and family he had always wanted. Refereeing kept him involved in sports, although not in football and not as a coach. Life had handed him some hard times, but Tommy took pride in the fact that he somehow managed to make the best of it.

After fourteen months in the navy, Bill Cameron received his discharge in June 1946 and returned to Sequoyah. "I came back not so much to get my diploma but because it was home," Bill said. After traveling halfway around the world, he arrived expecting to see change and bustle; much to his surprise, very few things at Sequoyah had changed. True, there were no longer tanks and halftracks out back in mock fights, and the POWs had been shipped home to Germany. The four thousand civilians and military police at Camp Gruber were also gone, leaving behind only one division and a caretaker crew.

The word "orphan" had been dropped from the school's name, which had been changed to Sequoyah Vocational School. Everything looked unchanged, with the grounds in spit-spot order and every building's windows sparkling clean. Girls and boys still wore uniforms, a familiar sight that made Bill feel at home. He met his youngest sister, Fannie, for the first time. At eight years old, she was no longer the baby who had waved at him from behind the screen door when he left with the agent in 1939. She joined in his joyous reunion with George and Ann Marie. They, too, had grown and changed.

Boots, the same happy playful dog, still had the run of the campus.

To Bill, the good news was that Sequoyah hadn't changed; the bad news was that life hadn't changed either. Classes were back to their prewar schedule, and despite being a veteran, he still had to ask for a pass to go into town and had to be in his bunk at ten o'clock. Tahlequah seemed to have just as many sailors, soldiers, marines, and flyboys, but the streets no longer had the county fair atmosphere. These ex-military individuals weren't in search of fun; they were attending Northeastern State College to get a degree under the GI Bill. Bill briefly thought about enrolling after he graduated from Sequoyah but dismissed the idea. In his time away, Bill had gotten a glimpse of the world, more than he would have in a normal lifetime, and Tahlequah had come to seem small. In the four years it would take him to finish college, he could see a lot more of the world. And he rationalized that his distaste for studying, tests, and homework was reason enough to steer clear of college.

For the time being, though, Sequoyah was home, its familiarity comforting at times, albeit at others stifling. The boiler-house whistle awakened him to do the same chores he'd done a hundred times. It signaled going to the same classes, listening to the same teachers. The students in those classes seemed so much younger, though he knew that many of them were his age. One good thing about Sequoyah was that the food was far and away better than navy food. The cooks baked cookies and made fruit pies. The chili on Saturdays and fried chicken on Sundays tasted even better than he'd remembered. There was fresh-baked bread, real eggs instead of powdered, fresh vegetables instead of canned, and genuine butter rather than the yellow-tinted lard served aboard ship.

Instinctively, Bill felt that at some point he would return to the military, but because he didn't know exactly what branch, he decided to stick around home for a while. One big draw was football. When he reported for practice on August 15, Bill discovered one big change at Sequoyah. Just out of the army, Major Emmett McLemore had replaced Jim Choate as coach and boys' advisor. In army tan gabardines and his khaki shirt starched with three sharp creases down the back, Coach McLemore looked to still be in the army. The only things missing were his epaulets and rank insignia.

"Fall in," McLemore ordered. Bill scrambled into position and assumed attention posture, his eyes following the major. Hands clasped behind his back, McLemore paced back and forth in front of the line as though reviewing his troops. "First practice is two o'clock this afternoon," he said. "I'll hand out assignments then. Starting tomorrow, we'll have two practices a day until classes start. If you want to play football for me, I suggest you make both of them."

Bill fought the urge to salute. McLemore had the self-assurance of an officer but the muscled build of a pro-football player. The prospect of being coached by McLemore excited Bill, and his enthusiasm escalated the more he learned about the man. McLemore had played football for Carlisle Indian School, Jim Thorpe's alma mater, and had then gone on to play four years for Pittsburgh State College. After graduation, he had joined the Oorang Indian pro-football team that Thorpe played for and coached. When the team folded, McLemore landed a position with the Kansas City Blues of the National Football League. He played a couple of seasons in the NFL, then returned to his hometown of Stilwell, Oklahoma, and coached high school football.

After one season, McLemore had left to join the army, which intrigued Bill: Why would *anybody* leave the NFL to coach high school football? And with McLemore's experience and coaching talent, why would he join the army? Bill figured that as good as McLemore was, he could have ended up at one of the big schools, such as the University of Oklahoma or Nebraska. The fact that a man such as McLemore had chosen a career in the military gave credibility to Bill's ideas about his own future—when he was ready to decide.

McLemore started Bill at fullback, saying it was the position he'd played at Pittsburgh State. Honored by the gesture, Bill loved the camaraderie and the competition that football provided. He had no problem with exhausting practices, and his extra efforts did not escape McLemore's attention. The look of respect he received was all the motivation Bill needed. On the field, Coach McLemore directed plays as though he enjoyed it, but off the field he was an exacting disciplinarian who kept his distance from the players.

Twelve-year-old Harris Cully arrived at Sequoyah in the fall of 1946. From Sasakwa, Oklahoma, in Seminole country, his sporadic attendance at school brought him to the attention of a concerned BIA field agent. The agent convinced his Seminole/Chickasaw father and full-blood Creek mother that if they wanted Harris and his siblings to get an education, they needed to get the children into an Indian boarding school. They enrolled Harris and two brothers into Euchee Indian School in Sapulpa, where they remained until it closed the following year.

The three boys then transferred to Sequoyah. According to Harris, his father was an accomplished jack-of-all-trades, despite having only two grades of schooling. "My dad could do electrical, plumbing, carpentry, and even mechanical work on a car. He made a living in construction, and I don't think in his entire life, he ever had to hire anyone to do those things. There wasn't anything he couldn't fix," Harris said.

Like so many other newcomers at Sequoyah, Harris came from a rural home and shared similar experiences, such as gathering wood to cook and heat with and hauling water from a spring two buckets at a time for the needs of eight or ten people. But unlike some of the boys he met, he had no trouble speaking and reading English. Harris spoke two languages. His mother, fluent in English and in Creek, had not wanted her children to forget their language, so she had made sure that they conversed equally in both.

16

Life Comes Full Circle
ᎠᏆ ᎠᏍᎭᏋ ᏍᏔᏓᏋ

1947

By the end of their second year in Okmulgee, Tommy's pay-grade had increased to SP-7, giving him an annual salary of $3,648. He liked his job: he had come to know many of his Creek families, and they were doing better. In addition, Dorothy's teaching job paid $1,678 a year; money no longer seemed a concern in May 1947. Eleven-month-old Jody had just begun to pull herself up to a standing position at the coffee table and would be walking soon. Jean and Jimmy had friends that Tommy and Dorothy liked. And Jean, set to graduate from St. Anthony's in less than a month, talked excitedly about college. She planned to be a teacher like her mother.

Twelve-year-old Jimmy told his father that he hoped they would stay in Okmulgee a long time so he could graduate with his friends. Tommy replied that life gave no guarantees but his fourteen years of seniority with the BIA meant that they had a good chance of remaining where they were. Early in his career, he had mapped out a timetable for his moves, but he had a family now; they owned a home and nobody wanted to move again. Bustling Okmulgee had a great deal to offer, including nearby Dripping Springs Lake and Okmulgee Lake, which provided all they could want for fishing, picnics, and family outings.

Almost simultaneously with everyone's agreement that they wanted to remain in Okmulgee, fate put a kink in the Thompsons' idyllic life. Not more than twenty-four hours after Jean graduated from St. Anthony's, with the ink on her diploma barely dry, a

LIFE COMES FULL CIRCLE

Department of the Interior notice arrived. From the Muskogee Agency it brought devastating news: "Effective immediately all Education Field Agent positions have been abolished. EFA pay grades have accordingly been adjusted to SP 6, $3,397 annual salary." But it was the next paragraph that hit like a bombshell. Tommy's new assignment was Jones Academy, with instructions to report at soon as possible.

Tommy read and reread the letter, absorbing the consequences: they would have to sell their home; Jimmy wouldn't get to graduate with his friends; and tiny, out-of-the-way Hartshorne was the last place in Oklahoma he wanted to go. Jones Academy was an all-male military school of mostly Choctaws but had no football or baseball teams, so the job was strictly as boys' advisor.

When Tommy broke the news to Dorothy and the kids, he joked with them that he feared for his life. He had to admit, when he was alone with his thoughts, that this situation challenged his core philosophy to make the best of whatever life handed him. Even Dorothy's stoic resolve seemed shaken. Tommy had no time or opportunity to lament, however; they wanted him at Jones right away. He reluctantly put up a For Sale sign in the front yard. With almost no houses for sale in Okmulgee, the first couple that came to look at it decided to buy.

Before the full impact of the reassignment had a chance to sink in, the BIA's contracted moving company arrived and loaded up the family's furniture and belongings. The Thompsons—minus Jean, who had returned to Tahlequah to get settled at Northeastern—arrived at their school-supplied apartment on July 31, 1947, with the moving truck pulling in right behind them. The movers unloaded quickly and disappeared. One glance at the small rooms, the tiny bathroom, and the worn cabinets in the kitchen and Jean burst into tears. Jimmy seemed dazed as he lay his baby sister down in his father's favorite chair to finish her nap. Surrounded by boxes and furniture, they hardly had room to move.

Protocol called for Tommy to make an obligatory call on Vice-Principal Jack McCarty. Tommy had heard that McCarty coached Jones's basketball team, which garnered statewide attention for doing well against college-level competition. Tommy introduced himself and shook McCarty's hand, then returned to the apartment, the disorder a symbol of the chaos this move had delivered to his family. The next day would be a far cry from the celebration with friends and neighbors in Okmulgee that Dorothy had planned for Jody's first birthday.

Wordlessly directing Jimmy to help him, Tommy cleared a path through the boxes to the kitchen, then moved out of Dorothy's way, for in all their moves, she had always brought order to the kitchen first. From the bedroom, Tommy could hear cupboard doors being slammed. He worked silently and with eye contact signaled Jimmy to do the same. By the following evening, Dorothy had set the kitchen in order enough to celebrate Jody's first birthday. Jimmy later remembered a simple meal followed by a store-bought cake from a McAlester bakery and presents that his mother had brought with them. "Jean not being with us was strange enough, but the shock of the abrupt move disappeared during the brief party," Jimmy said. "Dad tried so hard to make the best of it, how could we do anything else?" The minute they finished helping Jody open her presents, the three of them resumed unpacking.

Upon coming across the box with his office items, Tommy left to set it up but promised Dorothy that he would return quickly to help with the house. He strode across campus, the sparsely treed grounds offering little relief from August's blistering heat and high humidity. He had learned what little he knew about the academy from the BIA's records in the Muskogee office. Founded by Oklahoma's Choctaw Nation in 1891, it was named in honor of their principal chief, Wilson Jones. Since that time, it had been brought under the aegis of the Department of the Interior and was managed by the BIA. Jones Academy owned 540 acres of rolling hills divided into a cultivated section for crops, a hundred-plus acres in pasture for their Holstein herd, and the remainder in timber land. Vocational training would be part of his job.

The lone huge building constituted what there was of the school. McCarthy had said that it contained classrooms, dorm rooms, the kitchen and dining hall, and a few other rooms to support the operation of a school for almost two hundred boys. Tommy located his office in one of the small outside buildings. He opened the door and, greeted by hot musty air, left the door open. He retrieved a fan from the box and turned it on; the air movement picked up dust and added it to the mix. Trying to gather a measure of enthusiasm, Tommy unloaded his personal effects, placing the picture of Dorothy and the kids front and center on his desk. *How many times have I done this?* he asked himself, and the ready answer was, *Too many.* Dorothy had made no secret of her desire to settle down in one place. Truth be known, he was tired of moving, too.

As he finished hanging his Northeastern diploma on the wall, someone tapped on the opened door. It was Emmett McLemore, the coach and boys' advisor from Sequoyah, whom Tommy had met at a Sequoyah game the previous year. Tommy invited him in. McLemore sat down and glanced around, his eyes settling on Tommy's just-hung framed diploma. "Northeastern, good school."

"Very good," Tommy answered, anxious to get back to the apartment.

"We ended with a 6–2 season, not as good as I hoped, but not bad either. I think this season will be better. I lost six seniors, but everybody else is back."

"I read that." Tommy was unable to ignore his curiosity. "I'm surprised to see you here, since practice starts in two weeks."

McLemore ran his fingers along the sharp crease of his pants; he was clearly searching for words. "Oh, hell, I might as well come out with what's on my mind. I just found out Maude Parker, principal at Sequoyah, is retiring and Jack McCarty, vice-principal here, is going to take her place. Since Jack is also boys' advisor, BIA needed to replace him and they chose you. The truth is, Tommy, I would love to work at a smaller school. I think Jones Academy would be a perfect fit for me and my wife." McLemore stared at him as though trying to gauge his reaction.

"I'm not sure I understand, Emmett," Tommy said.

The major leaned forward, his hands clasped. "I took the liberty of talking to McCarty a few minutes ago. He's due at Sequoyah in two weeks but he said before he leaves, he would hire my wife as a dorm matron if I could work this out with you."

Tommy could not hide his surprise. "You *want* to come here?"

McLemore nodded. "Jack Brown is a wonderful boss, but Sequoyah is big and so are the responsibilities. Too big for me at this point in my life. Is there any chance you would consider switching positions with me? Take my job as coach and boys' advisor at Sequoyah and let me come here?"

Stunned as McLemore's words sunk in, Tommy had all he could do to answer calmly that he thought the switch would work out well for both of them.

Jimmy recalls being surrounded by furniture, crumpled newspaper, and half-filled boxes, when his father burst in, laughing. Dorothy rushed in; picking her up, Tommy twirled her around, then told them they would *never, ever* guess his news.

BIA records reveal that Tommy accepted McLemore's offer that day, August 1, 1947. Jack McCarty put the paperwork into motion by having Tommy and McLemore sign separate applications for transfer. That done, they immediately tackled the considerable paperwork involved with the myriad government channels. Among a dozen other papers that had to be signed was the customary affidavit of nonaffiliation, on which each man swore that he was not a member of any group or himself engaged in any attempt to overthrow the government of the United States.

McLemore took the applications back to Sequoyah for Superintendent Jack Brown's signature. Brown then forwarded them on to W. O. Roberts, the BIA area superintendent in Muskogee. Less than a fortnight later, on August 12, 1947, Tommy's transfer became official, with the proviso that he report to Sequoyah no later than August 15, in time to start football practice.

Still not believing how this serendipitous change had happened, Tommy left Dorothy and Jimmy to handle the movers; on the morning of August 15, he called on Superintendent Brown at his office in Cherokee Hall. "Well, Mr. Brown, if you recall, six years ago, I promised to come back for a personal tour." Tommy chuckled, unable to hide his enthusiasm. "I had no idea it would be as coach and boys' advisor, but I can't tell you how thrilled I am to have this job."

Brown stood up and shook Tommy's hand. "Not as thrilled as I am to have you here. Call me Jack, will you?"

Dorothy and the children arrived two days later and were followed by a moving van with their furniture. For the second time in two weeks, Jean (who went over between classes at Northeastern) and Jimmy unpacked boxes, although no grumbling or sad faces were on exhibit this time. Their apartment took up the entire ground floor of Unit A, the senior boys' dorm. It had a large living room, three bedrooms, and a good-sized kitchen and bathroom. Busy with his duties, Tommy happily steered clear of Dorothy for the first few days until she had the furniture in place and everything the way she wanted. "A bit of advice about women," he told Jimmy. "Never argue with them, and when they're upset, stay out of their way."

When finally he and Dorothy were able to joke about the kink in their plans turning out the way it did, she told him that only Providence had the power to work out a kink that big. She added that he had better stay put, because she would never move again.

Twenty-seven years had gone by since he had walked out of this school with a diploma in his hand and a pocket full of dreams. Coming back to this place that had left such a lasting imprint on his life gave Tommy pause to reflect. All those years ago, the three of them had been deposited like pennies their father no longer valued, and now here he was with his life coming full circle to the place where, as a sixteen-year-old, he had first dreamed of football playing a big part in his life. This was at last his chance to make a difference through football. Tommy shared his revelation with Dorothy. Understanding all that he meant, she nodded in agreement and told him that was the reason Providence had brought them home.

The buzz that one of the best athletes to graduate from Northeastern had replaced McLemore blew through Sequoyah like an Oklahoma tornado. A standout football and basketball player, a fleet-footed trackman, Tommy Thompson had taken football camps from Glenn "Pop" Warner and D. X. Bible, two of the best and winningest coaches in college football.

The news dispelled any lingering disappointment the boys had about losing a top-notch coach—but that was only part of the job. What about the advisor part, they wondered, the one that really affected them? McLemore had been distant and not that friendly on a personal level. After their brief euphoria about being coached by a super athlete, the boys wondered just what kind of man this Tommy Thompson would turn out to be.

17

Catch a Football or Milk a Cow
ᎦhᏫ ᎠᏥᏞᏫᏋ DᎮ ᏣᏍ ᎦᏌᎩb

1947

During the first few weeks of school, Sequoyah's new football coach beat a steady path between the cafeteria and main office, scouting recruits. Tommy could easily be spotted on campus in his khaki pants, baseball cap, and two-pocket white shirt with a pack of Lucky Strikes in each pocket. He seemed to be everywhere. At forty-three years old, five foot ten, and 190 pounds, Sequoyah's new coach launched into the job of his dreams with the energy of a new college graduate.

Out of Sequoyah's total enrollment of 350 students, half of them were boys; half that number, 60 or 70, were boys old enough to play high school football. Tommy wanted every one of them. It didn't matter whether a boy had ever seen a football or a game. If he managed to catch a pass, run without falling down, or possessed what looked to be a whisper of potential, Tommy recruited him.

First he tried a direct approach. "Come out for the football team; you'll have fun. I've got some good games lined up." He would smile and pat the boy on the back when he said it, but if he didn't get a positive response, Tommy used his big gun—dairy barn duty.

"What's dairy barn duty?" a few dared to ask.

He would then hand them Sequoyah's schedule to follow as he read to them: "Whistle blows at 6:00 A.M., boys with kitchen or power plant duty report as soon as they dress. Breakfast at 6:30 to 7:00. From 7:00 to 8:00 make bed, clean room, attend to personal hygiene, plus chores and assignments. Classes begin

COACH TOMMY THOMPSON AND THE BOYS OF SEQUOYAH

Former Northeastern athlete Tommy Thompson as coach after taking over gridiron duties at Sequoyah Vocational School, 1947. Permission granted by Jimmy Thompson.

8:15 A.M., lunch 11:30 to 12:45 P.M., and, after that, vocational training." He would make sure to tell them, "I assign that, too."

At this point he would turn his full gaze on them to make sure they were absorbing what he said. He could tell by their expression and demeanor whether he had their attention. Some would venture to ask, "What is vocational training?" With this, Tommy would think, *Excellent, I do have their attention.* "Oh, a variety of things, like agriculture, painting buildings on campus, carpentry, fence building. There's a lot of that and animal husbandry, you know, practical stuff." Tommy would then tell them that dairy barn duty was very different.

"Those boys have to report at 5:00 A.M. See, right there." Tommy would point to the time. "All you have to do is milk three or four Holsteins every morning, then hurry back and get yourself and your room cleaned up so you don't miss breakfast. Did I mention you have to milk the cows again in the afternoon and process the milk? Seven days a week, holidays included."

Tommy had a near-perfect recruiting record.

All the members of the previous year's squad, except the six graduating seniors, returned. They were already working out with two practice sessions a day. Ex-navy man Bill Cameron was one of them. Tommy considered Bill a gift from heaven. Cameron could tackle, he never fumbled the ball, and not many players could catch him when he sprinted for the end zone. Tommy kept him at fullback; because he had such a good grasp of the game, Bill was put in charge of helping the other players with their assignments. Tommy picked Bill's younger brother, George, another good player, as his first-string fullback.

Danny Whitekiller let Tommy know that he had been on the 1945 and '46 squads but Choate and McLemore had never given him much playing time. Tommy put him on the varsity squad, and Whitekiller turned in solid performances at middle guard and end. He admired and respected Coach Tommy and later recalled, "He was Indian like us, as well as our teacher. He taught us not just football but what we needed to know to be successful in life. He gave us confidence because he trusted us. We were his football team, and Tommy made us believe we were *somebody*."

Whitekiller recalled some of Tommy's football strategies, "like the three-step shift on defense where the tackles, guards, and ends line up about three yards from the ball. Depending on the play, we'd shift our formation to either a balanced line or single wing. It was fun because the opponent's defense wouldn't figure it out until we were running our play." According to Whitekiller, "Not all Indian schools had football programs in 1947. If people wanted to see Indian boys play, Sequoyah was the place they came. It had a good reputation as a boarding school and for its football program."

In 1947, coaches in northeastern Oklahoma set up their fall schedules the summer before by phoning each other. Tommy made it a point to get acquainted with every high school coach in the six surrounding counties. Excited by the talent of his returning players and determined to fill out his squad, Tommy allowed no eligible boy to escape his attention. He discovered several good prospects. Ninth grader Milo Yellowhead was one of them. A transfer from Liberty Mounds School, Yellowhead admitted up front that he had no experience. "But I want to learn," he said. Tommy liked his attitude and suggested he bulk up by eating more and working out in the gym. Tommy assigned Yellowhead the defensive middle guard position and advised him, "All you have to do is hit their center, then hit him again."

Tommy's interest in his players went beyond football. He eased boys into conversations and eventually got to know them well. Their stories sometimes broke his heart; Milo Yellowhead's was one.

Milo's mother, Lucy Long, had died giving birth to him. Fortunately, a kind couple had immediately rescued him: full-blood Euchee Kelly Yellowhead and half-Creek, half-Euchee Sarah Yellowhead had no children of their own. "They were good parents," Milo recalled. "Later, they filed papers to legally adopt me but ran into a snag, so the adoption never went through."

Milo lived with them until he turned six in 1936; they then told him that it was time for him to start school. The Yellowheads enrolled Milo in Euchee Indian School in nearby Sapulpa. At the same time, a neighbor family enrolled their six-year-old son, Clarence. After the registration process was finished, the boys' parents said goodbye and returned home. Upon seeing them leave, Milo and Clarence talked it over and decided they didn't like boarding school enough to stay, so they walked eight miles back home. When the boys encountered their astonished parents, the Yellowheads and their neighbors decided to teach the boys a lesson. They told Milo and Clarence to turn around and walk back to school, which they did.

Milo never knew the identity of his biological father, so he took the name Yellowhead. He told Tommy that he eventually learned he had an older brother and sister who were rescued by other families. After several years, the three of them found each other. "But we never became close, because not growing up together, we could never make up those missing years."

Another good prospect, Andrew Mouse, Tommy encountered in the main office on the first day of school. "Tommy offered me dairy barn duty or football. I jumped at the chance to play," Andrew said. Tommy asked him his last name; Andrew answered, "Mouse." Chuckling, the new coach told him he was too big to be a mouse—rat was more like it. Andrew recalled, "My nickname 'Rat' was born that day and stuck with me the whole time I went to Sequoyah."

Andrew had a story similar to Yellowhead's. His full-blood Cherokee mother died when he was a baby, and five years later his father died. Andrew went to live with his grandmother but, as he told Tommy, "She lived on an old lady's pension and barely had enough to support herself, let alone me." Tom and Julie Mouse, distant relatives of Andrew's full-blood Cherokee father, told his grandmother that they would give him a home.

"The Mouses were good to me," he told Tommy. They took him to church every Sunday and made sure he attended a small country grade school in Delaware County up to the fifth grade. They switched him to a public school in Jay, Oklahoma, for the sixth grade; he attended until he turned thirteen in 1945. Tom and Julie Mouse enrolled their teenage son at Sequoyah, but Andrew told Tommy that he had run away after three months because of the coach and boys' advisor at the time.

More than interested in that remark, Tommy wanted to know who the coach was and why Andrew had left. Andrew told him, "I really wanted to play football, but I was too small, so I asked Coach Choate if I could manage the team. He said okay, but then I found out his definition of managing was having me mark the lines on the field for every home game and drag the tackling dummies three hundred yards from the gym to the field and back again after practice. The dummies weighed more than I did. It would have been easier to play football."

Tommy learned that the final straw for Andrew had been that after he had done everything Coach Choate asked him to do, the coach refused to let Andrew go with the team to out-of-town games. Mouse ran back home to Jay and stayed the rest of the year. "And you're just coming back now?" Tommy asked. Andrew nodded.

"Lucky for me," Tommy told him. "You'll play plenty of football and go everywhere the team goes." It took only one practice session for Tommy to discover that the boy he nicknamed Rat had a natural talent for football.

Tommy liked Sequoyah's new principal, Jack McCarty, the man who had helped facilitate the job switch with McLemore. But he liked the principal even more after Jack phoned him to say that fifteen-year-old John Anderson was at the registrar's desk and the coach would definitely want this boy on his team. Tommy immediately set out to find Anderson, but before they had the chance to officially meet, he witnessed the boy's considerable boxing talent. A string of expert jabs by Anderson convinced a bully not to pick on any more kids. A violation of school rules, fighting automatically earned Anderson disciplinary action. Because the boys' advisor had the responsibility of administering it, Tommy's first encounter involved giving Anderson a spanking.

Anderson later recalled with a laugh, "I was taller than Tommy but I didn't weigh as much. He had me report to his office in the gym and gave me a couple whacks on the butt with a paddle he called the Board of Education. Afterward, he shook my hand and asked me to join the football team." Tommy recognized natural talent and asked Anderson whether he would be interested in joining Sequoyah's boxing team. Anderson said yes to both. The grateful coach of both sports paid a visit to Principal McCarty to thank him.

McCarty said he appreciated Tommy's interest because Anderson held a special place in the lives of McCarty and his family. The eldest of ten children, John and his siblings had anxiously welcomed their Choctaw/Chickasaw father home from World War II, only to witness his complete mental breakdown not long after. Their father had seen major combat in the navy; not receiving psychiatric help after returning, he turned to alcohol and disappeared from their life.

Anderson's Choctaw/Chickasaw/white mother somehow kept the family together. She made sure her children attended school.

As chance would have it, she enrolled thirteen-year-old John at Jones Academy the same year McCarty became vice-principal at the school. McCarty told Tommy that the minute he met John, he sensed that the boy had no direction and no father to guide him. McCarty and his wife took John under their wing and included him in their family's activities. Later when Tommy talked with Anderson, John told the coach how much McCarty's family had influenced and guided him. He said they kept him from making mistakes and their acceptance and affection helped him be a better person. Anderson's story deeply touched Tommy; it showed what a difference one person could make in someone's life.

Tommy was disappointed that new arrival Jay Whitecrow was too young to play, because with some bulking up he could be a good candidate for the team. Still, Tommy wanted to get to know the boy. He learned that Whitecrow came to Sequoyah for all-too familiar reasons. His Cayuga/Seneca father, Mayo Whitecrow, had been in the military, serving first as a scout for John Pershing when the general chased Pancho Villa all over Mexico, then again with Pershing in World War I. Whitecrow told Tommy that his father had a scrapbook of pictures and documents from the war. "Before he got sick, I'd sit on the floor next to him. He let me point to a picture, then he'd share that part of his life. I loved those times. I really loved my dad," Whitecrow said.

But Mayo Whitecrow fell ill, and the doctor admitted him to the hospital in Miami, Oklahoma. Distraught, Jay ran away from home to be close to his father. He told of living in a cardboard box by the Neosho River. Having no money, when he got hungry enough he would knock on a door and, if no one answered, let himself in, eat what he could from the icebox, stuff some food into his pockets, and sneak out. His father's condition steadily worsened until the doctors transferred Mayo to the veteran's hospital in Muskogee, where he died.

"I didn't get scared when he died, I got angry," Whitecrow admitted. The boy's story went straight to Tommy's heart. Mayo Whitecrow's death splintered the family. Jay's mother allowed other families to take his two youngest sisters and enrolled Jay and his younger brother at Sequoyah. One sister, Sally, later joined them. Jay later remembered his aunt driving him and his brother to Sequoyah in her brand new 1947 Cadillac. His aunt had bought him new pants to wear. "The legs were way too long," he said, "so my aunt folded them under and pinned them with safety pins just below the knee. There were some boys playing a game when we got there. I don't remember what kind of game, but I joined in, and it didn't take long for all the safety pins to come loose. I had a foot of pant leg hanging over my shoes. We all had a good laugh."

Jay told Tommy that he thought Sequoyah was one of the most beautiful places he'd ever seen, and for the first time in a long time, he felt safe and warm. He loved the food and was grateful to be there. Tommy was relieved when Anderson befriended Whitecrow, who quickly learned from him how to deal with bullies. "It was inevitable you'd come across a bully in a school as big as Sequoyah," Whitecrow said. "I didn't have John's boxing talent, but what I learned was it wasn't so important that you *won* the fight, only that you *fought* the fight."

Tommy identified with Jay's anger about his father. He kept a close check on Jay, who (not surprisingly) had several meetings with the "Board of Education." Whitecrow later remembered, "When I would hear Tommy holler 'Jay Whitecrow!' at the top of his lungs, I knew what was coming. Very seldom did he discipline you on the spot. He told you when you were going to get a spanking and how many licks you would get so you had a night or two for it to weigh heavy on the mind. When I first got to Sequoyah," Whitecrow recalled, "I had this weird idea that if I didn't break a rule [and get disciplined,] nobody would even know I was there. Finally, I began to understand I had to care about me before anyone else would. I was on a one-way path to nowhere when I came to Sequoyah. Being there turned my life around."

Thompson Gouge was also too young to receive Tommy's "catch a ball or milk a cow" offer. Though not eligible to play football, the full-blood Creek fifth grader met Tommy soon after transferring from Euchee Boarding School. It was a traumatic first meeting, in the middle of the night and with Thompson in terrible pain. Gouge later recalled, "The CQ must have notified Tommy because the next thing I knew he walked into my room. I was in bed with a nightgown on. Tommy wrapped me in a blanket and carried me to his car. He drove me to Hastings Hospital in Tahlequah, carried me right in the door and asked to see a doctor. He kept telling me not to be afraid, that everything would be okay and he would stay with me. It turned out to be appendicitis. Tommy did stay, just like a dad. The next day he went looking for my mom and stepdad. I don't know how he found them, because they were picking cotton. But Tommy brought my mother to the hospital."

The care and concern Tommy showed Gouge that night forged a father-son bond between the two. "My whole time at Sequoyah, Tommy treated me like his son, and I thought of him as a father," Gouge said later.

Coach Tommy began his first football season at Sequoyah with a game against Muskogee Central High School and the next against St. Joseph's. The following game, Sequoyah's traditional Thanksgiving Day rivalry with Chilocco Indian School, was called a grudge match by the *Tahlequah Citizen*; George Cameron compared it to an Oklahoma-Texas game. Chilocco had beaten Sequoyah the year before, 14–13. The 1947 game turned into a knock-down, drag-out between two all-Indian teams, neither of them willing to lose. The Indians of Sequoyah suffered some injuries but won, 7–6, and Tommy offered them congratulations for their "refuse to lose" attitude.

Their game drew one of the biggest crowds ever to see a Sequoyah game. In the locker room afterward, Tommy joked, "On my team I have a Deer, a Dirteater, a Locust, a Tiger, a Wildcat, a Hummingbird, a Dreadfulwater, a Bat, a Bighorse, a Yellowhead, a Weavel, and even a Rat. How can we lose?"

As he had done early in his BIA career, Tommy maintained twelve- to fifteen-hour days, six days a week. Sharing a common living room with the senior boys who lived upstairs turned the

Thompsons into instant surrogate parents, helping with homework and even playing checkers, which Tommy loved to do. And because they spent almost every evening together, Jean, Jimmy, and Jody viewed the boys as family. Dorothy is reported to have made no distinction between what she called "Tommy's boys" and her own children. She liked to make popcorn or a pie or cake and would divide it among her newfound family. Though his first football season ended with a 5-3-1 record, Tommy told Dorothy he couldn't be happier. He had the job of his dreams and an extended family he loved as though they were his own.

Dorothy shared his comment with Jean, who responded by sharing some news of her own. "I'm in love, Momma."

"Oh, dear," Dorothy said. "Wait a little while before you tell your father, will you?" Jean agreed, and it became routine that on Friday and Saturday nights, she would kiss her father on the cheek and breeze out the door. Tommy never failed to ask his wife if she knew where Jean was going and with whom. Dorothy replied truthfully. "Of course I know. She's with a friend."

As Christmas drew closer, Tommy figured out that Jean's friend was a young, good-looking, half-Cherokee fellow named Amon Baker. Baker had visited Jean at the apartment several times in the last few months, and although they acted properly, Tommy could see that they were smitten with each other. He went to his wife and asked whether they were getting serious.

Dorothy answered him, "You be nice to Jean's latest boyfriend."

Tommy knew very little about Baker except that he was a senior and had completed a tour of duty in the navy. He had two younger brothers at Sequoyah. Tommy checked his files and found out that Baker had joined the football team but left the team after injuring his knee. When asked about his plans after graduation, Baker said that he had already submitted his application to Northeastern and wanted to be a teacher. Tommy considered that a point in his favor.

Because this Baker fellow seemed to be serious about his daughter, Tommy decided that he should get to know the young man a lot better.

18

Cherokee Pied Piper
ᏣᎳᎩ ᎠᏓᏘᏃᎯᏱ

1947–48

Amon Baker didn't know quite what to make of Tommy's curiosity about him. When he called on Jean at their apartment, Baker's conversations ended up being as much with her father as with Jean. Though her father seemed very friendly, Tommy asked a lot of questions about the navy and about Baker's family and the teaching career he envisioned. Early on, Jean had warned Baker about her father and how defensive he could be with her boyfriends. She added that he was being so nice to Amon that it surprised her. More amazing to Jean and Dorothy was when Tommy invited Baker along on a basketball referee job.

Baker, who had come to like and admire Tommy very much, jumped at the chance. "Tommy was an athlete and a competitor at heart. He could have been a full-time referee, because every coach in northeast Oklahoma wanted Tommy Thompson to officiate for him. He was good at it and it was obvious he loved the game," Baker later said.

Visiting with him on the drive and getting to watch how he conducted himself during the game gave Baker great insight into Tommy, the man, the coach, the father, and the husband. "He was a man of integrity but very much in charge. Everybody respected Coach Thompson, including me." Baker recalled a game that took place in Westville, a small town just inside the Oklahoma-Arkansas border. Westville played a team from Stilwell; Tommy said at the time that the Stilwell coach had called him because the schools had a history of rivalry and their games sometimes got out of hand. A second referee had agreed to assist Tommy but failed to show up, because his car broke down.

Baker told the story. "The Westville gymnasium was standing room only, with about nine hundred hometown fans. Late in the first quarter, a Stilwell player got fouled. When the boy approached the line to take his free throw, the crowd went crazy. They started booing and stomping their feet. Some fans even hollered insults at the player. Officials today are used to that kind of behavior, but not back then and certainly not Tommy.

"As the player started to take his shot, the crowd got even uglier, screaming at the kid until Tommy held up his hand and blew the whistle. He signaled for the boy to give him the ball and then just stood there, one hand on his hip, the ball under his other arm. The players didn't know what to make of it. They looked at each other and at Tommy, like 'What's going on?' I had a seat right behind the players' bench, and they were doing the same thing. For a minute or two the crowd didn't seem to understand, but then it dawned that Tommy had stopped the game and wasn't going to start it until they stopped the noise.

"They quieted down a little, but there was still a buzz going around. Tommy walked over in front of the long side of the gym where the Westville fans sat. He raised the ball in the air and the crowd went dead silent. Tommy told them, 'This Stilwell boy is entitled to a free shot without you screaming insults and trying to distract him. I'm here to give him his chance. And you will, too, or I will clear the gym. There won't be anybody in here but the coaches, the players, and me.' You could have heard a pin drop. Tommy handed the ball back to the Stilwell player, and he made his shot.

"In the second half, Tommy called a Stilwell player for traveling. He blew his whistle and instead of the player tossing the ball to Tommy, he laid it on the floor and took off to the other end of the court. I don't know if he meant to be disrespectful or he didn't know what he was supposed to do. Tommy stood there as the boy took his position at the other end. One of the other Stilwell players realized the mistake and picked up the ball but Tommy blew his whistle and told him to put it down. This time, the crowd went silent immediately.

"Tommy pointed to the player who made the foul. He didn't yell, but he told him to bring the ball and hand it to him. He didn't sound mad or excited, but you could tell he meant what he said. The player brought the ball back and handed it to Tommy, and play resumed. After that, the crowd and the players behaved. There was no more trouble. It changed the tenor of the game."

Baker enjoyed the evening so much that when Tommy asked him along a second time, he accepted right away; he hoped it meant that Tommy had enjoyed it as much as he. That game, Baker recalls, was at Checotah High School, an hour's drive from Tahlequah.

As at the Westville game, Checotah's gymnasium was standing room only. Baker vividly recalled the game. "Not long into the first quarter, a heckler high up in the stands started giving Tommy a bad time. He would holler insults when Tommy blew the whistle. Tommy ignored the first few, but when the heckler yelled, 'You're a blind man, where's your dog?' Tommy blew his whistle and stopped the game.

"The crowd went quiet when he walked up to the edge of the court. Tommy pointed to the guy and said, 'You! Up there in the stands. Get down here.' Lots of people stood up so they could see the guy, and for a minute he didn't move, but then I guess he figured out Tommy didn't intend to start the game until he did. Everybody in the gym watched him make his way down to the floor. Tommy got right in his face and did all the talking. The guy looked scared to death. I was sitting right behind the players, but I couldn't hear what Tommy said. When he finished, he patted the guy on the shoulder and stood there until he made it all the way back to his seat. When the guy sat down, Tommy started the game. After that the game was about basketball, not the crowd. Tommy expected good sportsmanship and respect by the players and the crowd, and he had no trouble asking for it."

On the way home, Baker asked him what he'd said to the heckler. "Tommy told the guy he was being disrespectful and disrupting the game. And if he did it one more time, he was going to walk him to the door, and in front of the whole crowd, he'd personally throw him out." Baker viewed the incident as demonstrating Tommy's respect for the game and the players.

It became routine that at least once a month, Baker would accompany Tommy to a game. During their trips, Tommy talked about his philosophy of sports, how they helped prepare youngsters for life's challenges, and how they revealed a person's true nature. He believed that whatever strengths and weaknesses a person had, they would surface in sports.

As time went by, their conversations turned to marriage and family and education. "I don't think I ever met a happier man or anyone more devoted to his wife and children," Baker later said. But to Baker's question about his childhood, all Tommy revealed was that the uncle he was named after had left him an inheritance and another uncle had beat him out of it. He added that it had made life hard, especially for one of his sisters.

Baker remembered that as the only time in the ten years he knew Tommy that the older man sounded bitter and angry. Normally jovial and upbeat, he never spoke of his childhood again. "I often wondered if that was what gave Tommy his compassion for children," Baker said.

Baker would occasionally walk across Sequoyah's campus with Tommy. "It was like walking with a Cherokee Pied Piper," Baker recalled. "Kids followed him. They loved being around Tommy, and he loved them—big or little, it didn't matter. I can't even count how many times some little boy or girl would run up and holler 'Tommy!' He would laugh—Tommy had this high-pitched laugh that was so distinctive I can remember it to this day. He'd pick up the boy or girl and swing him around. You'd swear you were watching a father and his child."

About his later life Tommy spoke willingly, even recalling a disastrous trip the summer before he graduated from Northeastern. Before he and Dorothy left for Claremore, Tommy and Lewis Rabbit, a football friend he knew from Haskell, had taken the train to Chicago on the promise of a professional football career with an all-Indian team called the Chicago Indians. Tommy told Baker that after working out for three or four days with the team, he and Lewis skedaddled back to Tahlequah because the promoter didn't get financing and they darned near starved to death. Tommy remembered, thankfully, that he hadn't said a word about the offer to anyone but Dorothy.

In December 1947, Jean extended an invitation to Baker from her parents to join the family on Christmas Day to open presents and have supper. "That family had so much fun, and being included was wonderful," Baker later recalled. As suppertime neared, Jean convinced Baker that her father seemed in such a good mood, it would be a good time to approach him.

"I asked Tommy's permission to marry his daughter," Baker said. "After spending so much time with him on trips, I felt pretty sure he would say yes. Thankfully he did and then told me he was happy to have me in the family."

Amon Baker and Jean Thompson's wedding took place on January 9, 1948, at the First United Methodist Church in Tahlequah. Tommy gave his daughter away and afterward wiped away his tears with his handkerchief. Dorothy, who always had a way of making sense out of whatever confronted her husband and family, assured Tommy that not only would Jean remain a big part of their lives, but he now had another son.

19

The Chameleon
DLᎪCBᎾy ᎣᏢᏆᎾRT ᎫᏟᏍᏢ

1948

The new year that began with their daughter marrying Amon Baker continued smoothly for the Thompson family. Amon would graduate from Sequoyah in May and start classes at Northeastern in the fall. He and Jean, who was already a student at Northeastern State Teachers College, had an apartment nearby. Thirteen-year-old Jimmy, an eighth grader, had friends from public school and just as many at Sequoyah. For every boy living upstairs from the Thompsons' apartment, eighteen-month-old Jody had become their little sister. They vied for her attention, and she reciprocated with laughter and gibberish they only half understood.

Dorothy had come to admire Harry Truman. Nothing like his eloquent and sophisticated predecessor, Truman made it a point not to emulate Roosevelt, whom Dorothy had venerated. Dorothy claimed she admired Truman for being his own man and for how hard he fought against Republican Thomas Dewey for a second term. Though considered the underdog, Truman pulled off the most stunning upset to date in presidential history. His victory restored Dorothy's interest in politics and her allegiance to the U.S. president.

With school just out, June 1948 began with a typical evening for Tommy and Dorothy, as the senior boys from upstairs gathered in their shared living room. Six players (one of them the Thompsons' son, Jimmy) all lay on their stomach, propped up on elbows, with concentration etched on each face. Dorothy left to tuck Jody into bed, then returned to the living room, pausing to watch three checker games in progress. Tommy peered over the newspaper at her. "Dorothy Jean Thompson, don't you dare." About to point out a move to one of the boys, she instead answered a knock on the door.

It took all of Bill Cameron's courage to knock on the Thompsons' door that night. Mrs. Thompson invited him in. The sight of boys sprawled on the floor playing checkers and Tommy sitting in his chair reading the newspaper gave the appearance of one big family.

Tommy offered him coffee, but Bill declined. Heart beating fast, all he wanted to do was say what he had come to say and leave. He didn't want to break down in front of them.

Dorothy offered to leave the two of them alone, but Bill asked her to stay. "I came to say goodbye. I'm joining the army," he blurted out.

Tommy rose from his chair. "Bill, no! Please don't say that."

Bill took a deep breath and exhaled. Intent on doing this right, he had practiced on the way over. "Coach, I'm not the academic type. The thought of four more years of tests and studying—I can't do it. I've given this a lot of thought, and I believe the military will be a good career for me."

Tommy looked devastated. "What can I say to change your mind?"

Bill glanced from Tommy to Dorothy, his heart bursting with emotion. "It's really hard to say goodbye to you and Mrs. Thompson. You've been like parents to me, and I want you to know how much I appreciate everything you've done. You two have made a big difference in my life."

Dorothy brushed away a tear as she glanced at Tommy.

"I hate to disappoint you more than anybody, Coach," Bill said. "And I hate goodbyes, but I had to come by, since I won't be coming back to Sequoyah, not as home anyway."

"You can't hate goodbyes more than I do." Tommy's voice was husky with emotion. He embraced Bill. "Damn, I feel like I'm losing a son."

Bill blinked back tears. "We're even then, because I feel like a kid leaving home for the first time." He straightened his shoulders.

"I'm on my way to parachute school at Fort Benning, Georgia. I'll be there six months. Not sure where after that, but I'll let you know."

Bill hugged Mrs. Thompson and departed quickly, proud that he had let them know just how much they both meant to him.

Cecil and Rudell Shipp, George Cameron, Danny Whitekiller, Harris Cully, and John Anderson returned to school on September 2, 1948, after two weeks at Army National Guard camp in Fort Sill, Oklahoma. They joined the rest of the team for football practice the following day and learned from Tommy that they had two weeks to get ready for their first game.

In mid-September, they left by bus for Siloam Springs, Arkansas, to face a team whose players consistently made All-State. After four scoreless quarters of smash-mouth football, Siloam Springs scored their lone touchdown as the final whistle blew. The following week, the Sequoyah Indians had another away game, this one against Pawhuska, a public high school in the heart of Osage country. Sequoyah proved no match for Pawhuska's taller, heavier players; the Indians were outweighed at every position.

Back at Sequoyah, Tommy called his team together to figure out what they could do about having to face teams with a significant height and weight advantage. He shifted several assignments and urged his players to take advantage of their greatest strength—speed.

By making adjustments and shifting their emphasis to speed, the Indians won their next five games, four of them by shutouts. "The adjustments Coach made did it," Danny Whitekiller later recalled. "We played tougher and smarter." Tommy gave them added incentive by announcing that, for the first time in the school's history, Sequoyah would take part in the Oklahoma Athletic Association's Class C playoffs in District 12.

The Indians, with Coach Tommy Thompson, drew large crowds to their home games even though there was no seating and fans either had to bring their own chairs or stand on weed-covered sidelines. Because Sequoyah's field did not have lights, night games were played on Gable Field at Northeastern, many times drawing as many fans as the Northeastern Redmen. Even the *Tahlequah Citizen* acknowledged that "any game with the boys from Sequoyah guarantees a good turnout."

Tommy attributed their ability to draw a good crowd as the reason a group of Muskogee and Tahlequah political and business leaders issued the Indians an invitation. The group wanted them to play Riverside Indian School in an all-Indian football game as the opening event of the centennial. Planned as a huge two-day celebration, it commemorated one hundred years of progress by the Five Civilized Tribes: Cherokee, Choctaw, Creek, Seminole, and Chickasaw. Muskogee, the official host city, anticipated thousands of visitors from all forty-eight states for this important historical event. The all-Indian game would be Tahlequah's contribution to the celebration.

The two teams met on an October 1948 evening on Gable Field before a sold-out crowd in Northeastern's 2,500-seat stadium. Riverside's all-Indian team included Apache, Kiowa, Caddo, Comanche, and Delaware players. The crowd watched Sequoyah's Indians shut out their opponents, 38–0.

The following day, the centennial celebration moved to Muskogee, where an estimated crowd of thirty thousand people lined Third Street. The crowd watched a parade of floats, prancing horses, costumed native dancers, school bands, and civic entries from dozens of towns, plus all thirty-nine recognized tribes in Oklahoma. Days before, as a tribute to the tribes and the state, artists had painted huge replicas of each seal of the Five Civilized Tribes and the State of Oklahoma on the parade route's brick-paved street. Tommy's boys assisted with directing parking and traffic and as guides at the Indian Art Exposition, a collection of paintings, pottery, rugs, weavings, and artifacts from the Five Civilized Tribes.

Eight U.S. governors and several members of President Truman's cabinet attended the centennial, as did movie stars Adolph Menjou, Jack Oakie, Kay Francis, Gary Cooper, Bill Boyd, and Van Heflin. Prominent leaders from all five tribes and dozens of other tribes watched a rugged game of Cherokee ball, the game from which lacrosse descended. Afterward, a Keetoowah chief inducted Native

Oklahoman Van Heflin into the Keetoowah Society. Speeches and ceremonies received national radio coverage, and the festivities concluded with an army-navy show and a giant program of fireworks.

The Indians' five straight victories and shutout of Riverside raised hopes for a 7-2 season and a berth in the state playoffs. But in their next game against Morris High, the Sequoyah Indians lost 0–18 when right end J. D. Johnson broke his arm in the first quarter. The following week, they lost their last game of the 1948 season to Dewar, 14–18.

Two weeks later, on December 12, Sequoyah's basketball season began, a welcome antidote for football's disappointing outcome. In their first game on the home court, the Indians took on the Stilwell Panthers. Tommy and his son, Jimmy, attended as spectators, which was a radical change for Coach Thompson. Sequoyah's principal, Jack McCarty, coached the first game, then surrendered his coaching duties to Tommy the following day, saying his job took too much of his time.

Tommy relished the opportunity to coach his second-favorite sport. John Anderson, Andrew Mouse, Milo Yellowhead, and several first-string football players joined the basketball squad. Surprised at how easily they could switch from football to basketball, the team did not miss a step in the next two months, racking up one win after another.

Their spectacular 14-2 season earned Sequoyah a berth in the Northeastern Oklahoma Athletic Association's Class B playoffs for the first time in school history. The District 12 Class B championship would be determined in a three-game playoff.

In their first playoff game, Sequoyah defeated the Wagoner Bulldogs 44–29 on Wagoner's home court. A close 35–34 win over their next opponent, Stigler, advanced the Indians to the finals against the same school. In the third and final game of the tournament, Sequoyah defeated the Stigler Panthers for the second time, 42–31. The win earned them the District 12 Class B Championship trophy. Sequoyah's 363 total season points (as opposed to Stigler's 210), plus stories about their 16-2 record in local and eastern Oklahoma newspapers, went a long way in helping Tommy and his boys forget football season.

Tommy had no time off after basketball ended, though, because baseball followed almost on its heels. John Anderson showed his considerable athletic talent as pitcher and one of the team's big hitters. The Indians replicated their basketball season with a stellar record of wins, which earned them a chance to compete in the Cherokee County baseball Class B championships.

It was a two-game playoff this time: in their first game, against a Kansas team, Sequoyah's John Anderson pitched five innings and allowed two runs. With the Indians leading 3 to 2 in the sixth inning, Sequoyah at bat and bases loaded, Anderson blasted a triple that drove in the three runs. He then scored on a Kansas overthrow to third base. Their 7–2 win over Kansas advanced Sequoyah to the finals and a game against Westville, which they won. Sequoyah's trophy as District 12 Class B Baseball Champions went into the school's trophy case alongside their basketball trophy.

The end of the baseball season offered Tommy a breather and time to evaluate his second year at Sequoyah. His boys had made substantial progress. Many had never before taken part in competitive sports, which in his mind was fundamental in their journey to manhood. Most had arrived scrawny and out of shape. All of them, during the year, had put on weight and had no trouble playing forty-eight minutes of basketball or nine innings of baseball. Players on his football team routinely played a full sixty minutes—on offense and defense.

Aside from their accomplishments in sports, he could see other changes. Their teachers' weekly reports showed good effort and improvement but strongly suggested that they needed more class time. Vocational training, the one thing Tommy could not ignore, took as many hours a day as they spent in class. By preparing them to be farmers or to get a job in some trade, vocational training might be considered practical, but it was not farsighted. Mr. Brown agreed.

The two of them discussed the subject often; Brown said that he, too, regretted the time vocational training took away from studies. Practically speaking, however, he pointed out that if schools such as Sequoyah weren't self-sufficient, they wouldn't exist. Brown maintained, "Vocational training is so engrained in the system, only God could change it."

Near the end of the school year, George Cameron appeared at Tommy's office with a letter from his brother at Fort Benning. Bill wrote that there were three hundred guys in his class, and part of their training took place in gliders. He went on, "They take us up to 2,000 feet and cut us loose in a plane with no motor. That'll separate the men from the boys! I'm doing fine. Will let you know where I go from here. Hug Ann Marie and Fannie for me and be sure to read this to Coach and Mrs. Thompson. Tell them I sure miss them."

Consistently upbeat, charismatic, complex, and openly devoted to his wife and family and the boys in his care, Coach Tommy Thompson was not the sort of person one would think had a drinking problem, especially in view of the fact that he deplored his father's alcoholism. But according to Amon Baker, he did have a drinking problem. Baker described his father-in-law as being an "episodic alcoholic." Once a month he would buy a bottle of whiskey, drive someplace and park away from the school, and drink the entire bottle. According to his children and the students who knew he drank, Tommy did not ever disclose to anyone that he had an alcohol problem.

To the contrary, he made every effort to keep it secret; Dorothy aided him in doing so. Aware that a few of the boys knew, she occasionally had to call on them for help. Cecil Shipp later recalled, "Sometimes on a Saturday night on the way home from a movie in town, some of us would spot Tommy going into Blackhawk's Liquor. If he drank that night and didn't come home, Mrs. Thompson would send for Bill Baker, John Anderson, or me, to find his car and bring him back. After she had to do that a few times, we found out Mrs. Thompson put her foot down and insisted he not drink in his car. She made Tommy go to a motel."

THE CHAMELEON

Before 1948, Tommy would have bought his whiskey from one of Tahlequah's four bootleggers, who, according to Shipp, "might as well be listed in the Yellow Pages because everybody knew who they were." But in 1948 Oklahoma changed its laws, and with it no longer being a dry state, liquor stores such as Blackhawk's sold hard liquor as well as beer.

Thompson Gouge knew Tommy drank. "I don't remember any of us ever talking bad about him for it. He was good to us and we could count on Tommy. He made a big difference in my life. I was having a lot of trouble with a subject. I studied hard, but when I took the test I made a low grade. I did so poorly that I decided I shouldn't even be in school. I went to my room and started packing. Tommy found out about it and came up to my room. He told me if I gave up now, that later in my life when things got tough, I'd do the same thing. He said he didn't want me to be that way. Tommy told me to unpack, get out my book, and start studying. Because he told me he *knew* I could do it, I graduated from high school."

Danny Whitekiller spent five years at Sequoyah, four of them playing football, in daily contact with Tommy. Whitekiller had no idea that his coach had a problem with alcohol, which is testimony to Tommy's success at hiding it. When the subject was brought up with Whitekiller, he assumed that the problem must have taken place after he graduated.

According to Shipp, the boys did not talk among themselves about Tommy's drinking. Nor did they ever consider snitching on him to Superintendent Brown. "Tommy treated each one of us like his son," Shipp said later. "We viewed him as a dad. He was really the only father I ever had. Tommy had a way of making us feel special. It was obvious to us and to anyone that knew him that he loved *his* boys. And even as young as some of us were, we were aware enough to be thankful to Mrs. Thompson and his kids for sharing him with us. I guess you could say we covered for Tommy because we didn't want to lose him. We realized just how much of himself he gave to us."

Shipp said Tommy did what fathers do. "Every evening he stopped in the dorm library to see who was doing homework and who wasn't," Shipp recalled. "He'd get after anybody he thought was slacking, but if we had finished, he would sit down and play checkers or penny-ante poker with us. None of us realized it at the time, but looking back, there was a lot of fatherly advice slipped in those visits. He'd talk about football or basketball or life in general. He talked a lot about the difference between right and wrong and tell us, 'Be proud you're Indian. Be responsible for your actions. Respect your elders. Learn to get along with people.' And he never failed to tell us to behave ourselves around girls."

The boys maintain that not once during those visits did he ever smell of liquor or look or act inebriated. Bill Baker, however, recalled once seeing Tommy drunk. It happened on a Saturday in Muskogee. Bill left school without getting a pass and hitchhiked to Muskogee to visit his mother. Not finding her at home, he waited on her front porch until dusk and then walked back into Muskogee. There, parked at the curb in front of the post office, was Tommy's Chevy. Baker said he figured the coach had found out he'd left without a pass. "The minute I saw his car, I knew I was in trouble. My knees were shaking when I walked up to his car. Tommy was behind the wheel, chin on his chest like he was asleep. The windows were open and the car reeked of whiskey. I could have turned around and high-tailed it back to school, but I didn't. I tapped him on the shoulder and asked if he would like me to drive him home. Tommy said yes, 'But as soon as we get there I'm gonna paddle your butt for not getting a pass.'"

Tommy slept during the twenty-one-mile ride back to Sequoyah. It was dark by the time they arrived, so Bill parked the coach's Chevy in the lot near his apartment and knocked on the door. A worried Mrs. Thompson answered and helped him get Tommy into the apartment. She thanked Bill profusely. According to Bill Baker, "the big difference with Tommy was that he never drank in front of us and he was never abusive. In fact, he was the opposite. Tommy showed us every day how much he cared about us. We accepted him for what he was—a good man."

THE CHAMELEON

Looking back, the men who used to be Tommy's boys agree that he shouldered more responsibility than any other person they've ever known. Cecil Shipp recalled, "He worked six days a week, sometimes sixteen-hour days. I don't know how he did it, but once in a while I guess he needed to escape and liquor was his way of doing it. We knew Tommy as a father, a teacher, and a mentor who taught us about life. As our coach, he taught us to love sports and helped us become good athletes. The fact that he drank will never take away from Tommy's greatness."

Because he was a private man about that part of his life, how Tommy dealt with it in his various other roles remains a mystery. But interviews with his children as well with people who knew and had worked with him confirm that Tommy's episodic bouts with whiskey had no effect on his desire or ability to be a surrogate father, teacher, friend, or mentor.

Like a chameleon, he became whatever a child needed him to be.

20

Sacred Traditions
ᏚᎳᎢᏓ ᎯᏈᎾᎴᏆᎠᏪᎦᎢ

July 1949

As printed in the *Tahlequah Star Citizen*, July 1949:

> With stomp dances of pagan origin the Cherokees on July 19th celebrated the 99th anniversary of the birth of Redbird Smith, founder of the mysterious Nighthawk Keetoowah. Fires burned throughout the almost impenetrable rocky hills encircling Tahlequah as old full blood Indians and members of the younger generation gathered to dance to a melancholy chant and the sound of rattles and drum.
>
> Embers, kept glowing for hundreds of years and brought over the Trail of Tears from Georgia, gave birth to flames which centered innumerable dancing circles. Dancers followed a ceremony believed to have originated before the time of Columbus when the Cherokees were fire-worshippers. Organized by the Nighthawks, a secret tightly knit organization of male full bloods, the nighttime dances were open to all who cared to join in preserving ancient Cherokee customs, now fast-dying as young Indians turn to material civilization....
>
> The Cherokee stomp dance is said to be one of the few Indian ceremonies still performed spontaneously. It is no showy exhibition with preliminary advertising. In fact, few Tahlequahans know the exact dates and places for the dances. Experts say that the stomp dance is slowly slipping into extinction. This year's performance may be the last. (reprinted with permission by the *Tahlequah Daily Press,* successor)

SACRED TRADITIONS

Fields Smith, a Sequoyah student in 1949 and grandson of Redbird Smith, said in an interview, "The stomp dance is far from becoming extinct. Each of the seven clans hold ceremonies today that are just as viable and important as they ever were. Stomp grounds to the Cherokees are the equivalent of a church, a gathering place to pray and perform sacred ceremonies. In nineteen forty-nine and for many years after, the stomp grounds on my grandfather's land near Vian held the biggest stomp dance in northeast Oklahoma. Everyone came to it. Even today between two hundred and two hundred fifty people attend. Redbird Smith was born on July nineteenth, which is a big day for Cherokees. But now the biggest stomp ground is the one my Uncle Stoke Smith founded when he moved the sacred fire to his wife's allotment land twelve miles north of Vian. They have stomp dances there once a month, and as many as fifteen hundred people attend."

Fields provided his own perspective on the stomp dance described by the *Tahlequah Star Citizen* article:

> I was sixteen the summer of nineteen forty-nine, and I remember that July nineteenth like it was yesterday. For me, that day was always exciting but sad at the same time. A day like no other, part of it sacred to strengthen ancient beliefs and customs, part of it laughter and fun and competition. I got to see friends and relatives I hadn't seen for a long time. But even at sixteen, this stomp dance held great significance for me. It was the ninety-ninth celebration of my grandfather's birth. I looked forward to all of it, the stomp dance, the stick ball game, the wonderful food, but I felt sad, too, because my parents weren't there. Both of them died young.
>
> Redbird Smith had eight sons. My father, Samuel, was his second son. Dad was chief of the Keetoowahs for many years, and he loved this day; my mother [did,] too. He would have been in charge of the whole thing, directing preparations and greeting leaders from the six other stomp grounds. I remember really missing them that day.
>
> Three or four hundred people had arrived the previous day, most of them on horseback or in horse- or mule-drawn

wagons. A few came in cars and trucks but not many. It was an impressive sight, looking out over nine acres of stomp grounds and seeing hundreds of campfires with people gathered around them. No one ever knew exactly how many would come, but in the nineteen forties it was usually about five or six hundred people.

After my father died, two of his younger brothers became chief of the Keetoowahs, but in nineteen forty-nine Uncle Stoke Smith was chief. He was Redbird's youngest son. I'd been living with him and his family for four summers, since my mother died. I worked with his sons baling hay, plowing, and doing general farmwork. I liked being surrounded by family, more cousins than I could count and a slew of aunts and uncles close enough to borrow a cup of sugar or, if the breeze was right, smell an apple pie set in a window sill to cool.

I remember waking up early that morning, and, like it always seemed to do, it rained the night before. The air was cool and full of wonderful smells, campfire smoke, damp earth, weeds and grass. Because it was cool, the birds were chirping. Even they seemed excited.

I walked a quarter of a mile from my uncle's house to the stomp grounds. I wanted to watch the lighting of the sacred fire. Tradition says its embers have burned from ancient times when the Cherokees were fire worshippers, but in nineteen forty-nine, the sacred fire was lit by chosen fire keepers for each stomp dance. Three were chosen that year: my brother and two cousins.

They gathered in the middle of the stomp grounds around a circle of ashes eight feet in diameter and a foot thick, the remains of past fires. They lay down four logs, each one three feet long and about eight inches in diameter, placing them down in the ashes—one log pointing north, one south, one east, and one west. Where they came together at the center, the fire keepers left enough space to build the fire.

SACRED TRADITIONS

All of this is done according to Cherokee tradition. They light it like they've done for a thousand years. The main fire keeper rubs a flint rock against a sharp knife blade over a small pile of dried mushroom debris they gather from a tree. Most all of the trees in this part of the country have mushroom debris on them. The flint rock against the knife blade makes a spark that sets the debris on fire. The fire keeper adds twigs and sticks until it's burning good and then puts wood on it. They keep the fire going all day and night until the celebration ends when the sun comes up the next morning. The sacred fire is the center and focus of the celebration.

Seven large arbors surround the fire, each one constructed of large tree limbs with brush piled on top to create shade. Underneath are rows of split-log benches where clan members sit to listen to speeches in the afternoon and watch the dancing after dark. Each clan's arbor has a designated position around the sacred fire, its place symbolic and spiritual: the first arbor belongs to the Wolf Clan and occupies the south position, the east belongs to the Long Hair Clan, and north is for the Bird Clan.

The due west position is left open, and in between the three arbors are four more arbors, also at compass points: southeast for the Bear Clan, northeast the Paint Clan, northwest the Deer Clan, and southwest the Savannah Clan. Cherokee clans evolved from ancient times with their own customs and traditions, which we observed at the nineteen forty-nine stomp dance and are still observed today.

In addition to the sacred fire, there are four parts to the celebration—the speeches, the food, a stick ball game, and the stomp dance—all of them spiritual. The feast is served at noon, and except for the desserts that the women make at home, everything is cooked that day at the stomp grounds. Uncle Stoke and his three brothers [the other four brothers had passed away] butchered and cooked ten or twelve hogs in a deep pit barbecue and distributed the meat to each family's campsite.

For three days before the celebration, my cousins and I gathered firewood and piled it alongside a trench about twelve feet long, twelve inches wide, and fourteen inches deep. It was lined with rocks to keep the sides from caving in and [to] radiate the heat. My cousins and I went around the night before to our relatives' houses and borrowed six or seven big cast iron pots. Both men and women did the cooking. They'd build a fire in the trench and put the cast iron pot on top of it.

The food they cooked was unbelievable: chicken, hominy grits, white beans, brown beans, and as many different kinds of soups as there were cooks. Most of the soups started with carrots and onions, potatoes and greens from the garden. Some cooks added beef; others would add chunks of carp or catfish. Others added baked and shredded squirrel meat or *kanucchi,* which is ground hickory nuts formed into balls.

Two very large permanent tables held all the food. One table was four feet wide and forty-five feet long with a plank top. Poles buried in the ground every four feet supported its massive weight. At noon the table was loaded with platters of pork and beef and chicken, pans of Indian fry-bread, cornbread, plain biscuits, biscuits with green onions inside, even biscuits with beans baked in them. There were big bowls of home-canned green beans, sliced fresh tomatoes, and fried taters. Desserts were at the end of the big table: apple pies; peach, lemon, and raisin pies; and big bread pans of peach and berry cobbler.

The second table was made from two ten-foot logs cut in half and laid side by side, flat side up. This is the table for the cast iron pots of hot food. My favorite soup was the one with squirrel meat, and my second favorite was the one with kanucchi—they are delicious.

At noon, women and girls took their place and stood on the north side of the big table, men and boys on the south. We waited for the Feed the Fire ceremony. The main fire keeper approached the fire with a dead white chicken in his hands, white to signify purity. He placed the chicken in the fire and chanted in Cherokee a prayer of thanks to God. After the sacrifice and prayer, everyone helped themselves to the food.

People brought their own plates and utensils, but not all six hundred people showed up. A lot of folks cooked and ate at their own campsite with friends and relatives they hadn't seen since the year before. Campers had their own spot. They would bring a cook stove and leave it there. No one ever bothered someone else's campsite.

The food was and still is a highlight, and there was plenty of it that year. But no liquor; people drank water or pop or Kool-Aid but mostly water because of the heat. A few times, though, some man would show up drunk. If he caused any trouble, my uncles would sit him at the base of a tree and tie his hands together in back of the tree until he sobered up.

Speeches came after lunch. Usually every stomp ground leader gave one. Uncle Stoke didn't necessarily give the first one, but he gave the longest speech. W. W. Keeler, chief of the Cherokee Nation, gave a speech that day. The speeches are religious in nature, not political. Being Christians, the Cherokees talk about worshipping God, about how to raise children to be good Christians. People sit in the arbor of their clan during the speeches. Since a child inherits the clan of his mother, I am a member of the Paint Clan. But my father belonged to the Bird Clan and since they came from different clans, I could sit in either arbor. The speeches lasted for several hours and it was usually hot by this time. Still, people were polite and listened.

After the speeches, we played stick ball. Even though it is a Cherokee tradition that goes way back in our tribe's history, anybody can play, not just Cherokees. Men, women, young and old (that's how kids learn the game), and it's men against women. Players use a golf-ball size ball covered with shoe tongue leather. The way stick ball is played and scored has never changed since ancient times. Exactly one hundred feet straight west from the fire (the reason there is no arbor at the west position) is a twenty-five-foot-tall pole. It has a painted ring six feet down from the top and a carved wooden carp on the very top.

Men play with a three-foot-long stick in each hand. On the end of each stick is a leather stringed scoop [used] to pick up the ball from the ground and throw it at the pole. Men can't touch the ball with their hands. Women can *only* use their hands. Similar to basketball when, say, a female has the ball, her teammates can guard her. They can hold the opponents away with their hands against a man's chest or arms.

If a player hits the pole between the carp and the painted line, their team gets one point, six points if the ball hits the fish on top. Before the game starts, the scorekeeper etches a one-hundred-foot line in the dirt straight from the sacred fire to the base of the pole. Each time a team scores a point, the scorekeeper draws a line in the dirt at three-foot intervals (women's [are] marked on the south side of the line, men's on the north). The first point is three feet from the base of the pole, [so] six points (six lines at three feet apart) takes up eighteen feet. When one of the team's lines reach the fire (thirty-three lines at three-foot intervals equals about one hundred feet), the scorekeeper starts back toward the pole. For each point scored, he then marks a line through the existing one, making an X. The first team to get lines all the way from the pole to the fire and back to the pole is the winner.

People watch from the arbor of their clan; others stand in the shade of a tree. It might be ninety degrees, but it doesn't daunt the players. By the end of the game, any moisture in the ground from the night's rain is gone. To keep dust down during the stomp dance, selected individuals walk around with pots of water, flinging the water over the dirt with their hands.

SACRED TRADITIONS

Just before dark and the stomp dancing began, I remember Uncle Stoke and another leader giving a warning speech. Warning speeches are traditional. They're to make sure everyone understands the behavior expected of them during the stomp dance. As soon as it's dark, coal lanterns are lit and the dancing begins.

One man or boy (he has to be Cherokee) is asked to lead a dance. The first leader might be Uncle Stoke or one of his sons or brothers. Young boys are encouraged to lead. I learned to dance by age four or five and led many of them. After choosing six men or boys to answer, the leader dances as he sings or chants his song to God. After each line or verse, the six men sing or chant their answer. There is no music, per se, only a drummer that plays for his clan. He stands or sits next to the fire so he can study the dancers and adjust his drumming to match their dance.

Young girls are chosen to dance with shackles, which are actually turtle shells, around their ankles. They make a jingly sound to keep time with the drum. Some stomp dancers hold hands while they dance, and some dance individually. A member of any tribe can join in and dance around the fire, but they have to stay in back of the leader and the six chosen men.

The celebration ends the next morning. It is tradition that the medicine man from each clan cooks up a batch of herbs in a big pot of water. There are seven pots, but you don't have to stick with your clan, just line up. It is a cleansing ceremony to protect against evil. The medicine man ladles the liquid into your cupped hands. You can wash your hands with it or your face or both. Once that's done, the stomp dance is over and everyone packs up and goes home.

Fields went on, "Something special about the nineteen forty-nine stomp dance was Tommy came and brought Jimmy and Jody. Tommy was a celebrity. Lots of people wanted to shake his hand and visit with him. He was his typical self—friendly, laughing, and talking with everybody. Tommy took part in the stomp dance with Jody in his arms. The fact that he came meant a lot to me. I missed my parents, but I had all my cousins and relatives and lots of pretty girls to visit with."

Jimmy Thompson also recalled attending the Redbird stomp dance in 1949: "I was fifteen, and I danced until I couldn't dance any more. Dad danced holding Jody in his arms. She had both arms up in the air. It was wonderful to watch them. They were laughing and having the time of their lives. That stomp dance was the first time I'd ever heard my dad carry on conversations in Cherokee. At home he spoke English, but he could speak beautiful Cherokee. That day he wasn't a coach or a boys' advisor, he was a proud Cherokee man."

21

Ah-sky-uh—the Man
DᎣᏚᎠ, Ꮎ DᎣᏚᎠ

1949

Fifteen-year-old Forman Ross and his cousin Dave Simon arrived at Sequoyah a week before classes started. After registering and receiving their government-issue clothes, the two boys scouted out the campus. To the east of the administration building they came across an oblong field marked with white lines, with boys running up and down the length of it. "Neither of us had ever seen a football field, but we knew they were playing *some* kind of game," Ross later said. "We stopped to watch; then a man with a whistle around his neck ran up and asked what grade we were in."

When he heard "ninth grade," Tommy told them to go to the gym, get their football gear on, and hurry back for practice. "Just like that, my becoming a man began that day under the leadership of Tommy Thompson," Ross recalled. "He became a second father to me." Ross started as a scrub, being assigned sometimes at guard and other times at tackle on offense and defense. Ross remembered, "I was really excited about playing and anxious to learn the game. Tommy encouraged me, so I learned fast."

Unlike most boys, Ross at age fifteen had made the decision to enroll at Sequoyah. He was one year old when his full-blood Cherokee mother died; Ross's father, also a full-blood Cherokee, remarried not long after. The family lived on Ross's father's allotment land near small, rural Kenwood, Oklahoma. As Ross grew older, his relationship with his stepmother became ever more strained. "That factored heavily in my decision to leave home," Ross said later. "That and my father did not value education. He wanted my brother and me to be farmers, like him. My brother liked farming, but I wanted more out of life. When I finished the eighth grade, I transferred to Sequoyah."

Though he had attended Kenwood's small public school, Ross easily adjusted to Sequoyah's military lifestyle. "I liked the discipline. And I figured with so many kids, it was probably the best way to run a school that size. Every time the whistle blew, we knew what to do and how they wanted it done. We made our beds at the same time in the same way. We knew how to fold our clothes and hang our towels on the rack. None of that bothered me." According to Ross, Sequoyah's rules seemed fair. "They were made very clear, and we knew what to expect if we broke them. When we left our room in the morning, it had to be ready for inspection by the dorm matron. If for some reason the room didn't pass, the guy responsible got four hours of disciplinary duty on Saturday. To me, it seemed pretty straightforward."

Sequoyah's 1949 football season officially began on August 15. Ross met the other full-blood Cherokee members of the team: George Cameron, Everett Nave, Danny Whitekiller, Fields Smith, John Anderson, and Andrew Mouse. They understood the game and explained it in Cherokee. "Sometimes we would call plays in Cherokee," Ross later said. "It made Tommy laugh."

Milo Yellowhead also suited up the first day of practice. He recalled that after their two daily practices, Tommy assigned one group to bale hay and another to cut silage for the dairy herd and hog farm. The coach called it conditioning. In 1947, Yellowhead's first year on the team, he played defensive middle guard. The next year he alternated between end and half. The summer of 1949, he was at home and found out he would be taking over quarterback duties when a letter from Tommy arrived in July. Sanders, the previous quarterback had graduated; George Cameron would be Yellowhead's backup.

August's one hundred degrees and 70 percent humidity came as no surprise to the boys. End Rudell Shipp recalled, "It made our afternoon practice sessions brutal. There were no sideline machines blowing cool mist over us like they do today. No trainers handed

Forman Ross, a platoon sergeant and paratrooper with the 101st Airborne, earned the Bronze Star for combat in Vietnam. Permission granted by Forman Ross.

out ice water or fortified drinks. Tommy's practice sessions tested our stamina and endurance as much as they perfected plays." Between practices and vocational work, the boys were either in shape or off the team. Shipp later acknowledged that despite Tommy's demanding expectations, something about him inspired them to play their hearts out. "After practice we would work on a certain play on our own until we got it right, sometimes until we were about to drop. We knew Tommy expected us to be tough, and we tried our best to be," Shipp said.

Harris Cully went home to Sasakwa for the summer of 1949 and also received a letter from Tommy. "He diagrammed the plays he wanted us to learn and wrote instructions on how to run them," Cully recalled. "He expected three things from his players: be tough, be in shape, and come back ready to play. Classes always started the Tuesday after Labor Day, and if he could, Tommy would have a game lined up that Friday. He found out quick who was ready to play."

The 1949 season began as Cully predicted. Classes started on Tuesday, September 4, and three days later the Indians played their first game against Class B Morris High School. Morris had beaten them 18–0 the previous season after right end J. D. Johnson broke his arm early in the first half. After three weeks of practice and heavy farmwork, Tommy's boys felt they were ready and Morris would be a good test.

No one remembers why Tommy decided to drive the sixty miles to the game instead of traveling with the team on the bus as he usually did. Quarterback Milo Yellowhead, John Anderson, and a couple of backs rode with him. The rest of the team traveled on Sequoyah's embarrassingly ancient yellow bus the boys called Crackerjack. John Anderson later remembered riding in Tommy's Chevy and talking football. As they passed through the town of Fort Gibson, a car pulled out in front of them. Tommy slammed on his brakes, but not fast enough. "I'd never been in a car accident before and neither had the other guys," Anderson recalled. "None of us were hurt, but it shook us up quite a bit."

Meanwhile, in Morris, the starting time for the game had come and gone. After waiting for over an hour, the officials told

Lem Sanders, Sequoyah's bus driver and only adult with the team, that they had to either play or forfeit. With no coach, no quarterback, and minus several backs, the Indians took to the field; by the end of the first half, they had scored two touchdowns. They were well into the second half when Tommy arrived with the rest of the team. Sequoyah defeated Morris 22–6, and Tommy promised he would never again take his car.

Sixteen hours after defeating Morris, the Indians boarded Crackerjack again, this time heading east to Rogers, Arkansas, to face a powerhouse Class A team. Whitekiller recalls still being sore and tired from the Morris game, but the Indians played Rogers to a 7–7 tie. Ecstatic over their performance, Tommy told them that their tough practices were paying off. If they hadn't played the day before, he told them, "You would have whipped those Arkansas boys."

The Oklahoma Athletic Association ranked high school teams in the state as A, B, or C, according to their school's enrollment (A for the largest). Because Sequoyah had only 350–75 students, OAA ranked it Class C. The ranking irritated Tommy; he wanted to play up, understanding that if they wanted to improve, the Indians needed to play Class A and B teams. He tried to line up as many A and B schools as he could for their 1949 season but encountered resistance. A and B coaches did not want to chance losing to a C school, and winning over any team coached by Tommy Thompson was far from certain.

Tommy nevertheless prevailed; his nine-game schedule included seven A or B schools, two C schools, and one unfilled date. In addition to that official schedule, he talked the coach of the Class A Muskogee Roughers into a scrimmage with his team. The Indians had played tough against Class A Rogers, but that was an Arkansas team. This test would be against an Oklahoma A team. Tommy was clearly excited when he announced the scrimmage.

"Coach asked us if we wouldn't like to know how good we really were," Yellowhead remembered. Tommy told them that playing a team of that caliber would give them their answer. "He convinced us we were good enough to go up against a powerhouse Oklahoma

Class A team," Yellowhead recalled; "We went into that scrimmage feeling we could beat them." Sequoyah played the Roughers to a 7–7 tie. Tommy congratulated them and said it proved what he already knew.

"Our formations were simple single and double wing, no fancy stuff, just straight smash-mouth football," Whitekiller recalled. "Tommy used a seven-diamond defense. I was middleman, so my job was to plow over the middle and nail the opponent's quarterback." Whether on defense or offense, Tommy had a reputation for using trick plays, according to Whitekiller.

Yellowhead believed that Tommy invented the "lonesome end" play long before it showed up at West Point. "The minute the center snapped the ball, the other linemen ran to the right sideline," Yellowhead recalled. "With the whole line on his right, the center became an eligible receiver, referred to as the lonesome end. I'd pass him the ball; he'd sprint for the end zone. We practiced that play and did it so quick, the other team had no time to react."

Whitekiller remembered, "Sometimes when we received the other team's kickoff and Tommy didn't like our field position, he'd call in John Anderson to punt on first down. The other team didn't know what to think. Since Big John could punt fifty and sixty yards, they wouldn't have anybody back that far and ended up with lousy field position."

Never having the luxury of a deep bench, Tommy used trick plays out of necessity. And he wasn't averse to additional assistance. According to John Anderson, "He involved Mr. Brown, who would run up and down the sidelines yelling us on. And when we won, which we often did, Tommy coerced him into buying us dinner instead of our traditional peanut butter and jelly sandwiches."

Andrew Mouse, Sequoyah's first player to make Oklahoma's All-State high school football team, calls Tommy a great coach because "he instilled a winning attitude in his players." Mouse recalled Tommy's use of humor and sometimes psychology, especially when they played an all-white team: "If their tackle knocked one of us on our butt, he would say, 'What's the matter, that white boy hit you too hard?' Or if their guy outran us, he'd

Danny Whitekiller (*left*), and brother Dave (*right*), suited up for the start of the 1949 football season. Permission granted by Danny Whitekiller.

say, 'That white boy too fast for you?' It wasn't racial and none of us took it that way. It was a competitive thing, a private joke he used to motivate us."

After Sequoyah defeated Class B Morris and tied Class A Rogers and Muskogee, the Indians went on to beat Class B Westville. A week later, Class C Watts proved no match for them, earning Sequoyah the Eastern Class C Division Championship. Tommy began to wonder whether this could be the season he'd dreamed about. Cameron and Anderson remembered that the team had wondered the same thing. Tommy fueled speculation, telling them he believed they had a good chance to win it all. At that, the team leaders called a strategy meeting to give themselves every chance to win. They held several more strategy meetings over the next few weeks.

Forman Ross reminisced about those days. "Tommy never said he believed Indian medicine would improve our chances, but he didn't tell us we couldn't use it. Fields Smith and several other players had a Cherokee medicine man in their family to give us sacred tobacco. One of us would spread the tobacco over the ground and then we'd all chant a prayer before a game."

Whether because of attitude, preparation, or Indian medicine, Sequoyah racked up wins. The *Tahlequah Citizen* on October 6, 1949, wrote, "Sequoyah Indians Smother Ketchum 39–0 Score." The paper went on to describe the Indians' sparkling offense and stalwart defense: "QB Yellowhead passed for 3 touchdowns and, on defense, intercepted a pass and ran it back 43 yards for a 4th TD. The Indians scored three more times and ended the game with 363 total yards to Ketchum's 180."

Tommy's irrepressible smile broadcast his elation; he was living his dream. By promising Wagoner High's coach that his Indians would play on their home field, Tommy filled the vacant date in his schedule. On October 7, the Indians defeated Wagoner's Class B team 12–0.

The following week, the Indians again made headlines: "Indians Go on Warpath after Tribal Grid Foes." The article continued, "Already winners of the Eastern Division Class 4C Championship, Sequoyah has only three non-conference games before meeting the Class C winner of the western division."

In the first of these three nonconference games, Sequoyah defeated Riverside Indian School 18–0. A week later, on Friday afternoon in the nearby town of Jay, the Indians played their second nonconference game, resulting in a shutout of Class B Jay High School, 38–0.

AH-SKY-UH—THE MAN

The following morning while at work in his office, Tommy received a call from a very irritated J. B. Earp, superintendent of Jay High School. "I want to know just how old you play your guys, anyway. I see Andrew Mouse on your roster. He's from Jay, am I correct?"

"Yes, he is," Tommy answered. "Why do you ask?"

"He's thirty years old, that's why. I'm calling to let you know I've lodged a complaint with Mr. Anderson, executive secretary of the Oklahoma High School Athletic Association."

"Andrew Mouse is not thirty years old. He's seventeen," Tommy said.

Adamant that Tommy had committed a grievous error, Earp would not listen to his explanation. Tommy promptly called Andy Mouse's dorm and asked the matron to put him on the phone. "Get yourself over here, Rat. We're going to Jay."

Mouse remembers their Saturday drive to Jay and following his aggravated coach into Superintendent Earp's office. After an initial tense exchange, the two men ended their brief meeting with a laugh and handshake. It turned out that another Andrew Mouse lived in Jay, a thirty-year-old deaf-mute. Earp apologized profusely and assured Tommy that he would call Secretary Anderson first thing Monday to withdraw his complaint.

"Talk about the pot calling the kettle black," Tommy told Mouse on the drive home. When Mouse asked what he meant, Tommy explained that a couple of years before, Jay High School had had a complaint filed against them for practicing before August 15, OAA's authorized date. "To show you how serious the charge is, the secretary drove all the way from Oklahoma City to pay a surprise visit to the school," Tommy told Mouse. "It was still before the 15th, and there was the team practicing. The story goes that the QB let fly a bad pass just as the OAA official walked up and he had to duck or get clobbered. Every high school coach in three counties had a good laugh over that."

Sequoyah played the third nonconference game on October 23, 1949, against Cascia Hall, a Catholic high school in Tulsa. Cascia brought their A team to Tahlequah for the Indians' homecoming game. Cascia's big players had consistently been tough for the Indians. But after Sequoyah's first-half offensive showing and the crowning of Sequoyah's football queen and her attendants during halftime pageantry, the Indians finished off Cascia Hall, 30–6.

Excitement ruled the Indians' locker room. An upbeat Tommy warned the team not to let up, though, and he stressed the importance of focusing solely on the next game. Sequoyah had one remaining game that, win or lose, would not affect either team's conference standing. Against the Class B Fairland High School Owls on October 28, the game would be the Indians' final test before they faced either Oilton or Dewar for the overall District 4 championship.

The Indians traveled to the northeastern corner of Oklahoma. Tommy addressed the team on the bus. "Fairland hasn't lost a game this season. They're Class B, but that doesn't mean they're any better, it only means more kids go to their school. You've already beat B teams. Just remember, all sixty minutes of this game count."

Tough defense by both teams dominated the first half, but the Indians scored two touchdowns in the third quarter. The *Daily Oklahoman* headlined the victory, "Unbeaten Sequoyah Indians Top Fairland, 13–6." The accompanying story stated that defensive safety Milo Yellowhead played a crucial role in holding Fairland to their lone touchdown.

On returning to Tahlequah, the team learned that Class C Dewar had won the Western District 4C Championship. As the winner of the Eastern District 4C Championship, Sequoyah would now vie with Dewar for championship of the entire district. To Tommy, what was even more important than the district title was that a victory over Dewar would give them a shot to advance to the state Class C playoffs. Undefeated Sequoyah had the home field advantage over one-loss Dewar. In a championship game played on November 10, 1949, on Gable Field at Northeastern, the Indians defeated Dewar 21–6.

They were in the State Class C Championship playoffs, a first in Sequoyah's seventy-seven-year history.

Tommy told them that their first playoff would be a home game against Quinton High, a Pittsburg County school. On Thanksgiving Day, November 24, 1949, Sequoyah students, Tahlequah citizens, and a sizeable contingent of Quinton fans—two thousand in all—packed the stadium at Northeastern, delaying their holiday dinners to see the first contest for the State Class C Championship. Quinton's Savages came determined to advance to the semifinals, but Sequoyah's Indians were dead-set on stopping them. According to Whitekiller, Tommy told them, "Only you guys are out there in the huddle. I can't call in plays or adjustments so all I ask is, play smart and play tough."

"Milo called our plays," Whitekiller remembered. "All quarterbacks did in those days."

Defense ruled the first half with no score by either team. In the third quarter, Sequoyah's offense scored twice. Quinton answered with two touchdowns of their own but missed one conversion. The Indians ran over the Savages in the fourth quarter with three touchdowns, yielding a final score of 34–13.

Jubilant Coach Tommy couldn't stop smiling.

Back at Sequoyah, Mr. Brown addressed the student body. He thanked Tommy and the team for their talent and hard work and for garnering the school prestige in sports for the first time since the school's founding in 1872. After the assembly, Mr. Brown and Tommy led a noisy, excited student body to the cafeteria for their traditional Thanksgiving meal.

The team had one week to get ready for the semifinal round of the playoffs. No home game this time, it would be played on a neutral field. During the week, Tommy observed the varsity squad holding daily meetings after practice: skull sessions, the boys called them. Watching them in action filled him with pride. As they worked together on plays and strategies, everyone took part: first one boy would lead the group, then another. It was a display of teamwork and leadership, the very things Tommy had hoped to instill in them.

On Friday morning, December 2, the Indians piled into Crackerjack for the trip to Checotah, about seventy miles south, in McIntosh

County. The opposing team, Class C Grandfield High, would be traveling from the other direction, their hometown just north of the Red River on the Texas border. George Cameron remembered arriving in Checotah in Sequoyah's embarrassing bus: "With our equipment tied piled on top of Crackerjack, we looked like an Indian traveling circus."

Whitekiller recalled, "Grandfield had several players, veterans from WWII, that came back to high school for their diploma so they could enroll in college under the GI Bill. They were older and a lot bigger than us."

After arriving at Checotah High, Tommy and the team walked to their stadium to check out the football field. An old stadium, it had been built by the WPA, the principal told them. Two sets of wooden stands, each about thirty yards in length, sat midway down both sides of the field, and open grass surrounded the remainder of the field. Three hours before game time, fans had already begun to arrive, nosing up their old jalopies and pickups close to the stands. There were just as many people gathered around their cars as sitting in the stands. As they walked back to the gym, Tommy told the boys, "There'll be two thousand people here by game time. Let's give them a good game."

Grandfield scored the first touchdown in the opening quarter but failed to convert. Their opponents' tough defense forced Sequoyah to keep bringing in left end and kicker John Anderson to punt. Twenty seconds before the end of the half, Yellowhead scored the Indian's first touchdown with a quarterback sneak from the one-yard line. Anderson's conversion gave the Indians a 7–6 halftime lead. Grandfield scored another TD but again failed to convert. Indian halfback Chastine Keener intercepted a Grandfield pass and ran it back to the Grandfield twenty-five-yard line; and Yellowhead completed the play with a spiral to Whitekiller in the end zone.

Anderson's point after clinched the 13–12 win. The victory ignited playoff fever at Sequoyah; it started in the locker room and spread throughout the school. The chance to be Oklahoma's Class C champions presented a possibility never before dreamed of in Sequoyah's long history. The team's excitement leveled off, though, when the boys learned they would be playing Medford High, coached by Howard Welborn. Medford had already won the Class C state championship twice, in 1945 and 1946, with Welborn as coach.

The December 3, 1949, edition of the *Enid News Eagle* came out with the list of OAA's High School All-State players in Class A, B, and C. Grandfield and Dewar each had one C player. Medford had two. Sequoyah players were conspicuously absent.

There wasn't a player on the Sequoyah squad who underestimated the task in front of them or failed to recognize the opportunity for what it was—a chance to make history. According to Forman Ross, "All of us Cherokee boys called Tommy Ah-sky-uh, 'the man.' He taught us how to take orders and give orders, how to stand up to larger than normal tasks. Tommy knew us inside and out, our feelings, our strengths, and our breaking points. He was our coach, and the gridiron is how he taught us to be men.

"We wanted to win for Ah-sky-uh as much as for ourselves."

22

The Day Hell Froze Over
ᎠᎦᏛ ᏔᎴ ᏣᏯᏃᎿ ᏧᏂᏃᎸᏫᏍ

DECEMBER 1949

The anticipated big day arrived: Wednesday, December 8. After finishing their noon meal, Tommy and the team boarded Crackerjack for the trip to Enid, in north-central Oklahoma. As an ominous sign, impenetrable black clouds obliterated all evidence of the sun. Noontime was dark as bedtime as Coach Tommy gazed out the window, alone with his thoughts. Facing the biggest game with the highest stakes of his career, his thoughts careened from celebrating victory to acknowledging that this would be Milo's and Danny's last football game for him. Goodbyes came with the job, and graduation was six months away, but it hurt to think about how much he would miss them.

Usually noisy, today the bus seemed eerily quiet. Tommy shifted around and gazed back. Danny and Dave Whitekiller and the boys around them were whispering. *Knowing Danny, it's football strategy,* Tommy thought. Toward the back of the bus, Milo Yellowhead sat alone, staring out the window, but he was always quiet before a game.

On the other side of the aisle, George Cameron's hands mimicked football plays as he and two or three boys spoke in hushed tones. Tommy couldn't hear them, but they looked serious. Tommy reflected that it was too bad Bill Cameron had joined the army; he would have been a big asset. Students John Harlin, Raymond Carney, and J. C. Cooper, who took care of the equipment, sat together, uncharacteristically quiet. They suited up and practiced with the team, and all three of them had worked hard to help get the Indians ready for this game.

(Top left) Bronze Star recipient Milo Yellowhead's 1950 graduation picture. Permission granted by Milo Yellowhead. *(Top right)* Milo preparing for 1949 championship game. Permission granted by Milo Yellowhead. *(Bottom left)* John Anderson practicing golf, 1950. Permission granted by John Anderson. *(Bottom right)* Bill [Cameron] Campbell, visiting Tommy and Dorothy Thompson's campus home, 1952. Permission granted by Jean Campbell (Mrs. Bill [Cameron] Campbell).

Tommy turned back around, his eyes on the empty highway ahead. It narrowed into the distance until it disappeared. At the horizon, highway met a sky black as pitch with no car lights visible. Tommy mentally congratulated himself for his foresight in borrowing all-weather coats from the National Guard for his boys; they would need the warmth in this weather. A half-hour west of Tulsa, they crossed over the Arkansas River.

At 4:00 p.m., Lem Sanders turned Crackerjack into the campus of Pawnee Indian Boarding School. Tommy checked his watch and the sky, which was darker than he had ever before seen it, in all his years in Oklahoma. The principal had invited the Indians to have supper and spend the night in the dorm. That would leave a sixty-mile drive to Enid the following day. Excited Pawnee students greeted them, and the Pawnee boys showed Sequoyah's players their rooms. When they came down for supper, the Pawnee and Sequoyah boys sat together on the boys' side of the cafeteria. Tommy and Lem Sanders exchanged smiles upon observing their boys answer questions, a bit embarrassed at the Pawnees' admiration. The school's cooks outdid themselves, serving fried chicken, mashed potatoes and gravy, and green beans. They all got cookies for dessert.

The following morning, the skies looked just as menacing. A Pawnee boy brought in a radio during breakfast, and the forecast sounded bad. Thursday's *Daily Oklahoman* summed it up: "Light snow Thursday afternoon, more of the same Thursday night. Friday, rain in the northern half of the state, highs in the low 40s with a strong wind warning posted, gusts up to 50 mph."

After breakfast, Tommy and his boys thanked their hosts and said goodbye, departing amid shouts of "Good luck!"

Crackerjack arrived at the outskirts of Enid on Thursday afternoon. Tommy asked Lem Sanders to drive them to Enid High School to check out field conditions. Assuming they wouldn't be there long, Tommy did not retrieve the all-weather coats from the top of the bus. John Anderson remembered, "We stepped out of Crackerjack into a blizzard."

Whipped by an icy wind straight out of the north, sheets of snow came at them horizontally. The boys huddled into a tight circle. "C'mon, let's work out before we go to the hotel," Tommy told them. "Forget the weather. Run some routes. That'll warm you up."

"The paper predicted low 40s but with the wind it felt like zero," Anderson recalled.

It didn't take long for George Cameron to confirm Tommy's assessment of the field: very soggy, tough to run on. He sprinted to midfield and motioned for Tommy to join him. The coach couldn't believe what he saw there. For almost the entire length of the field, the left side was two to four inches lower than the right side. The previous night's rain had frozen, creating a ninety-yard-long ice rink. Tommy told them to avoid that side of the field and called it an injury waiting to happen.

By the time they finished their workout, the snow had turned to freezing rain. An hour in the miserable conditions proved to be more than enough. On the bus, Tommy repeated his warning about the ice, then gave the team some news to cheer them up: they had a big steak dinner coming at the hotel. Tommy sent them to their rooms to wash up, but they soon gathered in the dining room. Everyone's spirits seem to lift when the food arrived. He invited them to have seconds of steak, mashed potatoes, and corn; many of them did. Anybody who still had room for dessert had his choice of pie or cake. It surprised Tommy how many takers there were. After dinner, the boys didn't move. Instead, their expectant faces turned to him.

Tommy stood up. "No speech tonight. Tomorrow's game day; get a good night's sleep."

He and Lem Sanders shared a troubled glance. There was no need to burden the boys with the fact that the Medford campus was only thirty miles north—their opponents had doubtless played on Enid's field many times.

Friday morning, Tommy joined the boys for breakfast in the hotel dining room. "It's too cold to practice outside," he said. "I've arranged for us to work out in the Enid High School gym."

"Good idea," he heard someone mumble. A voice from the back remarked, "Coach, do you think God is mad at us?" Laughter followed.

"I don't know why he would be mad at nice guys like us," Tommy joked back. Someone else asked whether the game might be cancelled. "Nobody cancels a football game because of weather. We're going to play and so is Medford."

After breakfast, Tommy conducted a strategy session, going over the plays he had designed and answering questions. Whitekiller remembered, "Tommy didn't give any big motivational speech. He just told us to play our position and make sure we played all sixty minutes of the game. This was the last game I would play for Tommy," Whitekiller reminisced. "I wanted to end our season with the championship. We all did."

They arrived early for the two o'clock game. Despite the horrific conditions, there were 1,800 or 1,900 fans huddled in the stands of the Enid High School stadium. It was so dark at two in the afternoon that the stadium's lights had been turned on. Bouncing off a thousand bright yellow rain slickers and hundreds of black and green and red umbrellas glistening with rain, the lights turned the stands into a blurred, misshapen rainbow. Remnants of the previous day's snowstorm clung to empty benches as snow began to fall again. The snow came down not in horizontal white sheets like those of the day before but thickly enough to make it hard to see.

Tommy saw no sign of the Medford Cardinals.

Four officials stood huddled in a circle on the high side of center field. They resembled large stuffed bears in their oversized jackets and fur hats with earflaps. Tommy walked out to them and introduced himself, then returned to the sidelines. "They're a good crew. They're all from Oklahoma A and M. The referee warned about the ice. They don't want any injuries."

The Indians got their first look at their opponents when the Cardinals ran onto the field and lined up for the coin toss. Andrew Mouse remembered them being bigger than any Sequoyah players except maybe John Anderson. "They were white," Mouse recalled, "so Tommy made his usual joke about not letting those white guys kick our butts, then told us to play smart and tough."

The official tossed the coin, caught it, and slapped it down on the back of his hand. The Cardinals called it right and elected to receive.

Clad in an all-weather National Guard jacket, Tommy watched twenty-two players take their position, crouching in anticipation of the opening whistle. Driven by an erratic wind, the snow swirled first in one direction, then another. He had difficulty identifying his players. The Cardinals' offensive line closed ranks to avoid the lower half of the field.

John Anderson ran forward and kicked off, and the game was under way.

Players lunged and collided; they slipped and fell with no one touching them. Blurry figures leaped, and legs churned even while bodies didn't appear to make any forward progress. Tommy heard grunts as players slammed into each other. From the sidelines, the scene appeared surreal, a bigger-than-life glass Christmas globe shaken so that the thick snow inside swirled around. Certain that gripping the football would be like trying to hang onto an ice cube, Tommy observed that neither team could hold on to it during their first few possessions. The referees had a hard time when players tossed the ball right to them.

Five minutes into the first quarter, Yellowhead, as quarterback, fumbled on the Sequoyah thirty-yard line. He tried to fall on the ball, but a Cardinal fullback pounced on it first. Pacing the sideline, Tommy watched as Medford advanced the ball with three running plays into the end zone. His groan turned to a cheer when Sequoyah's defenders stopped Medford's conversion run short of the goal line.

The snowflakes became smaller and smaller, finally turning into hail that pelted the players and stalwart fans. A few minutes later the hail abruptly stopped and changed to freezing rain delivered by wind gusts. A deluge obscured the stands on the other side of the stadium and limited Tommy's view of the field to a twenty-yard patch right in front of him. Hearing a faint cheer, he silently acknowledged Medford's diehard fans. They had come to see their two-time state champs take on an Indian school they'd only just heard about.

On the field, Milo and his front four exchanged resolute glances, squinting through icy rain that stung their cheeks like frozen needles. Sopping wet jerseys clung to their backs. Every intake of icy breath hurt, and every exhale was visible. Cold, stiff fingers refused to bend or flex. All twenty-two players kept to the upper side of the field, jamming closer, with less room to maneuver. The many collisions were hardly felt by cold-numbed bodies. With four minutes left in the first quarter, Yellowhead sailed a perfect spiral to Anderson in the end zone.

Tommy held his breath as Anderson went up after it and, with single-minded concentration, brought the ball down to his chest. Stadium lights glistening off his helmet, Anderson triumphantly hoisted the ball high in his right hand. Tommy clapped and cheered at the soaking wet Cherokee Statue of Liberty look-a-like who bore a wide grin on his face.

Anderson tossed the ball to the referee, ran back, and positioned himself at the twenty-yard line to kick the point after. He wiped his face to no avail, as his wet sleeve left more water behind than it swiped away. Sequoyah's center, Mouse, snapped the ball; Cameron caught it and placed it firmly on the ground. Anderson took three long strides and slammed a solid kick. Ten Sequoyah players and Tommy on the sidelines tried with body language to *lift-lift-lift* the ball as it sailed straight toward the goalposts! Loud groans could be heard when it flew just under the bar.

Neither team could mount a sustained drive in the second quarter. At halftime, the players raced for their respective locker rooms. "We had no dry towels to wipe ourselves off with or dry jerseys to change into," Anderson recalled. "We were cold and wet and muddy, but we still felt we had a chance. With those conditions, it was anybody's game."

Tommy praised them for scoring. "We just need to do it again."

Andrew Mouse remembered that they weren't discouraged. "If anything, we were more determined than ever. We still figured we could win. Tommy made a few adjustments, but he didn't give us any big motivational speech."

According to Danny Whitekiller, "He didn't need to. Tommy could see how much we wanted to win."

Sequoyah came out for the third quarter into pouring rain and wind that lived up to the forecaster's warning. Both teams tried but couldn't advance ten yards in four consecutive downs. By the fourth quarter the fans' resolve had disappeared. Only a handful of people remained in the stands. To the Indians, a successful play meant hanging onto the ball and gaining a yard, maybe two, before getting hit by what felt like a freight train. Short by four yards, the Indians faced fourth down on their own thirty-yard line. Anderson punted and watched in horror as a gust of wind picked up the ball and sailed it backwards. It came down on Sequoyah's fourteen-yard line.

The Indians fought hard to stop Medford, but their opponents played with equal determination. It took the Cardinals five plays to advance fourteen yards and score. They failed again to make their point after. As time grew shorter, Tommy paced faster along the sidelines. Then he stopped, eyes on his players.

With a minute and a half to go in the game, it was Sequoyah's ball. The Indians still had a chance, and even through the curtain of rain, Tommy could tell by the way they moved that his boys weren't about to give up. He trotted along the sideline, his heart beating like a jackhammer.

Yellowhead called three running plays in a row. Each receiver clawed and fought his way and advanced to the Cardinals' fifteen-yard line, five yards short of a first down. Yellowhead's fourth-down play was a quarterback sneak. He bulled his way to the Medford ten.

At the ten-yard-line, Yellowhead faked left and lunged right. Up ahead, the lights in the end zone cut a yellow shaft through the sleet. He saw a narrow lane between a blur of bodies. With a minute left in the game, sixty precious seconds to pull off the biggest win in Sequoyah history or blow the chance of a lifetime, Yellowhead lowered his shoulders and lunged for the opening—

but his left foot didn't move! Held fast in ankle-deep mud, he flattened forward full out and landed on his belly. Milo fought to free himself and get up, but time ran out. The referee's whistle pierced the air.

The game was over: Medford 12, Sequoyah 6.

The Cardinals erupted with hoops and hollers at winning their third state championship in six years.

Faces numb from the windblown icy rain, the Sequoyah players stood panting, staring at each other in stunned silence. Some held back their tears; others cried openly.

Tommy watched as Yellowhead struggled to his knees and then slowly stood up, shoulders slumped, head down.

"I wanted so much to comfort him," George Cameron recalled. "Comfort everybody. But I didn't know what to say, so I didn't say anything, We played our hearts out, but it wasn't meant to be. I cried. I couldn't help it. I remember thinking it was so cold and yet tears felt hot on my face. All I could think was, we let Coach Tommy down."

Danny Whitekiller remembered, "We couldn't believe it. We were sick."

The description by Andrew Mouse all these years later is perhaps the most succinct: "That game, those conditions—it was the day hell froze over."

According to Milo Yellowhead, "Tommy believed we could win. So did I. We all did. He was quiet on the bus ride, but at the hotel he told us that every one of us gave all we had to give and no coach could ask for more."

On Saturday afternoon, Jimmy, his mother, and three-year-old Jody waited in their apartment at Sequoyah for Tommy to return from Enid.

Jimmy remembered the day well. "Mom and I had heard the score on the radio and the announcer talk about the terrible weather. The game was Friday, but Dad and the team spent the night in Enid. He wasn't smiling when he walked in the door. In fact, he looked exhausted, with dark circles under his eyes. You could see hurt and disappointment written all over him. Mom started to say something to him, but Dad held up his hand. These might not be his exact words, but he said something like, 'I doubt whether I will ever witness a game like that again in my lifetime. Those boys couldn't have played any harder or shown more courage. It breaks my heart they didn't win, but I've never felt as much pride as I did at that game.' Mom and I broke down," Jimmy said. "We couldn't help it."

23

Sequoyah Dreamboats
ᏏᏉᏯ ᏌᎾᏯᎵᏕᎢ

1949–50

The students, employees, and faculty welcomed Tommy and the football team back as though they had won the state championship. Mr. Brown honored them for achieving something no other team had done in the school's seventy-seven-year history: capturing the District 12 championship and winning all the way to the state finals. Mr. Brown made it known that Tommy and the Indians had brought Sequoyah statewide recognition and respect for their football program. Brown's words and welcome helped ease some of Tommy's disappointment and went a long way toward helping the boys get over theirs.

The 1949–50 basketball season, which began a week later, swept away any lingering negative thoughts. Tommy marveled at how quickly the boys returned to their usual upbeat selves. But this particular basketball season, he concluded that the girls from Tahlequah High had a lot to do with it. As football players, his boys received attention from the girls at Sequoyah and Tahlequah High, but for some reason that he failed to comprehend, the white girls from Tahlequah High swooned over the very same boys when they were on a basketball court.

They called the boys "Sequoyah dreamboats."

Tommy got the chance to witness firsthand the phenomenon that had started the previous season. The Indians' first game (on December 17, 1949) was at Tahlequah High, their crosstown rival. A capacity crowd filled the gym; many of the fans were teenage girls. In full, bouncy skirts and bright sweaters, they created a colorful and noisy cheering section. The Tahlequah girls applauded appropriately when their Tigers ran onto the court. But when Sequoyah's Indians stormed into the gym, the girls jumped up en masse and screamed and clapped for a full two or three minutes. Tommy watched in amazement and glanced at his boys to see their reaction. Grinning and casting brief glances at their admirers, they clearly loved the attention.

Admittedly, the boys looked sharp in their navy blue warm-ups. Sequoyah was the only team in Cherokee County (or, for that matter, any county in northeastern Oklahoma) to have matching outfits with long pants. Knowing that ever-frugal Superintendent Brown would consider such an expenditure frivolous, Tommy had matched Brown's frugality with resourcefulness and finagled the uniform purchase through the friend of a friend.

His boys knew to show up looking their best, showered, shaved, and with hair neatly combed when they boarded the bus. Sequoyah's players came from a half-dozen different tribes and had the dark good looks that girls evidently found irresistible. A Tahlequah teacher at the game told Tommy he'd even caught girls in his classes carving the boys' initials in their desks.

Because Tommy entered his squad in every tournament he could, the girls took the opportunity to form a fan club similar to the groupies who followed movie stars. They showed up at every game and trekked from tournament to tournament, exclaiming how much they loved basketball when what they really wanted was to catch the eye of one of Sequoyah's dreamboats.

Tommy noted that none of this escaped the boys' attention; their delighted reaction only served to encourage the girls. But he didn't wait for an unfortunate incident to happen. After their first game, he addressed the team, saying that he expected them to conduct themselves in a way that would reflect well on them and on the school. "Behave yourselves around girls because I'll be watching you." He emphasized good sportsmanship—win or lose, they were to shake hands with their opponents. "Be a good sport on and off the court." Tommy ended his talk with standard advice his boys knew by heart: "And always, *always* be a gentleman."

The boys did have good manners, which Tommy routinely heard praised by parents and chaperones at parties that his boys attended. On any given weekend, several Sequoyah boys would be invited to a party given by a girl from Tahlequah High. Tommy kept close tabs on them, making sure he knew where they were and with whom. Often, and always unannounced, he would drop in on the party. Nearly always, he found the kids dancing to phonograph records or playing games and having refreshments. Satisfied, he would thank the parents and leave quietly. Had there been no parents present, Tommy would have gathered his boys and taken them back to school with him.

Emulating the dress of popular movie stars such as Farley Granger, Montgomery Clift, and Frank Sinatra, Sequoyah's teenage heartthrobs on the weekends dressed in slim-legged Levis, loafers, and white T-shirts. Handsome, friendly, clean-cut, and athletic, they received many invitations. Every Saturday, several girls would drive their parents' car to Sequoyah to pick up boys they had met at a game. Unless each boy had let Tommy know ahead of time, his date had to pick him up at the Thompsons' apartment or at his office in the building next door.

Ever the jokester, he loved to tease. "This isn't the same girl you went out with last weekend. What happened to her?" Or, "This girl's a lot prettier than the one you went out with last week." Though most boys had been targets of Tommy's teasing many times before, they never failed to be embarrassed.

Tommy made very clear to the couple what time the girl had to have him back at the dorm. If he set the deadline at eleven o'clock, he would tell the girl, "That means eleven o'clock *sharp*. If you have him back at 11:05, he won't be going to any more parties for a while."

Like the advice he dispensed during his evening checker and poker games about behaving around girls, Tommy's warning came with a smile or a chuckle, but the boys knew he meant every word.

24

Ambassador in Trouble
SOʼbL OʼK⁴J ꟅPᴓLᴧᏮT

1950

Bill Baker and Nip Shipp tried to find out names, but no one could say for sure who lodged the complaints against Boots. All they knew was that he had disrupted a few classes during exams and study time, and the buzz at school was that Boots was in trouble.

Not sure how serious it was or what to do, they went to Tommy. "This is the first I've heard of it," he said. "Maybe it's just mean-spirited grumbling. I doubt anything will come of it."

Bill handed him a paper with two names on it. "We asked around and narrowed it to these suspects. We were hoping maybe you would . . ."

Tommy's phone rang. He told them he would check into it, and the boys left, feeling only slightly less worried. The mild relief didn't last long, though, for on the following day, Bill received a summons to come to Tommy's office. He found Nip and insisted that his friend go with him. Both sets of eyebrows shot skyward at the sight of a .22 rifle lying on Tommy's desk. "You wanted to see us?" Bill asked.

The coach's grim expression confirmed their worst fear. "I'm afraid we have to get rid of Boots." He shook his head as he said it, as though the words hurt.

"Why!" Bill and Nip cried in unison.

"I know, I know. It's not fair," Tommy said. "A teacher and some supervisory employee that complained before are at it again. They pressured the superintendent. They want Boots gone."

Tommy handed the .22 to Bill and gave him two shells. "I don't want Boots to starve or suffer a terrible death. The most humane thing you can do is take him out in the woods. One shot, quick and clean. Don't load the rifle until you're ready to use it. Understood?"

Tears stung as Bill silently absorbed the directive. Words failing, he stood stiffly, unable to move.

"Nip, here." Tommy tossed him a key ring. "Use my car. Bring back my keys and the .22 when you're finished." Tommy rose, a grim look on his face. "I am sorry, really sorry. I hate this as much as you do."

Bill numbly followed Nip out of the office as disbelief, hurt, and anger engulfed him. The slump of Nip's shoulders signaled that his friend felt the same. Bill couldn't believe he hadn't said anything; he should have spoken up for Boots. That Nip hadn't either, that they both had left without saying a word, seemed unforgivable. Bill rationalized that they had both been too stunned to speak up, but it didn't make him feel any better.

Tommy's Chevy sat in its usual spot in the parking lot. The boys spent a half hour searching, whistling, and calling to locate Boots. Finally, he bounded up to them, excited and wagging his tail as he followed them to the car. Nip opened the door; Boots leaped in and sailed into the back seat, ready for adventure. Bill and Nip exchanged silent glances.

Bill drove out the front gate and turned east toward Highway 10. Turning north on the highway, they followed alongside the Illinois River. Bill drove so slowly that the Chevy occasionally lurched. In the back seat, Boots bounded from side to side, barking at the sight of a cow or a horse. Forty-five minutes later, they reached the outskirts of Oaks, a small farming town a few miles north of the Cherokee-Delaware County line.

Bill turned off the highway and pulled to a stop. In front of them lay open fields dotted with thick stands of trees in the distance. He shut off the motor, and Boots sailed over the seat, landing between them. "He thinks we're going rabbit hunt—" Nip's voice choked off.

"I don't think I can do this," Bill said. He gripped the hair on Boots's back, hating to let go. "Damn those people. Boots never did anything to them."

"That's right." Nip shook his head. Tears streamed down his face. "And I'm telling you right now, I am not going to shoot Boots. I don't care if I get a spanking every day for a month; I can't do it. I won't do it." He wiped his face with his shirtsleeve.

Boot's odor filled the car: pungent dog breath and damp hair, mixed with the scent of grass and weeds he no doubt had rolled and romped in. He barked excitedly, ready to start their hunt. Bill pictured Tommy. The thought of lying to Tommy made him nauseous. Nothing made Coach madder than someone lying to him or stealing something. "So what do we do?" Bill stared at Nip.

Nip was looking intently out the front window. "I think I see a fence yonder. Must be a farm of some kind. We're thirty miles from school. Let's let him go. Some farmer around here is bound to take him in."

Bill shrugged, torn over what to do. "But Tommy told us to shoot him. You know how he feels about lying."

"But we never said we would do it." Determination crept into Nip's voice. "We didn't say *anything*, so how could we lie?" His expression said he'd made up his mind.

Bill glanced over his shoulder at the .22 wedged tightly against the back seat. The thought of aiming it at Boots and squeezing the trigger made him shudder. "I couldn't shoot him either, not in a million years." He took a deep breath and opened the door.

Boots jumped across his lap and landed front paws first in a clump of dry weeds. Ears alert and nose lowered to the ground, eighty pounds of wiggling energy scurried in a circle, trying to pick up a scent.

"Quick," Nip said, "let's get out of here."

Bill slammed the door and started the car. After backing up slowly onto the empty road, he stopped. They both stared at Boots. He looked up at them, head cocked, his tail suddenly motionless. Framed against distant bare sycamores and elms, he stood in a small patch of snow atop winter grass as though waiting to find out what game they were about to play.

Bill turned his eyes to the road ahead and floored the Chevy. He couldn't look back.

Tommy made his evening rounds and spotted his Chevy in the parking lot but saw no sign of Nip or Bill. A call to their dorm confirmed that they had returned, but the fact that they hadn't checked in with him suggested that they were either devastated or mad. *Probably both,* Tommy thought. He would not soon forget the look on their faces when they walked out of his office.

The following morning, he wondered just how long it would take for them to return his .22 and car keys. He dreaded the students' reaction when they heard about Boots—the hurt and sorrow the news would create. Several students had seen the boys put the dog in his car, with Bill carrying the .22, and some were likely to have figured out what was going on. Appalled at the request the previous day, Tommy had tried to rationalize that Boots would get old and sick and one day have to be put down anyway. But that was a weak excuse, for Boots was in his prime and would live for a long time. Every student at Sequoyah loved him. They talked to him and about him as if he were a person. To every student, Boots symbolized the dog they would have if they had a home and family. The sad truth was, the eighty-pound canine was guilty of nothing more than enjoying his campus home.

Revealing the truth would not ease anyone's pain, though, Tommy knew. A supervisory employee who lived on campus had lodged the complaints mainly because of the superintendent's rule that dogs could not run free. The employee's dog had to be on either a leash or a forty-foot exercise line when at home. Boots violated the rules, and the employee wanted him gone. Tommy had to admit that the man had a valid point. Boots's other detractor was a teacher who complained that Boots bounding in and out of his classroom distracted his students. That was also a valid point.

Tommy glanced at his watch and saw that it was 9:00 A.M., thirty minutes until his daily meeting with the dorm matrons and vocational teachers. He picked up his briefcase and started for the door as the phone rang. He answered and heard Mr. Brown's

The boys' advisor's weekly meeting with dorm matrons and dorm assistants. (*Left to right*) Mrs. Goudreau, Mrs. Hardridge, Miss Brady, Tommy Thompson, Joe Grayson, and Raymond Pope. Permission granted by Jimmy Thompson.

secretary. "The superintendent would like to see you in his office before your meeting," she said. Tommy walked toward the administration building, wondering whether Mr. Brown's request had anything to do with Boots.

To his relief, Jack Brown greeted him with a smile. "You will be happy to know that all those complaints about our old bus did not fall on deaf ears. We will soon retire Crackerjack." Tommy chuckled, not surprised that Jack Brown knew the boys' name for the ancient bus. "We've purchased one of the two hundred and twenty surplus buses from the Hanford atomic plant near Richland, Washington. At a very good bargain." Brown looked pleased.

"The boys will love that," Tommy said. "And a bargain, even better." Mr. Brown was known for being frugal. "When will it be here?"

"Unfortunately, that why it's a bargain." Brown explained that he and L. B. Hunt, auto-shop teacher, had to fly to Washington, and the two of them would drive it back. "We're leaving tomorrow afternoon," Brown said. "We should be back in about ten days."

Hunt, the auto-shop teacher and an excellent mechanic, was the best person to accompany Brown, because he had kept Crackerjack running. Sharp-cornered, a faded yellow rectangle, the bus looked very much like a box of Crackerjacks. There wasn't a Sequoyah football, basketball, or baseball player who didn't act embarrassed to pull up to an A or B school in it. The players at Rogers High in Arkansas had great fun razzing his boys: "All you need on top of that old wreck is live chickens and pigs and you'd look like a gypsy caravan." In the two years he'd traveled in the bus, Tommy had grown accustomed to seeing his boys try to hide by slouching down as they pulled up to a school. He would tell them to laugh it off and show their grit on the field.

Bargain or not and surplus or new, the bus was an unexpected purchase on the boys' behalf; retiring an operable vehicle ran counter to Mr. Brown's core philosophy. Tommy thanked him for the considerable time and effort and wished him a safe journey. He left for his staff meeting, then spent the rest of his day growing more agitated at Nip and Bill at their carelessness for not yet returning the keys and the rifle.

The 5:30 whistle blew for dinner. Tommy left his office and started for the cafeteria, grateful that he had something good to announce to offset the news about Boots. He figured Nip and Bill were avoiding him even though they knew he would have been waiting for them. Walking toward the cafeteria, Tommy saw a circle of boys up ahead. A full head taller than all the others, Nip stood at the edge of the group. Bill was beside him. Squinting into the setting sun, Tommy discovered the reason for the commotion.

In the middle of the crowd, Boots pranced back and forth, in and around the boys' legs as they tried to hug and pet him. Tommy recognized Fields Smith, Stanley and Sterling Speaks, George Cameron, Thompson Gouge, Everett Nave, and Jay Whitecrow. Harris Cully furtively poked Nip, who then nudged Bill. The two stood stiff and still, all but snapping to attention and saluting. As Tommy approached, all eyes were on him. Boots bounded up as though greeting a long-lost friend rather than the person who had ordered his execution. Tommy bent over and ruffled the dog's hair, then straightened to address Bill and Nip.

"I'll see you in my office in Unit B after supper." The group turned and hurried off en masse toward the cafeteria, with Boots trotting alongside. Tommy followed, mulling over conflicting feelings: relief at seeing the happy dog home and safe but perplexed with boys who had disobeyed an order. No matter that this particular order was one Tommy did not endorse; they needed to understand the importance of keeping their word. In addition, life involved choices, and choices had consequences. If he succeeded at nothing else, Tommy wanted every one of his boys to graduate with an understanding of and an ability to apply these basic values. Their success, and his as their surrogate father, hinged on their abiding by rules he hoped they felt were fair. And if they didn't, that they at least understood there would be a price to pay for breaking the rules.

But as he reflected on the matter, he realized that rules and consequences could not be applied to Boots. Loving the dog as much as the boys did, would he not have done the same thing at that age, he asked himself. After supper, Tommy waited in his office in Unit B. Nip and Bill arrived a few minutes later and walked in without a word. Bill placed the .22 on the edge of the desk. Nip put the car keys and shells next to it. They stepped back and stood at attention.

"Did both of you understand what I told you to do?" Tommy asked.

"Yessir," they said in unison.

"Then you lied because Boots is here."

They glanced at each other, silently begging the other to answer. Nip spoke up. "I couldn't do it, coach."

"Me neither," Bill said. "We drove all the way up to Oaks. Boots thought we were taking him hunting when he jumped out of the car. When we didn't get out, he just stood there looking at us like, 'What're you doing?'" Bill's eyes filled with tears; he glanced at Nip.

"We didn't lie, Coach," Nip said. "When you told us to shoot him we didn't say anything. We were too . . ." Too emotional to finish, he wiped away a tear.

"Coach." Bill paused, searching for words. "We took him up there to do what you said, but when Boots looked at us like he did, I realized I could never shoot him. He's . . . Boots. We let him go, thinking some farmer would surely want a beautiful dog like him."

Tommy stared at two sets of eyes full of pain. He had to cough to get rid of the lump in his throat. "You should have told me the truth the minute you got back. You know that?"

"Yessir." They nodded in unison.

"Do you think you should be punished?"

Bill answered, "If you think we should." Nip nodded in agreement.

Their answer went straight to Tommy's heart. They had heard his order and, knowing full well that their decision would have consequences, had made the choice their hearts told them to make. Tommy thought back to their meeting, when he had handed the .22 and shells to Bill and tossed the key ring to Nip. "Nip, you're right. Neither one of you said a word, so you didn't lie. Let me talk to Mr. Brown and see if we can find a solution. I'm not going to punish you, but I don't want you to make a habit of not coming clean. You know how I feel about that."

"Yessir, thank you, Coach." Their tense posture relaxed.

"I'm glad we straightened this out." Tommy said and told them they could go. He sat staring after them, unable to dismiss the gnawing feeling that he never should have given them the order in the first place. There had to be another solution. Tommy checked off ten days on his calendar to speak to Superintendent Brown when he returned—before Boots's detractors did.

But ten days went by and Mr. Brown and Hunt had not returned. Another week passed and still no bus pulled in. Three weeks later, on March 2, Tommy learned that they were back. He waited until the following day to call on Mr. Brown. Upon entering Brown's office, one glance told Tommy that he'd chosen a bad time; the superintendent had a terrible cold.

"Tommy, what can I do for you?" Brown asked in a raspy voice. His eyes looked watery, and he winced when he tried to stand.

"Jack, what happened?"

"Just about everything bad that could." Brown motioned for Tommy to sit down. "The flight and purchase went well, but a blizzard blew in just as we were about to leave. The folks up there advised us to stay put because they said it was a bad storm. They were right. It snowed every day for two weeks. Hunt and I tried staying in their barracks two nights, freezing half to death. We moved to a hotel. Our wives had to deposit money in our accounts to cover the checks we wrote for food and the hotel."

"And the trip home?"

Brown shook his head. "The weather improved enough that we figured we could avoid trouble if we came back through Arizona and New Mexico. Believe it or not, we got caught in a snowstorm in Arizona." He grabbed a tissue and sneezed into it. "We ended up having to shovel our way into an abandoned cabin, which is how I hurt my back. Then I caught this blasted cold." Jack gave a half-hearted grin. "I'm hoping one day all this will seem funny."

"I am so sorry." Tommy also felt somewhat guilty. Mr. Brown had bought the bus because Tommy had complained for two years about Crackerjack: it didn't have enough seats, and those it had were so close together that the boys smashed their knees against the seat in front of them.

"Mr. Hunt is servicing the bus today. It should be ready tomorrow," Brown said.

"I really appreciate it, sir." Tommy hesitated but decided he'd better tell the superintendent about Boots. "Jack, do you remember our talk about getting rid of Boots?"

"I remember very well," Mr. Brown said.

"Well, I didn't want him to starve to death or suffer, so I told Nip Shipp and Bill Baker to put him down. I gave them my .22, and they drove him up to Delaware County, but they couldn't bring themselves to do it." Jack Brown's eyebrows arched in an unspoken *why not*. "They let him go hoping that some farmer up there would take him in."

Brown sighed. "Where is Boots now? Although I can probably guess."

Tommy nodded. "He found his way back. Thirty miles in less than twenty-four hours. I have to be honest, Jack, I can't blame them. The boys love that dog. There isn't a student at this school who—"

The superintendent held up his hand. "No need to defend them. I know how the children feel, and I'm not sure I could have done it either. I will work out something with the individuals who lodged the complaints, but right now I have a favor to ask of you."

"Of course. Whatever you need." Tommy breathed a sigh of relief.

Mr. Brown's voice faltered. "I received a call from a reporter at the *Tahlequah Citizen* this morning about Wadie Miller. He was a student and CQ here a few years back. A wonderful young man. The boys in his dorm loved him like a big brother. They cried when he joined the army. We were told he was killed in action in Germany."

Brown looked stricken. "His body has been returned for reburial here. He didn't die in combat, Tommy. Wadie starved to death in a German prison camp." Brown swabbed his eyes with a tissue. "The article will be in tomorrow's paper, prison camp details and all. It's going to devastate the boys all over again. I need you to prepare them." He rose, clearly emotional.

Tommy assured him he would.

A check through the records revealed that George Cameron and Everett Nave were among the dozen boys who had been in Wadie's dorm. He invited them to his office and encouraged all the boys to talk about their friend. Tommy finally broke the news as gently as he could, saying only that Wadie died while a prisoner and not in action.

Gingerly changing the subject around to Boots, Tommy gave them the good news that the dog would get to live at Sequoyah for good—there was no question about his having to leave. As his presence had done since his arrival, Boots helped to soften the painful news.

25

Goodbyes Don't Get Any Easier
ᎤᏩᏌ Ꮅ ᏬᎵᏨᎠᎢ

MAY 1950

Nine girls and eight boys, Danny Whitekiller and Milo Yellowhead among them, made up the 1950 graduating class. Tommy and Dorothy sat alongside the other proud parents at graduation. Salutatorian Monroe Harjo's speech, *How the A Bomb Has Affected Our Homes*, presented innocently enough, infused an ominous note and served as a reminder of the persistent troubling news from Korea.

The superintendent congratulated the seniors and joked that this was his last chance to give them advice. Typical for Jack Brown, the advice was practical and heartfelt. "As you go from Sequoyah to assume your responsibilities as an adult, may you do so with determination to sell your services to others. Yours is a duty to set an example by action of good citizenship. Cooperate with others in every worthwhile endeavor. Our best wishes go with you for a successful and happy life."

After the ceremony, Milo and Danny came by Tommy's office. He had dreaded this moment: achievement and goodbye were opposite sides of the same coin. Milo would be joining the Marines in September. Tommy had suggested that he apply to Dartmouth, Grinnell, or Iowa, but Milo said that he liked the idea of being a Marine better. Danny reminded Tommy of his promise to his father, though, and said that he planned to go to college; he just needed a scholarship and had no doubt that he would get one.

Tommy rose and congratulated them, thinking how strong and confident they looked: gangly boys when they arrived, both were fine, handsome young men now. "I am so proud of you,"

Tommy said. "It's been a real honor and privilege to be your coach." He made them promise to keep in touch and embraced each one. "God, how I hate goodbyes." Tommy's voice was hoarse with emotion.

Both looking emotional, Milo and Danny took that as their cue to leave.

The moment was bittersweet as Tommy watched them walk away. Goodbyes weren't getting any easier.

Grateful to have a diversion, he turned his attention to setting up his football schedule. A full week of phone calls resulted in games against Class A Rogers in Arkansas, three B schools, and three conference games against C teams. Unable to fill three dates, Tommy phoned the sports editor at the *Tahlequah Star Citizen*. An article appeared the following day, stating, "Thompson is seeking three foes, preferably Class A or B teams. In their string of 13 victories last season, the Indians allowed no team to score more than 2 touchdowns. Thompson expects 19 lettermen to return from his 1949 team, which lost only one game, to Medford in the Class C finals."

George Cameron and Everett Nave came by Tommy's office to let him know that they and several other boys had gone to Wadie Miller's funeral. They both looked as if they had been crying. George handed Tommy an envelope addressed to "George, Ann Marie, Fannie Cameron, and Coach and Mrs. Thompson." From Fort Bragg, North Carolina, his brother had written, "I joined the 82nd Airborne. They call us devils in baggy pants. I got my glider wings at Fort Benning—I'm real proud of that. Three hundred one guys started the training. Four months later only 101 graduated. After six years at Sequoyah, getting used to the military was easy. Thank you for that, Tommy." Hearing from his boys and learning where they were and that they were well and happy helped Tommy get through painful goodbyes. Bill was right; the military seemed a good choice for him.

Tommy closed his office a week later. Using accumulated vacation and sick leave, he planned to be gone for six weeks. Earning spending money this summer would not be a problem for his boys. As the boys' advisor at Sequoyah, Tommy had received a letter from Green Giant Foods in Elkhorn, Wisconsin, seeking workers for their pea harvest. The company provided free housing and meals; if Tommy could round up a large enough crew, Green Giant would send a bus to Tahlequah to transport them. For his daily supervision of the recruits, Tommy would receive a salary.

He had no trouble finding takers: eighteen young men from Tahlequah plus John Anderson, Bill Baker, Nip and Rudell Shipp, Harris Cully, Ed Shangreau, Chastine Keener, and Everett Nave from Sequoyah. Tommy agreed to let sixteen-year-old Jimmy go along for the opportunity to earn serious money. All of the Sequoyah boys viewed harvesting peas as their best shot to earn enough money to buy a car. Dorothy gave Tommy her blessing to be away for six weeks, but she told him to see that the boys had some fun, not just work.

Green Giant's bus left Tahlequah in the early morning on June 13, 1950, and arrived late the following evening at the plant on the outskirts of Elkhorn. A small city in itself, the plant consisted of several huge buildings filled with canning machinery, plus two dormitories, each one housing two hundred to three hundred workers. Pickers from all over the country joined the harvest, along with local workers from Elkhorn and the surrounding area. The compound resembled a military base. In addition to the dorms, Green Giant had its own kitchen and laundry and a large cafeteria where all the workers and employees ate.

Tommy rode with his crew the first morning to the farm scheduled for harvest that day. "It had to be one of the largest," Nip Shipp recalled. "It covered five hundred acres, maybe more. The rows stretched so far in the distance, you couldn't see where they ended. No matter what direction you looked, all you saw were rows of peas. A nice German family owned the farm."

Tommy watched and listened with his boys as an employee demonstrated how to operate the huge shelling machines. Green Giant owned four of them, each one five feet high and ten feet long. A separate cutting machine harvested the peas, which were then deposited into a dump truck and delivered to the shelling area. Four boys fed the harvested peas into the shelling machine with pitchforks; then a conveyor belt delivered peas to a large bulk container in the front of the machine. Foliage, stems, and debris went to the back, where a roller crushed and packed it into oblong bales to be used for cow feed. The work was hot, heavy, and dusty.

Tommy stayed with his boys until he felt confident that they could operate the machines. Then he returned to the barracks and phoned home. Jody answered and, full of four-year-old wonder, asked half a dozen questions before agreeing to surrender the receiver to her mother. Dorothy asked about their trip and the boys and then told Tommy that Mr. Hunt had called for him. "I told him you were in Wisconsin. He didn't tell me what he wanted but said he needs to talk to you."

Tommy reached Hunt in his office at Sequoyah.

"I'm sorry to be the bearer of bad news, Tommy, but I was sure you knew Riley Chapman. He drowned in the Illinois River yesterday."

"Oh my God, how terrible!" Tommy responded. "How? Did he go swimming alone? I've told them a—"

"I know you have and, no, Riley wasn't alone. He went with three friends. They were trying to walk across the river but midway the water reached his chest and Riley panicked. One of his friends tried to save him and darned near drowned in the process. We had the fire department searching the river, but three fishermen found his body. Mr. Brown notified Riley's mother." Hunt told him that the boy who had tried to save Riley tearfully admitted, "Coach told us the river was dangerous. He warned us not to go there, but we didn't think anything would happen."

The boy's remark gave Tommy little comfort. Only fifteen, Riley had his whole life ahead of him. His mother had transferred him from Eufala because she wanted him to get a good education. Tommy shuddered at the image of the boy in the river; all of his preaching about its danger hadn't kept Riley Chapman safe. His mother would be devastated. Tommy's only comfort was that Jack Brown had been the one to notify her. No one would be more sympathetic.

GOODBYES DON'T GET ANY EASIER

Tommy broke the news to his boys that evening.

Harris Cully recalled, "Tommy was constantly after us [about] how dangerous the river could be. A bunch of us would listen politely and go swimming anyway. We'd snag a big log and ride it a few miles downstream, ditch it, then walk back and do it again. Coach would've tanned our hides with the Board of Education if he'd found out. Thankfully, nobody ever snitched on us."

During their second morning in camp, Tommy and his boys met some of the new recruits, members of the Ojibway, Kickapoo, Menominee, and Winnebago tribes from nearby reservations. They said they picked peas for Green Giant every year. The company paid by the hour, and harvesters could work as many hours as they wanted.

On hearing that, some of Tommy's boys started putting in ten-hour days.

Everett Nave recalled, "But not on Sundays. Tommy took us to Milwaukee one Sunday and showed us the sights. Another Sunday we went to a beach on Lake Michigan. Of course we wanted to go swimming. Tommy said okay, but after what happened to Riley, he insisted on going in with us. We swam and played volleyball."

With long hours of daylight, after work the boys would get up a baseball game and play until dark. Tommy joined in as a player, not a coach. After dark, they played cards in the German family's barn. Everett Nave reminisced about those games. "We'd play penny-ante poker or gin rummy or checkers. Tommy was the best checker player I've ever come across. That was such a fun summer."

Nip Shipp recalled, "I swear the German family ate six times a day; three meals and as many snacks. They always included us, giving us bologna sandwiches, pie, cake, and cookies—lots of cookies." But when they hauled out a tub full of cold beer to go with the snacks, Tommy thanked them but told them that since the boys were operating machinery, he didn't want his boys drinking.

Tommy's declaration came one beer too late.

Bill Baker later said, "I drank my first-ever beer, a Pabst Blue Ribbon. The German family assumed we were eighteen because that was Green Giant's minimum age. I was only fifteen, but I

(*Left to right*) Harris Cully, Everett Nave, and Rudell Shipp, at Lake Michigan during the Green Giant pea harvest trip to Elkhorn, Wisconsin, 1950. Permission granted by Everett Nave.

had made a photostatic copy of my birth certificate. It had a black background with white printing so I took some bleach and changed my date of birth. It looked so bad, I couldn't believe they accepted it."

Tommy and the boys ate with the other workers in the cafeteria. After dinner one evening, Bill Baker began to feel nauseous and soon had severe stomach pains. Tommy called the company physician. The doctor took one look at him and asked his age. "I could lie on paper, but for some reason I couldn't look him in the eye and do it, so I told him the truth," Bill said. "He gave me some pills, and the minute I felt better, the company sent me packing. Since I was the only one going home, I had to pay my bus fare back to Tahlequah. I ended up having to bale hay to pay for my ticket."

Tommy supervised not only the boys from Sequoyah but also the eighteen young men from Tahlequah. As he did at school, he kept as tight a rein on them as he did his own, making a bed check every night, eating with them in the cafeteria, playing cards or checkers every evening, and generally keeping them out of trouble.

Because several Tahlequah boys told him they planned on enlisting soon, Tommy made it a point every evening to turn on the radio for news. The situation sounded ominous. On June 25, 1950, North Korean troops crossed the 38th parallel. The U.N. Security Council asked for support, and the United States responded by dispatching troops and establishing a command site. On July 8, President Truman appointed General Douglas MacArthur commander of all U.N. forces in Korea. Nightly broadcasts reported divisions of the National Guard being mobilized. Tommy called Dorothy to find out whether she'd heard anything about Tahlequah's Company M. She had heard nothing so far, she told him.

Harvest wrapped up in the last week of July, and Green Giant handed out paychecks. Each one of the boys earned about $600 for their six weeks of harvesting peas. Jimmy Thompson, Nip and Rudell Shipp, John Anderson, and Everett Nave pressed Tommy to take them to buy cars.

"That was big money," Everett Nave later said. He bought a 1940 Pontiac. Nip and his brother each chipped in $200 and bought a 1937 Nash Lafayette. John Anderson bought a 1934 Plymouth, Jimmy Thompson a 1938 Plymouth. Tommy used his salary to buy a 1949 six-cylinder Ford coupe that he planned to sell in Tahlequah to make extra money. Everyone chipped in for a case of motor oil for the drive home and to use after they got back.

Everett Nave recalled, "It took three guys to drive my Pontiac home—one to steer, one to keep the floor shift in gear because it kept slipping out. And after dark, a third person had to dim and brighten the lights. My Pontiac used all twenty-four quarts of oil on the drive home. I sold it for fifty bucks as soon as we got back."

Cecil "Nip" Shipp and the 1937 Nash Lafayette that he and Rudell had bought with money from the Green Giant pea harvest, 1950. Permission granted by Cecil Shipp.

According to Nip Shipp, "We had a blast on the drive home. Some highways were deserted, and Tommy drove the lead car so he couldn't see that far back. We'd stand on the running board playing John Dillinger, pretending like we were shooting at each other. The Lafayette turned out to be a slick car. Rudy and I drove it for a couple of years after that summer."

John Anderson remembers teaching his sisters to drive his Plymouth, but only when he "could keep air in the tires."

Jimmy Thompson named his Plymouth "Hadicol" and drove it for all four years of college. Jimmy reminisced, "I loved cars and had always wanted a V-8, so I tried talking Dad into buying one in Wisconsin, but for some reason he liked six-cylinder cars. Not long after we got back, Dad and I were driving to Muskogee in the Ford coupe he bought. We came up behind a Sequoyah employee driving a brand new 1950 V-8 Olds. I told Dad, 'Look at that beautiful V-8.'

"Dad wanted to race the guy. I told him he didn't stand a chance, but Dad said he could beat him. When the guy realized Dad wanted to race, he floored the Olds and left us in the dust. I couldn't stop laughing, but Dad didn't think it was funny. He sold the Ford like he intended, and I don't think he ever bought a V-8 in his life."

The boys' armada of used cars rolled into Tahlequah on July 31, 1950, with Tommy's Ford coupe in the lead. He arrived to an incomplete football schedule and a country once again at war. With barely a chance to say hello to his family, Tommy saw his boys off the following morning for their two-week National Guard training at Fort Sill. Swirling about their departure were rumors that Tahlequah's Company M would soon be called up.

26

The Board of Education
ᎤᎾᏙᏗ ᎠᏂ ᏧᎦᏃᏢᏗ

1950

Tommy accompanied his boys to the National Guard armory in Tahlequah and returned to Sequoyah, hoping none of them got sick or hurt or pulled a stunt that would get them in trouble. At school they knew the rules and the consequences for breaking those rules. They were good kids, but every one of them could be a prankster if the opportunity presented itself.

Tommy believed in living by the rules: by the school's rules while at Sequoyah and, when away from school, by society's rules. Sequoyah had no specific rule about lying or stealing, but anyone who did broke Tommy's Rule. From countless warnings, every boy in his charge knew that he hated lying or stealing more than anything and that anyone caught doing either would meet the Board of Education.

According to Nip Shipp, Tommy had two Boards of Education: one in his office at the boys' gym, where most of the boys received their paddling, the other in his office in Unit B. Nip remembers each board being about two feet long, three inches wide, and three-quarters of an inch thick, with holes drilled in them.

Milo Yellowhead recalled, "We knew we would face some form of punishment if we broke a rule. It might be extra duty like shoveling coal at the power plant or not getting to take part in school activities or go into town. The worst was the Board of Education, and it didn't matter how old you were, what grade you were in, or if you were student body president. If Tommy thought what you did warranted a paddling, you got one. It may

THE BOARD OF EDUCATION

sound funny, but it seemed fair. We knew the rules and the consequences if we broke them. For me to learn at such a young age that my actions had consequences, good and bad, was a valuable lesson I took with me from Sequoyah."

Boys sneaking off campus without a pass or pulling off a midnight raid of the kitchen never failed to draw Tommy's attention. They ate supper at 5:30 P.M. with no snacks available afterward except from the school's store, which took money. With hunger always a factor, the boys occasionally pulled a night raid on the kitchen, coming away with a gallon of peaches or fruit cocktail or green plums. They made sure to leave no clues or damage a window screen breaking in or leaving, so that they could tap the kitchen again. Despite the care they took to hide their tracks, Tommy somehow always managed to catch them. When asked how, he told them that when he was their age he'd done the same thing—and most everything else they would ever think of.

Peanut butter ranked as the boys' number one favorite. The peanut butter served by Sequoyah's cooks came unhomogenized and in two-gallon containers. Two inches of oil covered the top and had to be thoroughly stirred into the stiff mixture for it to be spread on bread. No one ever learned how Tommy found out about their peanut butter sortie, but one midnight raid on the kitchen by eleven boys—including Nip Shipp, Danny Whitekiller, Thompson Gouge, Forman Ross, and Bill Baker—earned the entire group a session with the Board of Education. With each smack on their bottom, Tommy had them yell "peanut butter."

Afterward, Tommy opened a new two-gallon can of peanut butter and poured the oil off the top. Handing each one a spoon, he told them to finish all of it. Forman Ross remembers that the paddling plus two gallons of peanut butter split eleven ways cured them for a while, but they did it again when they got hungry. Growing-boy appetites combined with suppers served too early led to a lot of the meetings with the Board of Education.

At fifteen years of age, six feet tall, and 165 pounds, it was rare for Nip Shipp *not* to be hungry. When Tommy caught him stealing sweet potatoes, the coach made him return them to the kitchen and confess to Mrs. Meigs, the cook. She told Nip that she appreciated his bringing the potatoes back and asked whether he didn't get enough to eat. Nip told her the truth: he didn't care for the hominy at supper and didn't eat it. It was 7:00 P.M. and the cafeteria was closed, but Mrs. Meigs offered to fix Nip something to eat. He thanked her but declined, saying that he had an appointment with Coach Thompson.

Tommy reminded Nip that stealing was a bad thing and asked why he did it. Nip replied that it was because he was hungry. "I understand, Nip," Tommy said, "but a rule is a rule and you broke it." As he often did, Tommy bargained about how many licks they should get. "How about I give you five licks?" he asked Nip, who countered with four. Tommy gave him one hard swat and then told him if he yelled "sweet potato" with the next three, Tommy would call it even.

Thompson Gouge remembered that he had a few meetings with the Board of Education, too. "Tommy handed out discipline but he did it with sense of humor. I don't think I ever saw him use the board in anger. Not a one of us ever got mad at him."

Jay Whitecrow and Bill Baker earned an encounter with the Board of Education for their two-man night raid on the root cellar behind Home Three. Jay Whitecrow reminisced about their adventure: "There was a bunch of good-smelling apples stored in the cellar. Bill and I were able to pull the screen out enough for me to slip through. He was supposed to stand guard outside and warn me if somebody was coming. I'm in the cellar handing apples up to Bill and all of a sudden in comes this hand that's bigger than Bill's—a lot bigger. I put an apple in it and the hand disappeared. It came back—it was Tommy's hand, with a flashlight in it this time. He shined it around, which scared the tar outta me so I jumped into a barrel that had a few apples in it. Tommy waited a few minutes and shined the light around again. I could hear him laughing. It didn't take a genius to realize I wasn't going anywhere, so I told him I was ready to come out."

Whitecrow remembers Tommy's laugh as high-pitched and rapid like machine-gun fire, the most distinctive laugh he'd ever heard. "Tommy stood there laughing as I climbed out the window. He told Bill and me, 'You broke the rules. You know what that means. Tomorrow morning be in my office at 9:30.' We had all night to think about it. The next morning, sure enough, Bill got his paddling first and then me."

If peanut butter ranked number one, parched corn garnered second place as a favorite snack. Sequoyah boys years before had learned how to parch corn from an Osage student and passed down the skill. Because it required a campfire, it had to be done far enough away from campus buildings that smoke wouldn't lead anyone to find them. With no money to buy corn, the boys first had to raid the school's corn bin in a nighttime sortie.

Once the main ingredient was secured, they headed to Bald Hill, a half mile away from all school buildings. Next they located the wire screens they'd made in shop class and hidden in the trees. After placing a homemade screen over an open fire pit, they spread an even layer of corn kernels on the screen. After a few minutes, the corn either cracked open, like popcorn, or parched (turned brown). Because parching corn involved elaborate planning and execution, not to mention the risk of getting caught sneaking out of and back into the dorm, the boys parched several pounds at a time to make the caper worthwhile.

Parching large quantities created transportation and safe storage problems, though: how to get the finished product back to campus and, with that accomplished, where to hide it. Pillowcases took care of transportation but created another potential problem—discovery. Not wanting to risk the possibility of a dorm matron finding a pillow without a case, they had to slowly build an inventory of pillowcases from the supply room. All these measures, carefully planned and carried out, ensured a steady source of snacks during the week.

Nip Shipp remembers that Superintendent Brown got wind of their parched corn capers and tried to thwart them by replacing the school's wooden corn bin with a metal one with a padlock on it. The boys promptly cut a hole through the metal, and once again, their main ingredient became available.

Another illicit snack was wild onions, a traditional Cherokee delicacy that Forman Ross, Fields Smith, John Anderson, Andrew Mouse, George Cameron, Bill Baker, and Everett Nave often ate growing up. This was not solely a Cherokee event, though; half-Seminole Nip Shipp and boys from other tribes were invited to take part. This snack required a great deal of planning and execution. Boys first gathered the onions that grew along the banks of a half-dozen creeks near the school. Gathering them took diligent attention because crow poison looked very much like a wild onion, especially in the dark. The gatherer had to recognize that wild onions had round stems and crow poison stems were flat.

According to Bill Baker, "You can't cook wild onions without scrambled eggs." Eggs required a midnight requisition, the boys' term for a raid of the school's poultry farm. Baker and Shipp often led these after-dark forays. With eggs and onions procured, they needed a third ingredient, butter, which they lifted from the kitchen. As they did with the screens for parching corn, the boys hid their cooking skillets in the trees on Bald Hill. The hill provided the perfect hideout where the boys could gather after dark and enjoy a favorite snack.

Bill Baker recalled, "Half the reason we did it was because we were hungry; the other half was the adventure of it. When I look back, I realize the tremendous planning, teamwork, and implementation it took to pull off what we did. I will never forget those times. They were innocent fun."

Not every escapade resulted in getting caught and meeting the Board of Education. Fields Smith and Bill Baker served as Tommy's official barbers. Most Saturdays they gave haircuts in the basement of Unit B, which had two regulation barber chairs. On more than one occasion, Bill and Fields sneaked into the basement in Unit B and took turns spinning each other in one of the chairs. Each would spin the other as fast and for as long as he could take it, or until he felt dizzy and nauseated. Before their disoriented state wore off, the boys reported to the nurse at the campus hospital complaining they must be "coming down with something."

THE BOARD OF EDUCATION

The nurse issued each one a pass to skip class. Fields recalls spending the day in their dorm room, playing cards, reading comic books, or just lazing around talking. He said they knew better than to pull the prank very often, but it worked several times over the years.

The rare times when Tommy was away from school and boys broke a rule, Mr. Brown determined their punishment, though he left meetings with the Board of Education up to Tommy. When Nave and two other boys got caught three times one night trying to hitchhike into Tahlequah, Mr. Brown made all three write, "I will not leave the campus without permission," five hundred times.

And not all the infractions that Tommy discovered resulted in a meeting with the Board of Education. "He could be creative," Nip Shipp recalled. "Part of the fun with Tommy was seeing what punishment he would come up with." Nip was one of six boys who slipped out bed one night and sneaked off to town without getting a pass. Not surprisingly, Tommy caught them. He told them, "You realize I want to know where you go; that's why I ask you to get a pass." He added that had they asked for one, he would have gladly given it to them. "But since you didn't, I want you to dig a ditch six feet deep by three feet wide by six feet long."

Every day for the next ten days, in front of a large audience of snickering students, Nip and the other boys spent all of their free time digging. Nip remembered, "When we finally finished, Tommy made a big ceremony out of measuring the ditch to make sure it was exact. He gave all of us a piece of paper and told us to write, 'I promise never to go AWOL again.' He checked everyone's paper, [then] said to carefully fold it into a square and throw it in the ditch."

When they complied, Tommy told them, "This was to make you understand that a choice you made is why you've spent ten days of your free time digging. Learn from it. Okay, now fill the ditch back up."

27

You're in the Army Now
DhᏰᏫᎩ ᎤᏫD ZᏊ

AUGUST 1950

Despite the escalating conflict in Korea, classes, vocational training, and the daily routine at Sequoyah remained steady and on schedule. Superintendent Brown would have it no other way. In town, Tommy overheard people call Korea a containment operation, while others referred to it as a police action, which is what radio newscasters called it. But with enemies killing each other, it was what Tommy called war. Milo Yellowhead would surely be sent to Korea. So would Bill Cameron and the dozens of other boys Tommy hadn't been able to talk out of joining the military.

Once again, he faced boys not old enough to vote walking into his office and announcing that they had enlisted rather than wait to be drafted. Each encounter reminded him of the months after Pearl Harbor that he had spent lobbying boys to finish school and enroll at Northeastern or any other college. He hadn't been successful then, and Tommy hated to admit that he wasn't doing much better this time.

Curious and wondering whether he'd have enough players for a viable football team, he called coaches at a dozen high schools in eastern Oklahoma. They too were wrestling with players enlisting rather than waiting to be drafted, and several of the coaches asked Tommy whether the rumor were true that Tahlequah's National Guard unit would soon be activated. Determined to find out the truth, Tommy phoned Cecil Parkinson, commander of Company M, 279th Infantry.

YOU'RE IN THE ARMY NOW

Tahlequah's 279th Army National Guard Infantry Division, Ft. Hood, Texas, 1950. Corporal Cecil Shipp holds the guidon; his brother, Rudell Shipp, is in the back row, sixth from the left. Permission granted by Cecil Shipp.

But his call was too late, for Parkinson and the unit had just departed via convoy for Fort Sill. Somewhere on the highway in the camouflaged trucks and jeeps on their way south were Nip and Rudell Shipp, George Cameron, Andy Mouse, John Harlan, Ed Batt, Bill Adair, Monroe Harjo, Chastine Keener, Thomas Locust, Sequoyah Roberts, Lyman Vann, and Jim Justice. A third of his football squad would miss the first few days of practice. Tommy hoped that was all they would miss.

Except for dealing with the work that each new school year brought, he could do nothing but wait. A call from an excited Danny Whitekiller came as a welcome diversion; Danny had landed the scholarship he needed to attend Bacone College in Muskogee. "You're not going to believe how it happened, Coach, but this is the God's truth," Danny said.

"I could use some good news," Tommy told him.

"John Anderson went with me to the BIA office in Muskogee to see if they would help me get a scholarship. The office was already closed. John could see how disappointed I was so he talked me into checking out the campus anyway. We walked toward Bacone, but before we got to the buildings we saw two men marking the lines on their football field. One of them was Tuffy Stratton." Danny sounded breathless.

"Their coach?" Tommy chuckled. "Slow down so I can understand you."

"Sorry, but it was just like my first day at Sequoyah when I met you. Coach Stratton ran up to us and said he wanted us on his team. He offered us scholarships, room, board, tuition, books, everything. John told him he still had a year to graduate, but I said sure. Tommy, I'm going to college just like I promised my dad." His excitement was infectious.

Nor did his story surprise Tommy. He remembered their first meeting in 1947; from that day, Danny Whitekiller had given his all to every assignment. His "sure, I can do that" attitude didn't come from arrogance. It came from faith.

The call left Tommy smiling as he walked to his meeting with dorm matrons Ina Brady, Mary Penoi, and Rebecca Trent. Formerly Miss Goodman, Rebecca had married Rollie Trent, the manager of Sequoyah's farm. Mrs. Trent voiced concern about one new youngster, twelve-year-old Thomas Batson. "I took him to the hospital the minute I saw his toe. I asked him when he cut it and he couldn't remember exactly, just 'sometime last summer.' His foot is so badly infected, I hope he doesn't lose it to gangrene."

Tommy asked her to keep a close check and let him know how Thomas got along. "Assuming it's going to be fine," Tommy said, "I want to see him as soon as he's released."

Three weeks later, Thomas Batson walked into Tommy's office, limping only slightly. Tommy had him remove the hospital boot and looked at his foot. Seeing that the injury was no longer a worry, Tommy asked how it had happened.

Thomas's story was painfully familiar. When his Cherokee mother died, Thomas and his brother Owen remained with their alcoholic father, a white man. He forbade them to speak Cherokee and had little to do with them. After their mother died, he drank even more and seemed to lose all interest in them, even ignoring Thomas's foot when his son cut it on a half-buried tin can. The neighbors noticed Thomas's foot and how dirty and starved the boys looked; they met to plan getting the brothers into a foster home. Before they could do anything, the boys' father heard about the plan and straight away drove his sons to Sequoyah and dropped them off dirty, hungry, and barefooted.

"Well, I'm grateful your foot is okay and that you're here. What do you and your brother think of Sequoyah?" Tommy asked.

Batson put on the boot. His wide smile answered Tommy's question, but he said they liked their teachers and had made some friends. "The food is the best part. Those cooks are good!"

Tommy patted his own stomach. "You can tell I like the food, too. Thomas, I want you to know you can come to me anytime with a problem or if you just need somebody to talk to. Owen, too. I'd like you to let me know how you're getting along." Tommy wrote Mrs. Trent to be sure to notify him immediately if the boys' father showed up. *I have a few words for him,* Tommy thought.

The boys returned from National Guard camp on August 15, in time for the first practice. Nip Shipp was finally eligible to play; at six feet and 165 pounds, he was a perfect center. Milo's and Danny's absence created a void, however. Each of them had been a leader: one stoic and determined, the other enthusiastic and gregarious. They had encouraged their team with their unshakeable faith that winning came from planning, practice, and 100 percent effort. Thinking back to the championship game from hell, Tommy agreed that 90 percent of victories could be attributed to the boys' formula. But sometimes fate played a hand, as it had done in that game—the critical 10 percent being the weather.

In the midst of an already busy afternoon, Tommy received a call from Jack Brown that Hollywood movie star Burt Lancaster was in Tahlequah and had requested a tour of Sequoyah. Brown said that he would show Lancaster the campus but asked Tommy to give the star a tour of their athletic facilities. News of the movie *Jim Thorpe, All American,* being filmed at Bacone College had been in Muskogee's and Tahlequah's newspapers. The story described Bacone's campus as having been turned into a Hollywood version of Carlisle Indian School in Pennsylvania. From his son, Tommy had heard that Bacone students would be in crowd shots, while Danny Whitekiller had done a scene on the track with Lancaster and six other boys. Jimmy said that the scene had been shot three times and Lancaster had outrun the students all three times.

Knowing that Jimmy would never forgive his father if he didn't get to meet Lancaster, Tommy phoned their apartment to tell him of the news. Before Tommy could finish his sentence, Jimmy said he was on his way and hung up. Thirty minutes later, Jack Brown and Lancaster arrived. Brown remarked that they had created quite a stir during their tour of the campus.

"I'm not surprised." Tommy smiled at the study in contrast presented by Brown and Lancaster. Brown, impeccably groomed in a suit and tie, stood about 5' 8" and was very slender, with his dark hair neatly trimmed. Beside him, a good head taller, was a bronze, muscular Mr. Hollywood in casual slacks and a tight-fitting T-shirt. With his disheveled thick hair, Lancaster looked every inch the athlete he was portraying in the movie.

Brown thanked Lancaster for his visit and bade them goodbye. He exited as Jimmy Thompson arrived.

"Your son?" the star asked Tommy, who nodded. "Your dad being a coach, I bet you play a lot of sports," Lancaster said to Jimmy.

"Yessir, he taught me everything I know." Lancaster wanted to know what sports. Jimmy glanced at his father, then replied, "Football, basketball, baseball." Lancaster flashed the famous smile Tommy had seen in his films and told Jimmy to keep playing, that sports would prepare him for life.

Jimmy smiled. "My dad says that *all* the time."

Tommy asked Lancaster whether he knew Jim Thorpe and then said he had lettered at Northeastern. "I met Jim Thorpe at

Northeastern when he visited the campus. You actually look enough like him to be his brother," Tommy said.

"Probably why I got the part." Lancaster chuckled. He said he had just come from Sequoyah's Indian Weaver's shop. "I bought some blankets and tweed material for a couple of suits. Oh, and some Indian rattles made of turtle shells for my kids."

They toured the gym and facilities. As they walked, Tommy mentioned the camps he'd taken from Bible and Warner. Lancaster said he'd had the pleasure of meeting both coaches. He congratulated Tommy for the previous year's great season and said that Coach Stratton told him about the Indians winning their way into the state finals. Tommy came away from the meeting a fan of Lancaster's. He described Lancaster to Dorothy as a genuine athlete who happened to be a good actor.

Fierce heat and high humidity greeted students when they returned to classes on the Tuesday after Labor Day. Three days later, Tommy, eleven starters, and six reserve players climbed aboard Sequoyah's new bus and headed for Rogers, Arkansas, for their first football game of the 1950 season. After the bus pulled up in front of Rogers High School, co-captains John Anderson and Mose Weavel jumped off quickly, almost daring the Rogers players to say something about the bus. Whether it was the heat and humidity or losing two first-stringers to ankle injuries early in the second half, the game ended in a lackluster 6–6 tie.

The next day, Saturday morning, Tommy opened the *Tahlequah Citizen* to a headline he had hoped never to see: "Tahlequah Guard Unit Mobilized." The accompanying story confirmed his fear. "Captain Cecil Parkinson, Commander of Company M, 279th Infantry Regiment announced that starting tomorrow, local Guard members will eat breakfast, dinner, and supper army style. All members are ordered to report to the armory ASAP." The article went on to say that the 279th would leave in ten days and join up along the way with the other Oklahoma units that made up the 45th Division. Eight weeks of training would follow at Camp Polk in Louisiana.

Just as it was sinking in that a dozen of his boys were all but gone, a panicked George Cameron appeared at Tommy's door. "Coach, a corporal at the guard unit just told me that I'm one month short of my three-year commitment. Unless I can prove some way that I'm not seventeen, I have to go." He said that to his knowledge, he'd never had a birth certificate.

Tommy rose and told George to follow. "Maybe your dad has it. If you're not seventeen, it won't matter whether you're one month short or not." They drove to Andy Cameron's house in Stilwell only to learn that all eight children had been delivered at home by a midwife, so none of their births had been officially recorded. But George's father produced the next best thing: the family Bible. Tommy waited beside George as Andy Cameron opened it. "Here it is. George was born July 19, 1932."

"I'm eighteen?" George looked crestfallen.

The obvious lack of feeling between father and son disappointed Tommy as much as being unable to spare George from leaving. Back at Sequoyah they shook hands, then Tommy hugged him. "Okay, George, since you have to do this, be a good soldier and take care of yourself. But promise me you will come back as soon as you can to get your diploma."

As he watched George walk away, it occurred to Tommy that if he didn't act fast, John Anderson, Nip and Rudell Shipp, and the other boys who were underage would also be on their way to Camp Polk. Every one of them had listed a false date of birth; Indian boys lying about their age was common as far back as when Tommy had been a student at Haskell. Twenty-five years earlier or in 1950, being in the National Guard meant good money and excellent training.

Tommy called Mrs. Penoi, the dorm matron in Unit A, and asked about the boys. Anderson, the Shipp brothers, and the others had already left for the Guard armory. Next, he phoned the armory to confirm that with proper documentation of their age, he could get them released. A corporal told him that he needed to submit a letter requesting release for each underage boy, along with a copy of the boy's birth certificate. If Tommy could find everyone's birth certificate in his Sequoyah file, getting the boys released would be simple. If not, he realized he would have to go to Oklahoma City and dig through the records.

Tommy hurried to the registrar's office. There he found Nip's and Rudell's birth certificates, submitted in 1943 with their applications by Galeena Walkingstick, the social worker from the BIA's Wewoka Agency. But John Anderson's and several others were not there. While he was busy gathering dates and information on his list of boys, the school secretary apologized for interrupting and handed Tommy an envelope. The return address, "R. E. Peppy Blount, Congress, State of Texas, House of Representatives, Austin," told Tommy that the letter concerned Nip and Rudell.

A cousin of the Shipp children, Peppy Blount was the son of Alma Shipp Blount, younger sister of the children's father, James Shipp. She and her husband had visited the boys at Sequoyah during the summer. Blount's letter began by thanking Tommy and went on, "My parents returned singing your praises. I am pleased beyond expression to know that Rudell and Cecil have the advantage of participating in competitive athletics under your guidance." It went on to explain that Blount was unit commander of the 49th Armored Division. His outline of requirements for obtaining a release for someone underage matched what Tommy had learned. At the end of his letter, Blount wrote, "If the signature of a legal guardian is required, please contact me post haste."

Tommy typed a generic letter of request and asked the secretary to obtain photostatic copies and leave them on his desk. Soldier Sanders agreed to run the afternoon practice in Tommy's absence.

Leaving a note for Dorothy that he would likely miss supper, Tommy raced to his car.

28

Where's a Medicine Man When You Need One?
ᎢᏳ ᏄᎸᎯᏳ ᎠᏎᎸ ᎦᎮᏍ

1950–51

A little before midnight, Tommy returned to his office with a folder of birth certificate copies. Someone had put the *Muskogee Phoenix* on his desk, its front-page headline in bold letters: "Indian Students Leave with 45th Division." The article continued, "Call up of the 45th Division has cut deeply into the student body of Sequoyah Indian Training School. Principal Jack McCarty said Thursday that twenty-three of Sequoyah's seventy-one male high school students have been mobilized. Indian youths comprise approximately half of the Tahlequah unit. Sequoyah's football team, defeated in the Class C finals last year by Medford High, will lose nine players."

His boys were on their way, like it or not. Tommy prepared the letters and attached a birth certificate to each one. He would personally deliver them to the armory in the morning. As he walked across the dark campus to the Thompsons' apartment, Tommy thought about the boys about to leave: George Cameron, Monroe Harjo, Ed Batt, John Harlan, Andrew Mouse, Chastine Keener, Tom Locust, and Sequoyah Roberts. Would they come back to get their diploma, he wondered, or had he seen them for the last time?

They had been the heart of his team the previous season, along with Danny and Milo. But the others had made a pact to pick up this year where they left off—and this time win the championship. After fighting so hard the previous year, they deserved another chance. But they were old enough, by the slimmest of margins, that their fighting might be in Korea. The next morning, Tommy handed his letters to Captain Parkinson at the Tahlequah armory. The commander signed the release forms without blinking an eye and, at the end of their meeting, said the boys were welcome to come back when they reached legal age. Tommy asked whether he knew where the called-up boys would be assigned after basic training.

Parkinson answered, "Hokkaido, Japan, for more training. After that, I'm not sure."

Tommy left his office pretty sure he knew what the commander's final comment really meant. Korea.

He was relieved to see Nip and Rudell Shipp, Forman Ross, and John Anderson back and suited up for afternoon practice. Dave Whitekiller, Danny's younger brother, was ready to play, as was freshman Bill Baker, Amon's brother. Eligible for the first time, Bill looked as if he could run. Tommy asked him to race the squad's two fastest players. When Baker beat both of them, Tommy assigned him a running back position.

The team diligently practiced twice a day but for some reason failed to produce results in their games. When John Anderson broke his leg in a game in which neither team scored, the Indians' morale sank to an all-time low. Exasperated, Tommy told Dorothy that he needed something, anything, to pull them out of it.

She reminded him how much fun he and Jimmy and Jody had had at the Redbird Smith stomp dance. Tommy needed no further suggestions. He consulted Jack Brown, who gave his permission and said that a stomp dance at Sequoyah would be another first in the school's history. Tommy called Fields Smith into his office to help organize and plan. He asked Fields to lead the first dance.

The event took place on a Saturday evening in late October and was a scaled-down adaptation of a traditional stomp dance, according to Fields. The entire student body attended, except for students who were ill and those being punished for an infraction. Mr. Brown and most of the school's employees and faculty and their families came.

Fields Smith chose Thompson Gouge, William Francis, Harris Cully, and three other boys to *answer* in his first dance. They danced in a circle around the fire to a rhythmic drumbeat. With

Tommy circulating in the crowd urging boys and girls to "get in there and dance," it didn't take long for them to join in—football players among them. Full-blood Creek Thompson Gouge led the second dance, which Jimmy Thompson joined, his enthusiasm drawing more and more students down to the fire.

By 8:30 P.M., stomp dancers had come to outnumber bystanders. Nevertheless, Mr. Brown subtly signaled Tommy that it was time for students to return to their dorms. With so many dancing, Tommy hated to see the evening end. The stomp dance created excitement that invaded the locker room, the brief change coming none too soon.

The team from Riverside Indian School in Anadarko in southwestern Oklahoma arrived at Northeastern's Gable Field for Sequoyah's homecoming game. Riverside's sole loss to non-Indian Grandfield High gave Tommy a goal for his team: "Beat Riverside and you'll be the champions of all Indian Schools." The *Tahlequah Citizen* likened the rivalry to Army/Navy or Oklahoma A and M and the University of Oklahoma. Playing with renewed energy, the Indians did so well that Tommy put in his second string to give them playing time. Only when Riverside intercepted a pass from the quarterback, George White, and threatened to score did Tommy send the first string back in to finish the game, with a final score of 19–7.

Despite a good finish, the Indians' 1950 season ended on December 5 with a dismal 3-4-2 record. They had twelve fewer players, nine of them lost to the National Guard and the other three to injuries. Tired, discouraged, and worried about his boys in the Guard, Tommy gave the football squad a day off and spent his evening with a bottle of relief. The following morning, he appeared at his office wearing the telltale clip-on sunglasses to hide his bloodshot eyes.

Basketball season began on December 12, with Stilwell coming to Sequoyah's home court. Because most of the basketball squad had been on the football team, Tommy had no idea what kind of season to expect. To his surprise, his keyed-up team outplayed

Stilwell from the first whistle and came away with a whopping 64–36 win. Tommy viewed their spirited play as an indication that they'd put football season to rest. Over the next month, Sequoyah's dream team defeated Eufaula, Checotah, Westville, and Sallisaw.

In mid-January, the weather turned bitterly cold. Storm clouds parked over Tahlequah for two weeks, delivering snow, sleet, and freezing rain. The boys' grumbling about the weather brought back images of Wahpeton Indian School in North Dakota to Tommy. He described Wahpeton, the school, and the weather in detail and then told his players, "We have a nice warm gym. Be thankful."

Saturdays were extra-duty days, and Tommy was at his desk early preparing assignments for boys who hadn't received the required merit points or had broken a rule. Most were older boys. Tommy believed in discipline, but (as he did with the Board of Education) he disciplined with humor. Lots of teasing accompanied amusing punishments for infractions Tommy considered trivial. Serious assignments usually involved labor; these he gave to boys who knowingly broke a rule. When his phone rang, Tommy assumed that the call was from a dorm matron telling him a boy was sick and couldn't make the meeting.

The call was not what he expected. A concerned-sounding matron reported that sixteen-year-old Choctaw Henry Bell had not shown up the previous night for bed check and still had not returned this morning at 9:00. Tommy's first thought was that Bell would meet the Board of Education for this serious infraction when he did show up. At the meeting, he asked whether anyone had seen Bell. No one had.

When Henry Bell didn't show up Saturday or Sunday, Tommy notified the police. Fear replaced displeasure, and he summoned some of Bell's friends into his office. They admitted to having seen Bell leave the National Guard meeting with two Guard friends. As the truth unfolded, Tommy learned that the three boys had begun drinking as they drove around. A few hours later, all three—the inebriated Bell and his friends—had gotten into an argument, and Bell had demanded they stop; he wanted out. Intoxicated enough to impair their judgment, Bell's friends had stopped the car and let him out. After they sobered up, neither one his friends could remember where Bell got out.

After ten days of searching, the police issued a statement: "Due to the bitter weather the victim has most likely perished therefore the search has been called off." Tommy had no intention of giving up. Saturday's extra duty for everybody became teams of boys searching a hundred yards off each side of the highway for thirty miles from Sequoyah to Vian. When that produced nothing, he organized a search of the woods in a large radius around Tahlequah.

"All that search produced was a half-dozen bootleg stills," Nip recalled. "The guys making the whiskey must have heard us coming and thought we were Feds. We could hear them smashing jars. It's a wonder we didn't get shot."

After two more weeks of searching, Shipp figured that Tommy would surely give up, but he wouldn't hear of it. He intended to consult a medicine man and said he should have done that in the first place. Tommy asked Shipp to drive to Stilwell with him after school. Nip waited in the car while Tommy consulted Jasper Smith, a Keetoowah medicine man and a cousin of Nip's fellow student Fields Smith. Tommy returned to the car with the message that Jasper wanted "to study on it for a night" and for Tommy to come back before sunrise the following morning. Nip recalled that he had to keep from laughing. After all the searching they and the police had done, he remembered wondering, why in the world would Tommy believe that Jasper would know where to find Henry's body?

Tommy stood firm and insisted that they drive back before dawn the following morning. Nip waited, half asleep in the car. "Tommy came out, and the first thing he said was, 'I told you so.'" He said Jasper gave him directions to a bridge in Cherokee County and from there exactly in what direction and how far from the bridge Tommy would find Henry's body. The fact that Cherokee County had dozens of bridges all pretty much alike reinforced Nip's skepticism, and he told Tommy that he believed they were wasting their time.

WHERE'S A MEDICINE MAN WHEN YOU NEED ONE?

Tommy replied, "Medicine men have powers other men don't have."

Back at Sequoyah, Tommy wasted no time in gathering a search party. Nip, Everett Nave, Bill Baker, Fields Smith, and Jay Whitecrow set out with Tommy in his Chevy following Jasper's directions to the bridge. Nip's skepticism dissolved when Tommy told them, "There it is!" and pulled up beside a bridge that was exactly where Jasper had said it would be. The boys followed behind as Tommy paced off the distance through the snow in the direction Jasper had told him. Exactly in the spot where the medicine man had said it would be, they found Henry Bell's remains partially covered with snow.

Tommy, Fields Smith, Bill Baker, and the other Cherokee boys weren't at all surprised, though Nip was astonished. "Ever since Bell disappeared, Tommy was obsessed about finding him," Fields Smith later said. "What hurt him the most was the thought of Henry dying alone in the woods." Tahlequah's police department took charge of returning Henry's body to Mississippi. Only after he learned that Henry had a Christian funeral and was buried beside his Choctaw family could Tommy put the tragedy to rest.

He returned to his coaching duties and basketball, grateful for the distraction. During the next two months, with faithful crowds that included the boys' smitten fans, the Indians racked up one win after another and ended with a spectacular 14-2 season. The jubilation over that for Tommy disappeared as May approached, though, heralding the end of another school year, another graduation, and goodbyes aplenty to boys who, if he had done his job right, were prepared to take their place in society. After four years at Sequoyah, Tommy's family had come to recognize the depressing effect that graduation had on him.

Tommy sought out John Anderson before the graduation ceremony. Both emotional, they laughed about their first meeting and Anderson's encounter with the Board of Education. John's plan to enroll at Bacone put a dent in Tommy's melancholy. He told John that he would come watch him play.

The last straw for Tommy came when Amon and Jean graduated from Northeastern. They had teaching jobs waiting for them at

Seneca Indian Boarding School in Wyandotte. The school was only sixty miles away, but to Tommy their move was symbolic; they were leaving home for good.

Not able to hide how depressed he was, on Sunday evening, after attending Sequoyah's and Northeastern's graduations, he told Dorothy that he had "business in town."

Her sad eyes told him she knew what he was about to do.

"Don't worry about me," Tommy said. "I'll be okay tomorrow."

29

Fish-Eater, Blanket-Ass—Hut!
DGꞱ ᎫՏβⱺᎩ, ᎤᏗᏕ⸱ ᎫᎢᏢ--hut!

1951–52

September's school preparation duties consumed Tommy's days: checking to make sure new arrivals got settled, recruiting eligible boys for the football team, scheduling vocational duties. Eleven incoming freshmen agreed to try out for the team. Elmer Fish was one of them. Elmer's older sister and four younger brothers arrived with him, but the other boys weren't old enough to play. Elmer was Creek, he said, though his mother had some Cherokee blood. He had been eight years of age when his parents divorced. Elmer and his siblings had attended several Indian schools, but the space in their ages had prevented them from attending the same school at the same time.

    Elmer could run like a deer, and Tommy saw that he would be a great addition to the squad, especially on offense. And at 150 pounds, he would be able to hold his own on defense. Tommy started him at right end. Fields Smith, Everett Nave, and Jay Whitecrow from the previous year's squad returned. Though small in stature and weight, Fields quickly grasped the complexities of the game. He was fast on his feet and had an accurate arm. Tommy gave him the quarterback position. Tommy looked forward to having Whitecrow, whom he assigned as guard, on the team. Smart, inquisitive, and gregarious, Whitecrow had earned more than his share of encounters with the Board of Education. Tommy viewed him as a good kid and felt that football would be an excellent outlet for him. Everett Nave, a 140-pound junior, had the attitude Tommy most admired. He would go after anybody, regardless of size. Tommy kept him at guard.

At the first practice the following week, Tommy glanced up from his clipboard when he heard somebody shout, "Hey, coach, need a good football player?" Tommy burst out laughing at the sight of George Cameron striding toward him.

"You bet I do!" Tommy embraced him, then introduced George to the new players. Tommy insisted he have supper with them.

Dorothy ended the meal with a big slab of pie. "Like old times," she told him.

Taller and heavier, George was visibly happy to be back. He told them that at the time he left Camp Polk, he had still harbored hatred of the Japanese because of Pearl Harbor. "Hokkaido, Japan, was the last place on earth I wanted to be stationed. After I was there a while I met some nice folks who lived near the base I realized how wrong I was."

When George rose to leave, Tommy told him to get his football gear and come to practice the next day. "You're my halfback." Tommy had thirty-nine names on his 1951 roster, eighteen from the 1950 team. Twenty-one new players presented a football coach's perennial challenge to get boys involved and anxious to learn. Next would be drills in basics with practice sessions and repetition until each knew his position and felt at ease handling the ball. Becoming a cohesive team could take as much as half the season in learning leadership, working together, and trusting each other—new concepts for many of them. Always important to Tommy was weaving life's lessons into the game he never tired of coaching.

At the beginning of each season, Tommy could count on a newspaper reporter showing up in search of a story. He didn't like what he read in an article in the *Tahlequah Citizen* on September 4, 1951: "The Indians, coached by Tommy Thompson, are a hustling scrappy outfit, but too light. They've been getting their share of knocks."

Though this was correct, Tommy didn't like seeing it in print for their opponents to read. Tackle Nip Shipp at 172 pounds and

The Cameron brothers. (*Left to right*) Bill, George, and Dave Cameron, circa 1951. Permission granted by Mrs. Bill [Cameron] Campbell and Mrs. George Cameron.

back Chastine Keener at 175 were his only heavyweights. Smith, the quarterback, weighed 130 pounds; his three running backs, averaging 141 pounds, would be going up against guys 50 and 60 pounds heavier. With his penchant for making the best of things, Tommy counted on speed, timing, and execution to make up for the lighter weight. They had nine games scheduled: seven against Class A and B schools and two against C schools.

At midseason, the Indians had a 2-2 record against Class A opponents and a single win against a Class C school. The next school on their schedule, Checotah High, was a big Class A public high school with an all-white team. Tommy stressed to his linemen that the key to bringing down a big player was to "tackle low, knees and below." He told them to welcome the challenge.

Checotah High School's bus arrived at Sequoyah on Friday, October 26, 1951. Tommy greeted the coach and stood chatting with him as the team filed out of the bus. "Where's your Q-B and running backs?" Tommy asked him.

"I didn't bring 'em," the coach answered. "I need them to be in good shape for the playoffs. Can't afford my best players getting injured."

Heat rushed to Tommy's face. "You're *saving* them for the playoffs?"

The coach shrugged. "Didn't figure I'd need 'em anyway."

Tommy fought down the impulse to tell the opposing coach what an arrogant jerk he was. Instead Tommy said, "We'll see about that," and strode toward the field. He was even madder at game time upon observing that Checotah used more second-string players in the first quarter than starters. Tommy paced his sideline, jaws clenched and a frown creasing his brow. Bill Baker remembered, "Coach looked ready to explode. That's as mad as I'd ever seen him. We pretty quick figured out why and poured it on. At halftime we were up fifty to zero. Tommy was still fuming in the locker room. He told us, 'I want you to teach that arrogant jerk a lesson. If you do, forget peanut butter and jelly sandwiches. I'll buy steak dinners for everybody.'"

One of the players suggested, "If we beat 'em by a hundred points, how about a steak dinner and a movie with a date?"

FISH-EATER, BLANKET-ASS—HUT!

"Done!" Tommy shouted and raised his fist. "Now get out there and show that guy how big a mistake he made underestimating us."

By the end of the third quarter, every Sequoyah player had scored at least one touchdown. The Indians ran rampant over Checotah in the final quarter. The final score was 108–0. After the game, a euphoric coach treated his entire team to a steak dinner, and the next night, he drove them and their dates in the school bus to the Thompson Theater for a movie.

Eastern Oklahoma newspapers had a field day over the game: Class C Sequoyah annihilating Class A Checotah. They compared it to David destroying Goliath. In his office Monday morning, Tommy answered his eighth call. Jack Brown's terse "good morning" told him this wasn't another call congratulating him.

"Thomas, I just hung up from speaking to Checotah's superintendent. He is very unhappy with us and so is his coach."

Jack had never before called him Thomas. "You mean they're unhappy with *me*," Tommy said, making no attempt to hide his sarcasm.

"Really, Tommy, a hundred and eight to zero?" Jack's 'zero' sounded like *zeeerow*.

"I am not sorry, Jack," Tommy replied. "Their coach didn't bring his best players, because he said he was saving them for the playoffs. When he said he didn't figure he'd need them anyway, I had to either play them into the ground or kick his arrogant ass. I chose the high road."

Jack Brown burst out laughing and couldn't stop, which triggered Tommy to do the same. It took several minutes for the two men to pull themselves together. "Okay, I understand why you did it," Jack said, "but I don't want this getting any bigger. I would appreciate your writing an apology to the superintendent with a copy to their coach." Tommy started to object, but Brown interrupted. "I didn't say you have to mean it. You gave them a giant lesson in humility. Their coach has been made to look like a fool by the press. A short letter, please?"

Tommy reluctantly agreed, then typed a three-line apology on Sequoyah stationery and dropped it in Monday's mail.

COACH TOMMY THOMPSON AND THE BOYS OF SEQUOYAH

On November 2, 1951, Sequoyah defeated Coweta 27–0 and won the District 12 championship, in Class B this time. The Indians had played their next opponent many times: Cascia Hall, a large Class A Catholic high school in Tulsa, with all white players. George Cameron later recalled, "Coach warned us before the game not to call them 'fish-eaters,' which we did in private, joking around." The game was on Cascia's home field, with the first quarter going their way. Sequoyah had the ball.

George Cameron remembered, "We broke huddle and lined up. Just as our center was about to hike the ball, one of our guys, in a voice loud enough that everybody heard, said 'fish-eaters.' There we were staring at them across the line and them staring back at us. We didn't know what to expect, but the minute our center snapped the ball, all hell broke loose. They blocked and tackled us double hard. They'd whomp us two times before the referee could blow his whistle. When our receivers caught a pass, Cascia players would yell 'Get that blanket-ass.' When they caught one, we'd yell, 'Run over that fish-eater.' We never knew who said it, but we paid for that remark."

Cascia Hall trounced Sequoyah 26–6. The Indians' football season ended November 28, 1951, with a victory over Class A Rogers High School on the Rogers home field.

Jack Brown appeared unannounced at Tommy's door shortly after the season ended. "You will want to see this." He handed Tommy a copy of *Life* magazine. "Page seventy-three," Brown said, and told Tommy goodbye. The date of December 3, 1951, told him it was the latest issue; he wondered why Brown was so sure he would want to see it. Tommy sat down and flipped to page 73. The article was about a letter written in October by a soldier returning to his combat unit in Korea. A brief paragraph explained the magazine's reason for printing it: "During what was officially described as a 'quiet' period on the Korean battlefront, John W. Harper, a Marine Lieutenant in a line company, wrote this letter to his father, a Marine Lieutenant-Colonel in World War II. It [the letter] was not intended for publication, but *Life* was given permission

FISH-EATER, BLANKET-ASS—HUT!

to publish it unedited as a small masterpiece of reporting on life in the front lines at a time when nothing was supposed to be happening."

Reading on, Tommy discovered the reason that Jack had personally delivered the magazine. Harper's letter recounted a fierce fight for a ridge held by the North Koreans: "Dear Paw: [When I returned,] . . . I discovered that one of the squad leaders—an Indian boy named Yellowhead—had conducted a wild, one-man Banzai charge during the assault, killing a number of gooks and collecting four or five prisoners. For this, he was recommended for the Bronze Star by the platoon leader present."

Milo's name produced the instant image of a soaking-wet mud-covered boy fighting with everything he had, to do what was expected of him. Tears stung and pride surged through Tommy. The news came as no surprise, simply confirmation of what he already knew: serious, conscientious Milo Yellowhead, a warrior on the football field, had proved himself, in Korea, a warrior still. A knock on his door made Tommy hurriedly wipe his eyes.

Thomas Batson entered, his serious expression a sign that he had something on his mind. Tommy hoped that whatever was concerning him today had nothing to do with his father. Tommy rose. "Thomas, good to see you." They shook hands, an act that was Tommy's first lesson for every new boy. He motioned to a chair. "What can I do for you?"

Thomas glanced around the office before looking Tommy in the eye. "You said I could come talk to you anytime I wanted, even if I . . ."

"You can tell me whatever is on your mind," Tommy said.

"Well, sir, I'm on the baseball team, but the season doesn't last very long." Thomas looked embarrassed. "I'd really like . . . I was wondering if there was any way after the season is over that somehow I could still play."

Relieved and touched by the boy's heartfelt request, Tommy told him that he'd come to the right person. He studied Thomas as he thought of some options. The boy was a natural in the outfield and a smart defensive player. His batting average had steadily increased. Tommy said, "You know our season starts three months from now. And you've seen how busy I am with advisor duties. I could sure use an assistant coach. Would you be interested?"

"Really?" Thomas grinned. "You bet I would."

Tommy added, "Did you know that every summer I coach the American Legion baseball team?" Thomas shook his head. "I need an assistant then, too. You can ride with me to the games so we can talk strategy. What do you say?" Thomas looked as though a genie had just granted him three wishes. "By the way, I bet you'd like to earn some spending money." The boy nodded. "There are so many things around here I need help with," Tommy told him. "We'll get you a job here at school."

Thomas sprang up from his chair. "Thank you, sir, thank you!"

"No need to call me 'sir.' 'Tommy' or 'coach' but not 'sir,' okay?" Tommy grabbed the boy's hand, pulled him close, and hugged him. "I'm glad you came to me. We're going to have fun." Thomas's step had a spring to it when he exited. It had taken courage for him to come and ask for something he needed—maybe a father's assurance that he cared.

Tommy returned to the open magazine on his desk. He read and reread the soldier's letter praising in black and white the courage of an Indian boy named Yellowhead. Milo had shed tears after the football game from hell—not for himself but shouldering the blame for their loss. Reading about him brought back just how much Milo had touched Tommy's life and then moved on—as Thomas Batson would do one day. Goodbyes would always be part of Tommy's job, but he reflected on how good it felt to celebrate Milo's courage and Thomas's joy that somebody needed him.

The first two months of 1952 failed to deliver the bitter cold temperatures and snow of the previous winter. Spring seemed to be poised on the horizon. Tommy walked across campus to his apartment, the sounds of construction filtering into his awareness. He'd promised Dorothy he would check on Jody, who was sick with a cold. The sitter answered the door and said that Jody had had a good lunch and was down for a nap. He tiptoed into her room and touched her forehead; sleeping peacefully, she felt cool to his touch.

Curious about the noise, Tommy walked toward it and found a huge truck in the process of lowering a house onto a foundation. He figured Jack Brown had purchased another government surplus house. A few years ago, the superintendent had bought four of them for employees whose job required them to live on campus. They cost almost nothing, and the school's building crew brought the houses up to standard with new plumbing and wiring, hardwood floors, and a coat of paint inside and out. Principal Jack McCarty and his family lived in one of them.

The moving crew settled the house onto the foundation. Tommy waited until the truck driver turned off the motor, then asked whether he could look around. He peeked through window openings at a good-sized living room and kitchen. The house had three bedrooms, one bathroom, a breakfast nook, and what looked like the beginning of a basement inside the foundation.

All four of the surplus houses had been occupied when Tommy and Dorothy arrived in 1947. But because his job required Tommy to live on campus, Mr. Brown had offered him the ground-floor apartment in Unit C at no rent. It had been a good arrangement, but while looking at this house sitting under huge oak trees, Tommy knew instinctively that Dorothy would jump at the chance to live in it.

He walked hurriedly to the administration building and tapped on Mr. Brown's open door. "Tommy, come in," Mr. Brown said.

"I just saw the surplus house being delivered and was wondering if it has been spoken for," Tommy said.

"No, it hasn't. Are you interested in renting it?"

"I am. I know Dorothy would love to be in a house with a real kitchen and a basement."

"Understandable," Brown said. "The rent is twenty-five dollars a month, which we can deduct from your salary if you like. I suggest you talk to Alaska Davis, building foreman. See what needs to be done and tell him you'll be living in it."

"Thank you, Jack," Tommy said and shook his hand. There had been no waffling—the decision had been rendered in true Jack Brown style. Tommy walked back to the house and talked to Davis, who said he would start on it as soon as he finished a small project for Mr. Brown. Davis figured no more than two months would be needed to get it ready for them to move into. A small problem was the missing roof over the breakfast nook; it needed to be a hipped roof, he said, to match the main roof. But he had framed only gable roofs. He assured Tommy he would find someone to do it.

Tommy told Dorothy the news that evening and mentioned what Davis had said about the missing section of roof. She reminded him that his son-in-law had been a journeyman carpenter before coming to Sequoyah. Dorothy said she would ask Amon whether he would do it.

Alaska Davis's crew began their preliminary work at the end of March. Amon and Jean drove down from Wyandotte over three successive weekends, which was time enough for Amon to frame and finish the roof over the breakfast nook. The construction crew returned and finished their work and turned over the house keys to Tommy in early May, a week before graduation.

Tommy lost six seniors from his football team in the 1952 graduating class: George Cameron was one of them. Tommy dreaded saying goodbye to George and all his boys. Back at Sequoyah for only a year, George had already told Tommy he was going to join the army like his brother. According to his family, Tommy took graduations "badly."

He helped with the move, but Dorothy, very much in charge, needed no help directing the movers. He knew this would be a good time to keep out of her way. He prudently did not mention the promise that Portia Vaughn had coerced him into making at the graduation ceremony. There would be time enough for that after his wife had their house in order. As she had done with every move, in her own way and her own time Dorothy transformed the house. They were comfortably established in their new home under the oaks as summer settled over the campus.

30

Make a Promise, Dance the Two-Step

ᎾᏍᎢᎤᏝ ᏗᏞᎤᎩ ᏝᏞ ᎢᏬᏝᎤᎡᏝ

1952

Ordinarily, Tommy gladly welcomed any boy who wanted to play football, but he had serious reservations about Bill Baker when Bill showed up in the fall of 1952. In a freak spring accident, while cleaning the bread-slicing machine in the kitchen, Bill had cut the end off his middle and ring fingers up to the first joint. Tommy worried about damage to his hand because practice could get as rough and tumble as a real game.

He did not expect to see Bill the first day of practice in a uniform saying he wanted to practice, but the boy came up to Tommy and showed him his hand: the ends of his severed fingers were covered with a metal cap taped on at the joint. "They're aluminum," Bill said. "I made them in shop this summer, and Mr. Hunt welded them into a flare so I can jam them over the joint." Tommy wanted to know how his fingers felt. Though it had been five months since the accident, Bill admitted that the ends were still sensitive. "I want to play anyway."

Tommy stared at 135 pounds of determination, a trait he longed to see in every one of his players. "Okay, but only long enough to see how they work." The aluminum caps worked so well that Tommy agreed to let Bill take part in the full practice. Over the next three weeks, he did so well in practices that the fourth week Bill Baker played in the Indians' first game of the season.

The Sunday after that game, Tommy and Dorothy had a surprise visitor. Bill Cameron showed up en route to Fort Ord in Monterey, California, from his assignment in Korea. He told them that

Sixteen-year-old cool dude Bill Baker in front of his dorm, August 1952. Permission granted by Bill Baker.

he had come to see his family and that included them. Dorothy insisted he stay for supper.

Tommy could see few traces of the boy he had first met. A confident young man, Bill Cameron talked proudly about his new assignment escorting the bodies of Indian soldiers killed in battle to their home for burial. Bill paused to retrieve a pack of Lucky Strikes from his pocket. "Your brand, coach, if I remember," he said.

Tommy chuckled. "So you were paying attention back then."

Bill offered each of them a cigarette, then lit one himself.

Tommy asked about Korea, whereupon Bill's expression turned pensive.

"I was there last winter with the Third Division. I've never been that cold. One afternoon I stood up out of my foxhole and looked across this valley. Snow four feet deep. I was hungry and cold, no cigarettes, and ten thousand miles from home. I remember thinking if I was going to die that day there was only two things I wanted. To see my mother and hug and kiss her. And see Sequoyah one more time. That's why I came, and I can't tell you how much I needed to see you."

Bill cleared his throat, a smile replacing his thoughtful expression. He asked about his brother.

"George got his diploma like he promised, then said he wanted to join the army," Tommy told him. "You know me—I tried to get him to go to Northeastern, but he wanted to follow in your footsteps. About now he's on his way to Fort Benning, Georgia, for jump school."

Over coffee, their talk turned to sports. Bill asked Tommy whether he thought the football team would get into the playoffs this season.

"Are you kidding? I *always* believe we'll get in the playoffs." Tommy laughed.

Bill asked about a few buddies, then rose; he said he had to get going. "I've wanted to say this for a long time but never did. I figure now's a good time. I've met a whole lot of people in my travels, but my Momma and the two of you are the number one, two, and three people I want to be around in my next life." No longer shy, Bill kissed Dorothy on the cheek, embraced Tommy, and quickly departed.

Only after Andrew Mouse walked onto the practice field a few days later did Tommy cheer up. "Are you back? You better not be just visiting."

"Nope, I'm back from the army to get my degree." Andy grinned. "And play football for Tommy Thompson."

Tommy scanned the boy. He had forgotten Rat's fair skin and curly red hair. "You sure you're Cherokee, Rat? You look more like an Irishman." They hugged each other.

"Irish?" Rat laughed and asked Tommy in Cherokee what position he'd be playing. Tommy answered in Cherokee that the plan was to switch him to any position where he was needed.

They talked again after practice, and Tommy told him his name would always be Rat. Andy said he figured as much, since every letter he received from Tommy at Fort Polk began "Dear Rat."

Andrew told Tommy that the Sequoyah boys had stuck together like family during the six months of boot camp and afterward, when the Forty-fifth Division went to Hokkaido. But from there, Rat said, everybody scattered: some to Korea, some to Germany. "I was in the Korea group. Serving as a forward observer for my mortar platoon. I'm considering a career in the army, coach."

Tommy grinned. "We need to have a serious talk about that."

Andy added talent and commitment to the team. Watching him play showed how much he loved the game. He played in Friday's game against Westville. The Indians started out by scoring three touchdowns to Westville's one in a mistake-free first half. Five minutes into the third quarter, the referee blew his whistle, and Tommy watched from the sidelines as twenty-two players dropped to their knees and crawled around in search of "Bill's finger." When it was found and returned to him, Bill came out and taped the aluminum cap back on. With the score 21–6, Tommy wanted him to sit out the rest of the game, but Bill begged to finish the game. After a final score of 37–6, a triumphant Bill raised his hand. "How 'bout that? All fingers present and accounted for."

Out of their next six games, the Indians lost to two Class A schools by a total of 13 points and trounced three B schools by a total of 89 points. Class A Rogers High beat Sequoyah in the last game of their regular season. The loss didn't matter, though, for the Indians made the playoffs.

In high spirits, Tommy surprised Dorothy and the boys by bringing home a Philco television for their new house, the first and only TV at Sequoyah. It came with two narrow transparent strips of plastic the width of the screen, one blue and one green. Adhering the blue strip to the top and the green one to the bottom was supposed to give the illusion of color to the black-and-white picture. Nip Shipp later recalled that they didn't fool him: "They just looked like plastic strips to me."

The other accessory that came with the Philco was a wall-to-wall floor covered with boys, so many that six-year-old Jody had to climb over and around a human obstacle course to cross the room. With the addition of the television, the Thompsons entertained even more boys than they had done at their apartment. Providing the boys had finished their homework on Thursday nights, they watched the Lone Ranger, cheering when Texas Ranger John Reid donned his mask and, with Tonto, set out to punish wrongdoers throughout the Old West. What they formerly had to pay ten cents at the theater to see, they now could watch for free in the Thompsons' living room, with popcorn supplied by Mrs. Thompson.

Turning his attention to their upcoming playoff games, Tommy determined that their losses had mostly been to schools with a significant weight and height advantage. He shifted Nip Shipp and Andy Mouse to tackles and played them side-by-side in an unbalanced line, then assigned 180-pound Chastine Keener at fullback. The team was as ready as it could be, and for the third time in his six years at Sequoyah, they were in the District 12 playoffs. Their first game would be in Spiro, a small town to the south almost on the Arkansas border in LeFlore County. A public school, Spiro had a reputation for having a solid football program.

Tommy assigned Bill Baker as right linebacker. What he lacked in weight, he made up for with speed. Baker recalled the game: "In the first half, quarterback Fields Smith called a play that gave me the ball. I shot across the line and got trapped by a two-hundred-pound right guard. That guy hit me so hard, he broke off my front tooth and knocked me out cold." Two Sequoyah players carried Baker off the field and stretched him out on the ground behind the benches.

Sequoyah defeated Spiro 14–7, but all that Baker remembered later was waking up back at school as Tommy was saying the cooks were fixing steaks for the team to celebrate their victory. Bill had a liquid supper, for his mouth was so swollen that he couldn't eat solid food for several days.

Their win gave the Indians the District 12 Class B Championship for the second time and advanced them into the state quarterfinals—giving them a second chance to win it all.

The boys responded with extra practices and strategy sessions. Tommy wanted to take part, but he felt responsible for Bill's getting knocked out by "that Spiro steamroller" and insisted on taking Bill to his dentist. Bill left the dentist's office with a gold cap over his broken tooth, which Tommy said looked so good he would likely have to fight the girls off.

Tommy forgot all about the promise he had made to Portia Vaughn at the graduation ceremony. When she called in the middle of playoff fever and reminded him, he tried to put her off, but Miss Vaughn would accept no excuses. She replied, "Am I correct in believing that Tommy Thompson is a man of his word?" That was all she had to say.

Nearly eighteen at the time, Jimmy Thompson recently recalled his father's reluctance to tell his mother about the promise. Tommy waited until after supper and made Jimmy promise to stay at the table and back him up. Jimmy remembered, "My dad was this big authority figure in charge of discipline at school. As a coach he'd get after players if they didn't do what he said. But around the house, Momma was the boss."

Remaining at the table after supper, with both of them smoking a cigarette, Tommy complimented Dorothy on the dinner and then said he had something to confess. "Before you say no, please hear me out. Miss Vaughn believes the boys should learn to dance, that it's a necessary social skill. And if I want them to be successful after they leave here, they need to know how to conduct themselves in social situations."

Dorothy stubbed out her cigarette a little harder than usual and asked point-blank, "Thomas Fox Thompson, what did you promise?"

"That I . . . that all of us would attend Miss Vaughn's dance lessons and Friday night dances." His wife started to protest. "Dorothy, you love the boys as much as I do, and they love you. They look at you as their mother. You want them to feel at ease in social situations, don't you?" Before she could answer, Tommy asked Jimmy what he thought about the idea. Jimmy answered truthfully that he loved to dance.

Jimmy recalls that the four of them took lessons and attended the dances and that his mother didn't stay upset very long. Tommy coerced twenty or thirty of his boys into coming, and Miss Vaughn matched that number with girls. Sometimes they danced to records, other times to Sequoyah's swing band, which was directed by Miss Vaughn. Dorothy took part in the lessons reluctantly at first, but Jimmy recalls that his father had such a good time dancing and was so good at it that it seemed more like a party. Tommy's enthusiasm won out. The boys found out learning to dance wasn't hard and it was a great way to meet girls.

Tommy thanked Dorothy profusely for her unwavering patience with him. His wife had long ago come to understand that he thrived on being a father to any and all boys in need of one. Though she may not have matched his enthusiasm at first, Dorothy grew into the role of surrogate mother. She liked that the boys felt at home in the Thompson house even when Tommy was refereeing a game. They came bringing homework or just wanting to talk. John Anderson reminisced about those days: "We called her 'Mrs. Thompson,' but she was like our mom. She'd watch television with us. She fussed over us when we got sick and always remembered our birthday. Mrs. Thompson was a wonderful mother."

Dorothy's priorities were, in order of importance, Tommy, her children (which included the boys), and her teaching career. Her greatest fear was that if his drinking problem became known, Tommy's image would be tarnished and cost him his job. Coaching and being surrogate father were, she knew, the heart and soul of Tommy Thompson. If those roles were taken away, it would destroy him.

As far back as Jody Thompson could remember, her father's drinking was a forbidden subject at home. Mentioning it would set off her mother quicker than anything. One of Jody's earliest memories at around six years of age was overhearing a telephone conversation between her mother and Superintendent Brown. Jack

Brown called and either intimated or asked Dorothy directly whether her husband had a drinking problem. Jody remembers her mother calmly denying it, but after Dorothy hung up, she launched into a "royal temper fit."

The intensity of her mother's anger frightened Jody. "I don't remember ever seeing her that mad," Jody recalled. "She stormed around the house the rest of the day."

The children believed that rather than attribute any blame to her husband for his drinking, their mother chose to blame it on his workload and commitment to his boys. Jean Thompson Baker later stated, "It never would have occurred to her to let Daddy's drinking shake her admiration and faith in him."

Dorothy maintained that Tommy's unmistakable devotion to his boys and Sequoyah should warrant Jack Brown's overlooking one small defect in an otherwise perfect gentleman.

31

Second Chances Are Hard to Come By
WPᏆ ᎣᏞᏟᎣᏞᏚᎯ ᎠᲚᏞᏬᏀ

1952

Tommy rarely delivered lengthy motivational speeches before a game. Given that quarterbacks called plays in the huddle, more often than not he used the pregame time to cover practical aspects: what situation called for a run, how to spot a blitz or an opponent's defensive back out of position, a good opportunity for a long pass. He didn't feel the need to motivate his boys. Five minutes with them in the locker room before any game, it was easy to see that they were ready and wanted to win.

Tommy looked forward to being in the playoffs. He was excited but more reflective and grateful this time. He didn't view it as the pinnacle of his career but rather the reward for a successful season. A second chance at the state championship, how often did that happen? Not often, he knew. In sports, as in life, second chances were hard to come by.

Tommy waited in the locker room assigned to them by the Okemah High School coach. When his players filed in, Tommy held up his hand for quiet. "At the hotel last night, I happened to glance down, and on the floor in the dining room I found a notebook." He held it up. "This is a scouting report. Somebody has outlined every one of our plays. You know what that means? Okemah will be ready for every play we run." Angry protests circled the locker room. He waited until they settled down. "There are three ways we can handle this. Get mad, be afraid those white guys will kick our butts, or [figure] that they are so afraid of us they hired somebody to give them our game plan." Tommy pumped his fist in the air and hollered, "So, how're you going to take it?"

All twenty-two players jumped up, pumping their fists and jeering. Sequoyah's team manager, Sterling Speaks, always energetic, circulated among them egging them on.

"That's the way I want you to take it," Tommy shouted. "Maybe they thought we were a bunch of upstart Indians from a school nobody ever heard of. Well, they must not think that anymore. They know those upstart Indians won their way into the state playoffs twice in four years." Tommy laughed as jeers turned to cheers; his players made it clear that they would take on the devil if he had on a helmet and a football uniform.

Remembering a sixteen-year-old's dream of football playing a part in his life, Tommy could hardly believe how good it felt to be living that dream.

The Indians trotted onto the frozen field and formed a circle for the coin toss. Light snow swirled around as the referee told them to have a good game. In the first quarter, Okemah's defense came at them with a knowing swagger, successfully stopping run plays and knocking down QB Smith's passes. In the second quarter, Tommy watched his boys anticipate Okemah's defense with good blocking on runs and Smith making shorter passes out to the flats.

In the second half, the Indians' speedy defense thwarted every Okemah attempt to score, holding them to a field goal. The final score was Sequoyah Indians 13, informed opponents 3.

The boys relived the game on the noisy bus ride back to Tahlequah.

But once at school, Tommy turned his attention to their next game. He phoned Warren Wheatley, *Muskogee Phoenix* sports reporter, to find out who their next opponent would be. Wheatley told Tommy that they would play the winner of a game scheduled the following day between Skiatook and Stroud. The game was in Stroud.

Knowing only that both were public high schools in northeastern Oklahoma—Skiatook in Osage County and Stroud in Lincoln County—Tommy decided it would be worth the drive to see the teams in action. He left the following morning for Stroud, a small town on the main highway, halfway between Oklahoma City and Tulsa. Skiatook's players, as was true of the majority of teams the Indians had played, were taller and heavier, but Tommy drove back to Sequoyah, telling himself that his boys' speed could offset their disadvantage.

He called a meeting in the gym the following evening after supper. Tommy held up the sports page of the *Muskogee Phoenix* and pointed to Warren Wheatley's article. "It's official; we're playing Skiatook. Their game against Stroud was a bust. Neither team scored, so according to OAA rules, Skiatook gets the win for their two penetrations into Stroud's red zone. Our win over Okemah gives us home field advantage." He filled them in on what to look for. "Despite the fact they didn't score, Skiatook's two senior backs, Walter Butler and J. D. Hill, could pose a threat. Watch for them to explode off formation on spinners." He pointed to his two guards. "Your job is to guard them."

Skiatook's team arrived Thursday afternoon for Friday night's game on Gable Field. On December 4, 1952, the *Tahlequah Citizen* hyped the game: "Skiatook Tigers are bigger but Sequoyah's Indians are willing. That seems to be the story as Coach Thompson prepares his fine Class B squad for the Skiatook heavy eleven, a team that has a habit of going far in the state playoffs."

Perfect football weather and abundant pregame press produced a crowd of 2,500 fans ready to witness an exciting semifinal battle. They weren't disappointed. Sequoyah sent the crowd into frenzy in the first quarter when quarterback Fields Smith connected with fullback Chastine Keener on a seventy-six-yard pass play. Smith then kicked the point after. Skiatook end Billy Jack Swan then slipped by two Sequoyah defenders and streaked thirty yards into the end zone. Their conversion tied the game at 7–7 as the first quarter ended. Both teams scored in the second quarter, leaving the score tied at 14–14 at halftime.

In the locker room, Tommy congratulated his team for playing tough. He made a few adjustments that he said would help neutralize Skiatook's height and weight advantage. The Indians went back on the field and in the second half gave the locals plenty to cheer about. Sequoyah scored two touchdowns and shut down Skiatook's offense by repelling four attempts to get in the end zone. The final score was 28–14.

Playoff excitement swept through the school for the second time. One team stood between the Indians and the state championship—the deciding game against Tonkawa High. Tommy warned them up front that Tonkawa's championship track team made up their backfield. "So it's going to be speed versus speed." The Indians had a week to prepare.

Three days of solid practices ensued, but when Wednesday's practice session ended, Bill Baker approached Tommy on the sideline. He said he didn't feel well and hadn't felt good since Monday.

"Maybe you're coming down with something," Tommy said. "Go to bed after supper and get some rest. I'll check on you in the morning." About to get into bed that night, Tommy received a call from Ina Brady, Bill's dorm matron. "I took Bill Baker to the campus hospital, and Dr. Allison examined him. Bill has an advanced case of mumps. They've dropped and he is in a great deal of pain. But bless him, Tommy, he asked me to tell you how sorry he is he won't get to play Tonkawa." Bill was a competitor, so his expression of disappointment came as no surprise to Tommy.

Bill was a fast broken-field runner and would be missed. The next morning, Tommy studied his reserve list and spied Ed Shangreau's name. An Osage boy who also had speed, Shangreau would take Baker's place.

The final game for the Class B state championships required the Indians to travel to the Stillwater campus of Oklahoma A and M University, home of the Cowboys. Every one of his boys loved out-of-town games, preferably towns more than a hundred miles from Tahlequah. Nip Shipp recalled, "When a high school team had to travel more than a hundred miles for a game, the state paid for the hotel. Staying in a hotel and eating in the dining room, we were in tall cotton."

Fields Smith, the quarterback, remembered arriving in Stillwater early on Thursday afternoon. "After Tommy got us settled into the hotel, we toured the stadium and went out on the field.

SECOND CHANCES ARE HARD TO COME BY

The 1952 football team played Tonkawa for the state championship at Oklahoma A and M stadium in Stillwater. Not all the team's members have been identified; those that have been include the following. (*First row*) #80, Rudell Shipp; #10, Fields Smith; not in uniform, Sterling Speaks, team manager. (*Second row*) # 63, Bill Baker. (*Third row*) #31, Jay Whitecrow; #30, Jimmy Ollis; #75, Cecil "Nip" Shipp; #83, Everett Nave; #70, Andrew Mouse. Permission granted by Bill Baker.

Somebody had brought along a football, so we started playing touch ball. I don't know how it happened, but I sprained my ankle, real bad. Tommy got this stricken look on his face and told me to sit down. He sent for a stretcher, and they hauled me into the Cowboys' training room."

Smith recalls that Oklahoma A and M trainers Tiny Smith and Billy Brizee iced his ankle. Once it was numbed, they held him down while the head trainer pulled his foot into position and stabilized it. Afterward they moved him into a room with a bed. Tommy brought him a radio and a newspaper. "Coach told me not to get up for anything except to go to the bathroom," Smith said. "And to rest my ankle as much as I could because the team was counting on me."

A and M trainers took Fields his meals, and he stayed down that night and Friday until just before game time. He later described how they prepared him for the game: "The trainer iced my ankle again and taped it from the bottom of my foot up to the top of my ankle. He told me it wouldn't hurt, but it might give out on me." The trainer wished him luck, then warned him not to let anyone else remove the tape.

The 2:00 P.M. game began under sunny skies with a cool breeze: perfect football weather. A and M's stadium dwarfed the crowd of a few hundred people, most of them Tonkawa fans, whose school lay thirty-five miles northwest of Stillwater.

At 5' 6" and 130 pounds, Fields Smith could only gawk at the size of Tonkawa's players, all of whom were muscular and a good head taller. Tonkawa had thirty-five players on their bench. Sequoyah had twenty-two.

Center Everett Nave snapped the ball, and the game was under way. Both teams' defenders held steady, with neither team able to score in the first half. On the first play of the third quarter, Tonkawa's quarterback, Marion Ernest, faked a pass, then ran sixty-three yards for a touchdown. On Sequoyah's next possession, Fields Smith hit David Simon three times for fifty-four yards. At Tonkawa's eight-yard line, Field spiraled a ball into the end zone only to see it slip through the receiver's hands. Sequoyah remained scoreless.

A Tonkawa receiver fumbled on their second possession of the third quarter. Harris Cully pounced on the ball and put Sequoyah on the offense. Smith bulleted a pass to Rudell Shipp in the corner of the end zone for six points, but their point-after attempt failed. Both teams scored a second touchdown in the third quarter, making the score 14–13.

With Tonkawa in possession of the ball again, their quarterback handed off to a running back who smashed his way through Sequoyah's line and streaked into the end zone. Smith recalls that that touchdown changed the momentum of the game.

Four times in the fourth quarter, Sequoyah fought to get into the end zone, but each time, Tonkawa's big defenders either broke up the play or halted the Indians' drive at the goal line.

SECOND CHANCES ARE HARD TO COME BY

With six minutes and eight seconds left in the game, Tonkawa scored their fourth touchdown, making the final score 27–13.

On the sidelines, Tommy watched as one by one, like dominoes, Fields Smith, Harris Cully, Foreman Ross, Nip and Rudell Shipp, Ed Shangreau, Elmer Fish, Jay Whitecrow, Everett Nave, and Andrew Mouse turned toward him with disappointment on each face. They had said from the beginning that they wanted to give him the state championship because of the 1949 game from hell.

But this game bore no resemblance to that one. His boys weren't half-dead from exhaustion, and the weather hadn't helped beat them. They had played a good game, holding their own until the fourth quarter against bigger, heavier players. Their stats were almost even with Tonkawa's. Thirty years of football contributed to Tommy's perspective: this was football at its best. And how many times in his career had he reminded boys that if they learned only one thing from this game of football, it should be how to win and how to lose?

Smiling, Tommy ran onto the field and congratulated his boys. He shook hands with Tonkawa's coach and players, his boys joining him. He heard "Good game" from both sides.

The *Muskogee Phoenix* ran a picture of Tommy and some of his players accepting the state Class B runner-up trophy. In the accompanying interview, sports reporter Warren Wheatley asked Tommy how the loss would affect his plans for next season.

Tommy laughed. "Next season, I expect every player on the team to be six inches taller and weigh at least fifty pounds more." He nodded at Wheatley. "They played a good game, and the way I look at it, this is just one loss in a winning season. It wouldn't occur to these guys or to me to give up. We'll be back in the playoffs next year."

Epilogue

> The Oklahoma summer night vibrates
> with a soft wind that carries the song of the whip-poor-will.
> The night is a shelter made of darkness,
> made of sound.
> The darkness is feminine. It goes out,
> goes out forever it seems, to give refuge to those whose stories
> are too painful for the harsh light of day.
> —*Kim Campbell, daughter of Bill [Cameron] Campbell*

Tommy remained at the school and the job he loved until his sudden death on Saturday, June 14, 1958, at age fifty-five. From 1952 to the time of his death, Tommy's football teams continued to earn praise and prestige for Sequoyah, but the state football championship eluded the coach, who never gave up believing that his boys would win.

His obituary in the *Tahlequah Citizen* reported that Tommy died from a stroke, though later opinion attributed his death to an aneurysm or pulmonary embolism. On Saturday morning, the day before Father's Day, Tommy and Dorothy sat having breakfast in the nook of their campus home. He told her how much he was looking forward to Father's Day and the whole family being together. She rose and took his empty cup to the kitchen. As she began to fill his cup, she heard a crash. Dorothy rushed back into the nook. Tommy lay dead on the floor.

Jimmy Thompson later recalled that a week before, as he walked across campus with his father, out of the blue Tommy said to him, "I want you to know, son, I'm not afraid to die." If he had

EPILOGUE

experienced a premonition of his death, except for that lone comment Tommy gave no indication of it.

His family and the boys who had worked with him the day before on a physically taxing project believed that the project contributed to his death. Tommy had enlisted a group of boys to help him drain and dismantle a large abandoned pond near the campus homes of several employees on Friday morning. He told the boys that he'd seen a colleague's three-year-old daughter playing near the pond and feared she might drown.

Tommy worked alongside his boys for most of the morning, muscling big boulders into wheelbarrows and hauling them away. Once that had been accomplished, the drained space needed to be filled with dirt. Matching shovel for shovel with boys one-third his age, Tommy helped transfer a truckload of dirt into the former pond. They finished in the late afternoon, and everyone was exhausted from a day of hard, heavy labor. Tommy died eighteen hours later.

Shock swept through Sequoyah, through Tahlequah, and through the sports world of eastern Oklahoma like a freak storm on a sunny summer day. Comments such as, "No, not Tommy Thompson! He's too young and energetic, too full of life," were heard over and over. His funeral was a Tahlequah phenomenon. The First United Methodist Church had no empty seats; its doors were opened wide, and the crowd outside was as large as the one inside. Mourners stood shoulder to shoulder in the churchyard all the way to the street.

Retired seventy-one-year-old Jack Brown and his wife, Nola, sat up front behind Dorothy and the children. The friendship between fellow Masons Tommy Thompson and Jack Brown had remained strong and loyal to the end. An intelligent and extremely perceptive man, Brown made it a point to know everything that went on at his school. Since nothing escaped him, Brown no doubt would have been aware of Tommy's alcoholism. Perhaps, as Dorothy so desperately wanted, Brown respected Tommy's commitment to Sequoyah and his boys highly enough that he chose to view Tommy's struggle with alcohol as she did: "one small blemish in an otherwise perfect gentleman."

After thirty-two years as the superintendent of Sequoyah, Jack Brown retired in 1956. On the right is the director of vocational education, Amon Baker, son-in-law of Tommy Thompson. Permission granted by Amon Baker.

EPILOGUE

Dorothy was inconsolable over Tommy's death. Jean, Jimmy, and Jody acknowledged that it was a loss from which she never fully recovered. Dorothy outlived Tommy by thirty years; she passed away in 1988 at age seventy-nine. For the first fifteen of those years, she visited his gravesite every day, seven days a week. When anyone dared to ask her why she made the daily pilgrimage, she would answer, "Tommy was and always will be the love of my life."

Unable to reconcile her grief, only when her doctor said that crying every day for fifteen years was destroying her did Dorothy cease her daily visits. Still, whenever one of "Tommy's boys" returned from the service or visited her, the first thing she did was take them to the cemetery.

Jack Brown retired from Sequoyah in May 1956 after thirty-two years as superintendent of the school that remained always close to his heart. He left a legacy of excellence and caring. His industrious, decisive leadership not only guided the Sequoyah Orphan Training School into the outstanding institution that it became but also set a standard that other Indian boarding schools aspired to meet. He continued to be a spokesperson for Indian education into his retirement. Jack Brown died in August 1987 at the age of one hundred years and three months.

Tommy's eldest daughter, Jean Thompson Baker, became a teacher like her mother and taught throughout her adult life. In the later years of her career, Jean was the principal of Owen School in Park Hill, Oklahoma, a suburb of Tahlequah. She and Amon had four daughters and four grandchildren. Jean died in December 2003 at age seventy-four. Her funeral was held at the same First United Methodist Church as her father's.

Jody Thompson attended Northeastern University and spent her career with Indian Health Services. She married Cherokee Knotchie McCrary, Jr., also a graduate of Northeastern University, who taught biology and chemistry at Sequoyah for thirteen years. They had two sons and four grandchildren. Jody passed away in June 2005 from complications of diabetes at the age of fifty-eight.

After graduating from Northeastern, Tommy's son, Jimmy, married fellow student Kendall Magnon Wood. With both of them

EPILOGUE

holding teaching credentials, they left for Arizona and taught Navajo children for five years. They divorced years later. Jimmy worked for thirty-six years for the Bureau of Indian Affairs. He has five children and thirteen grandchildren. Retired now, Jimmy Thompson and his wife, Zereta, live in Muskogee, Oklahoma. The Bible that belonged to Rose Gritts, Tommy's mother—the same Cherokee Bible that Tommy found in his flour sack the day his father left him at COTS—now belongs to Jimmy's son. Named for his grandfather, Thomas Fox Thompson III lives in Missouri.

Sequoyah's four-legged ambassador, Boots, lived out a long and happy life as ambassador in residence, his last few years with a committee of three boys to feed, bathe, and groom him. At Sequoyah reunions, graduates still share stories about their adventures with Boots.

Tommy absorbed twenty-seven years of life experiences before he returned full circle to the orphanage that had made an indelible imprint on his heart and character. Every written account and firsthand interview about Tommy Thompson confirms that he went back because he had a mission he could no longer ignore: to be a father, mentor, coach, and teacher to boys who, like him, had no choice but to be there. But unlike Tommy, who had spent his childhood with a cold and elusive father, his boys never doubted his love for them. He was the one they could count on in good times and bad.

Only after his first few years at Sequoyah did Tommy speak about his struggle with alcohol, and then it was only with Dorothy and his son-in-law Amon Baker. Amon later recalled, "Tommy checked himself into a hospital two different times for rehabilitation. Each time, he came out believing he was cured, but it didn't last, and no one felt more disappointed than Tommy. Still, in all the years I knew him, there was never a time when a boy needed Tommy that he wasn't right there for him." Baker added, "He was so set on not letting his boys down [that] you could say in that respect Tommy did conquer his problem. His episodic drinking remained the pattern throughout his life, and he fought to the very end to keep his secret."

EPILOGUE

Although he worked at Sequoyah for only twelve years, from 1947 to 1958, Tommy accomplished his goal of making a difference. Only nineteen boys are featured in this story, but the abundance of consistently similar accounts makes clear that Tommy touched the lives of all of the boys in his charge, regardless of age. There were no boundaries to his resolve that every boy leave Sequoyah ready and equipped to take his place in society.

Tommy left a legacy of honorable men whose stories this author is proud to have told. Grandfathers now, they readily acknowledge having used the guidelines he instilled in them to make the best of whatever life brought their way. The guidelines served them well. Nine of the nineteen boys whose lives are traced in this story graduated from college and went on to achieve advanced degrees. Of the ten who did not obtain a college degree, six experienced long and successful careers in the military, and two received a Bronze Star. Some either divorced or were widowed and married for a second time, but eleven of the nineteen are nearing or have already celebrated fifty years of marriage. In addition, several of Tommy's "boys" returned to teach or work at Sequoyah.

In 1994, Northeastern State University posthumously inducted Tommy Thompson into its Athletic Hall of Fame. Almost all of the men in this book belong to the Sequoyah Alumni Association (SAA), established more than fifty years ago. Sequoyah's Hall of Fame, established to honor individuals who have contributed to the school's preeminence in Indian education, posthumously inducted Tommy in 2004 and Jack Brown in 2005. Cecil "Nip" Shipp and Stanley Speaks were both inducted in 2004.

Tommy would be proud of the sports programs that are currently active at Sequoyah. The boys' and girls' basketball teams have won the Class 3A state championships—the girls for three consecutive years (2004, 2005, and 2006) and the boys in 2005. In December 2007, the Lady Indians participated in an invitational tournament of female high school basketball teams sponsored by Nike and played in Phoenix, Arizona. They placed fifth out of thirty teams from all over the United States.

The school's football spirit remains high. Sequoyah has won the district championship two years running and made it to the

EPILOGUE

semifinals in the state championship. The Indians' 2008 quarterback was awarded a full athletic scholarship to Ole Miss, and one of their tackles received a full athletic scholarship to Dartmouth.

In December 2006, Sequoyah and the Cherokee Nation celebrated the opening of an $8.5 million multipurpose facility and gymnasium on its campus. Architecturally outstanding and a state-of-the-art building, "The House Where They Play" stands as a symbol of pride in Cherokee heritage and a vision of the future. An Indian-only high school now operated by the Cherokee Nation, Sequoyah has Indian students from almost every tribe. Vocational training is a relic of the past: a visionary school and tribal leaders have incorporated into their curriculum the academics that had been deficient in Tommy's day. Innovative alliances with universities in language, science, math, and engineering programs are meant to prepare Sequoyah students for college and advanced degrees in various fields, including medicine and law. Elective classes in Cherokee are taught by linguists, aided by computer programs, and encouraged with music, contests, and language clubs.

In the more than fifty years since this story ended, we have witnessed immeasurable change, which is all the more evident when we contrast it to the world and mores of Tommy's era. Definitions of success and happiness, of heroes and accomplishment are different. Truth be told, there is little in our lives that hasn't been redefined. We've learned to multitask and expect to view news as it happens, but somewhere in the transition to our high-tech warp-speed world, we've seen something precious slip away—an unhurried pace and an appreciation of simple pleasures and traditional virtues. We no longer have time to hear the whip-poor-will sing Mother Nature's song. Amazingly, the boys of Sequoyah have managed to hang on to some of their past. They say they still live by the basic values they learned from their surrogate father, and many have passed these on to their children and grandchildren.

It has been my privilege to get to know these men: to laugh with them about peanut butter raids, lament nearly losing Boots, and hurt with them over a game that, but for the weather, they might very well have won. I am honored that they felt free to

EPILOGUE

share with me their triumphs and their sorrows. Sadly, since the beginning of this project, seven people in the story have died: Jean Thompson Baker, Jody Thompson McCrary, Thomas Batson, Thompson Gouge, brothers George and Bill Cameron, and Jay Whitecrow.

Though a few "boys" have moved away from Oklahoma, they still call Sequoyah home. And every May they return to celebrate each other and their school and in the process honor the man whose uncompromising love turned them into a family.

In Tommy's day, Sequoyah's football field was a hundred-yard patch of weed-covered, baked hard dirt with a four-foot drop from one end zone to the other. There were no bleachers for the fans who came to watch and no lights for nighttime practice or games.

In 1960, two years after Tommy's death, a group of Sequoyah students and employees began a construction project. Using the school's heavy equipment under the guidance of Amon Baker, they created a new football field, planted it in grass, and installed a sprinkler system to keep the grass lush and green. The BIA then came in and built bleachers and installed lights. Former and present students, Tahlequah and Muskogee citizens, and friends who either knew Tommy or only knew of him attended the dedication of Sequoyah's new football field. Doc Wadley, Tommy's long-time friend and fellow teammate at Northeastern, acted as the master of ceremonies.

They named the new field the Tommy Thompson Field—a fitting memorial to a man for whom football was a metaphor for life.

Postscript

Life After Sequoyah

John Anderson attended Bacone College in Muskogee, then was drafted and spent two years in the army. After twenty years working in the Oklahoma and Texas oilfields, John enrolled at the University of Science and Arts of Oklahoma and in 1962 earned a B.A. in sociology. He has been married for fifty years to Zenia Poemoceah, a full-blood Comanche; they have three sons, five grandchildren, and three great grandchildren. John lives in Chickasha, and his passion is golf. A ten handicapper, he plays golf every day and thinks nothing of playing twenty-seven holes in a day. Not fully retired, he is in charge of grounds maintenance for Chickasha's six schools.

Amon Baker earned B.S. and master's degrees in education from Northeastern College and then began a career with the BIA that spanned thirty-four years. Seventeen of those were spent at Sequoyah as a teacher, as the director of vocational programs, and as superintendent (1973–81). Amon remains the president of Sequoyah's school board. He married Jean Thompson; they have four daughters and four grandchildren.

Bill Baker majored in electronics at Muskogee Junior College for two years, then joined the army. At Fort Sill, he went to guided missile school. From there, he went to Caribou, Maine, where he was in charge of all supplies pertaining to the Nike control system. Bill completed college, earning a degree in electronic engineering. His forty-year career was spent in research, development, and electronics design for several major U.S. companies. After retiring in

POSTSCRIPT: LIFE AFTER SEQUOYAH

1999, Bill designed and built his home on eight acres about twenty miles south of Tulsa. He built his dream shop, complete with an electronics lab and a machine shop to restore classic cars. Bill, with three sons from a first marriage, has been married to Sue for more than thirty years and after adopting her son, now shares four sons and eight grandchildren with her.

Thomas Batson rodeoed all over Oklahoma and Texas before moving to California, where he met and married part-Choctaw Peggy Jean. Thomas worked at a variety of jobs, including vending machines, electronics, and construction, until his wife wanted to move nearer to her family in northeastern Texas. Thomas and Peggy were married for forty-six years; they had one son (Thomas, Jr.) and Peggy's daughter from a previous marriage. Thomas passed away in Westville, Oklahoma, in 2006.

Bill Cameron received his GED while in the military. Bill made the army his career for many years. He was discharged in 1967, then returned to Tahlequah, where he worked at Sequoyah for the next twelve years. Married for almost fifty years, Bill and part-Cherokee Jean Hooper, have a son and a daughter and two grandsons. Bill passed away in June 2008. His military funeral was conducted at Fort Gibson. Decades back in the Cherokee tribal rolls, the Camerons were sometimes listed as Campbell and other times as Cameron (name mixups on the Dawes rolls were not uncommon). Bill believed that Campbell was the right name although George, because their father went by the name Cameron, claimed Cameron. Bill officially changed his name to Campbell while in the military, but for the sake of consistency in the story of his life, I have elected to call him Bill Cameron throughout the chapters.

George Cameron spent four years in the army and then returned to Tahlequah. He married full-blood Cherokee Louise Fixin in 1958 and farmed the land allotted to his mother. George so loved Sequoyah that in 1994 he wrote *Sequoyah Orphans' Training School*, a memoir of his eleven years at the school. George suffered from

POSTSCRIPT: LIFE AFTER SEQUOYAH

severe arthritis and was confined to a wheelchair the last few years of his life, but he remained active in the community and Sequoyah, spearheading the Veterans War Memorial that graces the school grounds. George and Louise had two sons and two daughters, followed by ten grandchildren and one great grandchild. George passed away in October 2005.

Harris Cully attended Northeastern College and after working at various jobs began his career with the BIA. He turned to the Guidance Department at Sequoyah and, taking advantage of being back in Tahlequah, completed his B.S. degree in education at Northeastern. Harris retired in 1993 from the BIA after thirty-one years. His specialty was adult vocational training programs and employment assistance. He married Elsie Harjo, who is half Seminole and half Creek; he and Elsie have a son, a daughter, and five grandchildren.

Elmer Fish earned a B.S. degree in education in 1958 from Northeastern College and was immediately drafted and spent two years in the army. Elmer worked for an oil production company in Tulsa for twenty-two years, until they closed the doors, then spent fifteen years at a Dupont plant that produced pipe for gas pipelines. He has been married to Mattie Osborne, a full-blood Pawnee, for sixty years; they have two sons and three granddaughters and live in a suburb of Tulsa.

Thompson Gouge attended Haskell Institute in Lawrence, Kansas, then spent twenty-five years as a procurement officer at the Riverside Indian School in Anadarko, Oklahoma. For fifteen of those years, Thompson, an expert archer, taught archery after school to Anadarko's Boy Scouts. He founded the Riverside Warrior Society to help Indian boys appreciate and retain their heritage. Thompson married Lutie Goombi, a full-blood Kiowa, soon after he graduated from Sequoyah. They had four children and six grandchildren. After Lutie passed away, Thompson remained a widower until 2001, when he married Shirley Howery from the Caddo tribe.

POSTSCRIPT: LIFE AFTER SEQUOYAH

In 2004, while teaching stickball at an Indian conference in Dallas, Thompson suffered a slight stroke but remained involved working with Indian children until he passed away on March 5, 2007.

Andrew Mouse enlisted in the army and married and had a son while at Fort Sill. When his young wife died unexpectedly, Andy's infant son went to live with his adoptive parents and Andy went to Berlin as part of the Sixth Infantry Regiment. He spent eighteen years in the army as a machinist, on two different occasions playing on the All Star Army football team. One game against the Third Armored Division took place in Berlin's Olympic stadium in front of 80,000 people. After the army, Andy worked in Dallas as a machinist. His second marriage ended in the 1980s, whereupon Andy got in his car and headed east on I-30 with no particular destination. He stopped in Charleston, South Carolina, and has lived there for over twenty years. In 2000, Andrew married Bobbie Smith, a graduate of the University of South Carolina Law School. An advocate attorney, she represents children's interests in divorce, custody, and abuse cases.

Everett Nave left Sequoyah in 1953 and spent ten years in the navy, where he received his GED. After the navy, he worked ten years for Texas Boots in Tennessee. When his mother became ill in Oklahoma, Everett returned to Tulsa to take care of her. Working in a variety of jobs, he stayed in Tulsa for twenty-five years. Divorced, he married a second time and adopted his wife's daughter. When that marriage ended twenty years later, he returned to Tennessee and reconnected with Geraldean Sisco, who had worked at Texas Boots when he was there. Married since 1995, they live in Tennessee. Everett has an adopted daughter and two granddaughters. In 2003, his granddaughter Amanda became Miss Oklahoma Teenage America and competed nationally in Orlando. She graduated from the University of Oklahoma in 2008 with a B.S. degree in microbiology.

Forman Ross enlisted in the army as a private. He did three tours in Korea, served in the 101st and 82nd Airborne Divisions, and

POSTSCRIPT: LIFE AFTER SEQUOYAH

spent two years in Special Forces. As a platoon sergeant and part of the 101st Airborne Division, Forman was awarded a Bronze Star for meritorious service during his eleven-month tour in Vietnam. Paratrooper Ross made thirty-five jumps in 1965 alone and a total of fifty in his career. He later saw action in the Dominican Republic. Forman retired as sergeant first class in 1982 after a distinguished twenty-seven-year career in the military. He was married to Sequoyah graduate Emma Proctor for forty-seven years, until her death in 2008. They have twin sons and two daughters, one a graduate of Notre Dame, the other of Tulsa University. They have seven grandchildren. Forman's great-uncle John Ross was a former chief of the Cherokee Nation. Forman is a member of the Sequoyah school board as well as his hometown's Kenwood school board, where he was instrumental in the building of a veteran's memorial. Every year Forman organizes a Kenwood reunion of his Sequoyah brothers and their families.

Cecil "Nip" Shipp received an athletic scholarship to Northeastern, where he earned his B.S. degree in education and a master's degree in teaching and completed advanced graduate studies in education administration. After two one-year teaching jobs in Arizona and Missouri, Nip returned to Tahlequah. Working for the BIA, he became the football and basketball coach at Sequoyah and taught social studies; he later became the boys' advisor and academic guidance counselor. Nip became principal in 1970 and held the job for eleven years, during which he intermittently filled in as superintendent (between BIA permanent appointments) for two or three years. After a twenty-one-year career, Nip left Sequoyah in 1981. He worked nine more years for the BIA, the last six as tribal operations officer at the Tahlequah agency of the BIA. Nip met and married Eva Nell Wheeler from Tahlequah while he was a junior at Northeastern. They have one daughter, Susan. Nip and Eva recently moved to central Florida to be near Susan, her husband, and their two grandchildren. Nip was inducted into the Sequoyah Hall of Fame in 2004, along with Tommy Thompson and Stanley Speaks. In February 2009, Cecil was inducted into the Northeastern State University Athletic Hall of Fame.

POSTSCRIPT: LIFE AFTER SEQUOYAH

Rudell Shipp enlisted in the army after graduation. He spent three years with a guided missile unit in Germany, then returned to Fort Sill for training with Pershing and Corporal missiles. While stateside, he married Althea Gowen, a redheaded Irish girl and the sister of a soldier friend. Althea returned to Germany with him; she died in the fall of 2002 of emphysema. Rudell completed a distinguished eighteen-year career in the army, most of it overseas working with nuclear missiles. A dedicated army man and the top noncom in his division, Rudell retired with the rank of master sergeant in 1980. He has owned a nightclub for thirty years in Lawton, Oklahoma. It is one mile from the main gate of Fort Sill, the largest artillery center in the United States. Rudell has three stepsons and eleven grandchildren.

Fields Smith had a football scholarship at Bacone College, but the morning he planned to register, he woke up with Bell's palsy. The left side of his face became paralyzed, and he did not fully recover for three months. Unsure whether his scholarship was still viable and no longer certain that he wanted to go to college, Fields worked for two years, then was drafted into the army. He married Mary Alice Collins, and they had three sons. Mary died of cancer in 1984. Fields later married Juanita Smith, who had a son and a daughter. Over the years, Fields operated heavy equipment for a construction company, was a road supervisor for Sequoyah County, and was the track superintendent at Blue Ribbon Downs in Sallisaw, Oklahoma. Fields and Juanita have four sons, a daughter, and thirteen grandchildren.

Stanley Speaks earned B.S. and master's degrees in administration at Northeastern and began his career as the superintendent of Intermountain Boarding School in Brigham City, Utah, the largest boarding school in Box Elder County, with 2,100 students. While Stanley was still a student at Sequoyah, he was asked by Dorothy Thompson what he wanted to do when he grew up. When he answered that he wanted to teach Indian children, Dorothy advised him to go to work for the Bureau of Indian Affairs. Stanley

POSTSCRIPT: LIFE AFTER SEQUOYAH

followed her advice and today is the northwest regional director of the BIA, headquartered in Portland, Oregon. He supervises the 128 employees in his regional office and is in charge of twelve other agencies with approximately 700 employees. The agencies work with forty-four tribes in Oregon, Washington, Idaho, western Montana, and southeastern Alaska, providing the necessary services and support to aid tribes in becoming self-sufficient. Stanley and his wife celebrated their fiftieth wedding anniversary in 2006. They have two sons and two grandchildren. Stanley was inducted into the Sequoyah Hall of Fame in 2004, along with Tommy Thompson and Cecil "Nip" Shipp.

Sterling Speaks dropped out of Sequoyah in 1953 after his sophomore year and joined the army. Trained as a cook, Sterling spent five years in the military. He married Anna Faye Wildcat, a 1955 graduate of Sequoyah. After being discharged, Sterling returned to Tahlequah with Anna so that she could complete college at Northeastern. After graduation, Anna went to work for the BIA, her first assignment at the Navajo Reservation near Lukachukai, Arizona; Sterling took a job as assistant head cook. They remained in Arizona for ten years. In 1972, they returned to Tahlequah. Sterling discovered that his childhood friend Nip Shipp was principal of Sequoyah and Amon Baker was the superintendent. They hired him as assistant cook, and Sterling became head cook two years later. He remained at Sequoyah for ten years, until he retired. Sterling and Anna Faye have three sons, a daughter, and nine grandchildren.

Jay Whitecrow dropped out of Sequoyah in 1953 and spent three years in the army. He returned to Sequoyah and graduated, then attended Northeastern for three years. A summer job in Tulsa designing fixtures for an oilfield supply and maintenance company ended up lasting ten years. Jay moved to Louisiana to attend Southern University, graduating in 1972 with a B.S. degree. For the next twenty-five years, he taught and was involved in the prevention and treatment of American Indian substance abuse, for fourteen

POSTSCRIPT: LIFE AFTER SEQUOYAH

years serving as the executive director of the Tulsa facility, the only all-Indian treatment center in the United States. Jay has five children, fourteen grandchildren, and five great grandchildren "scattered from New York to Oklahoma." He passed away in October 2008.

Danny Whitekiller graduated from Bacone College in Muskogee, then served twenty-two months in the army. Danny attained a B.S. degree in education from Northeastern and for the next ten years taught at three schools, intermittently acting as principal, recreation advisor, and coach. One of the three was Seneca Indian School in Wyandotte, the same school he had run away from. For more than thirty years, Danny worked for the BIA as an adult education specialist and as a housing officer. He then worked for the Department of Defense, the Indian Health Service, and the Department of Health, Education and Welfare. He ended his distinguished career in 1990 as the administrator of W. W. Hastings Indian Hospital in Tahlequah. Danny married Ellen Faye Cochran in 1957; they have two sons, a daughter, three grandchildren, and two great-grandchildren.

Milo Yellowhead joined the Marines in September 1950. Six months later, Infantryman Yellowhead landed in Pusan, South Korea, assigned to the First Marine Division's Fifth Regiment, and received his weapon and ammo. Overnight he found himself in the middle of the fighting. Corporal Yellowhead earned a Bronze Star with Combat "V" for meritorious service on September 21, 1951, in Korea. He left the Marines in 1953 and worked for a steel company in Tulsa for five years. He met and married Ollie Foster in 1956, and they moved to New Mexico. Milo worked for Homestake Mining Company for thirty years, until he retired in 1988. He and Ollie have two daughters and five grandchildren—four boys and a girl. According to his wife, perhaps because of his early childhood, the most important thing to her husband is family. She claims, "Milo was made for retirement. He plays golf but has plenty of time to spend with the family."

Further Reading

Bloom, John. *To Show What an Indian Can Do: Sports at Native American Boarding Schools.* Minneapolis: University of Minnesota Press, 2000.

Cooper, Michael L. *Indian School: Teaching the White Man's Way.* New York: Houghton Mifflin, 1999.

Ellis, Clyde. "We Had a Lot of Fun, but of Course, That Wasn't the School Part: Life at the Rainy Mountain Boarding School, 1893–1920." In *Boarding School Blues,* edited by Clifford E. Trafzer, Jean A. Keller, and Lorene Sisquoc, 65–98. Lincoln: University of Nebraska Press, 2006.

Frei, Terry. *Third Down and a War to Go: The All-American 1942 Wisconsin Badgers.* Madison: Wisconsin Historical Society Press, 2005.

Jenkins, Sally. *The Real All Americans: The Team That Changed a Game, a People, a Nation.* New York: Doubleday, 2007.

Lomawaima, K. Tsianina. *They Called It Prairie Light: The Story of Chilocco Indian School.* Lincoln: University of Nebraska Press, 1995.

Oxendine, Joseph B. *American Indian Sports Heritage.* Champaign, Ill.: Human Kinetics Publishing, 1988.

Perdue, Theda. *The Cherokee.* New York: Chelsea House, 1989.

Reyhner, Jon Allan. *American Indian Education: A History.* Norman: University of Oklahoma Press, 2006.

Skolnick, Manny, and Sharon Skolnick. *Courage Is Like a Wild Horse.* Lincoln: University of Nebraska Press, 2001.

Szasz, Margaret Connell. "Through a Wide-Angle Lens: Acquiring and Maintaining Power, Position, and Knowledge through Boarding Schools." In *Boarding School Blues,* edited by Clifford E. Trafzer, Jean A. Keller, and Lorene Sisquoc, 187–201. Lincoln: University of Nebraska Press, 2006.

Watkins, T. H. *The Great Depression: America in the 1930s.* Boston: Little Brown, 1993.

Acknowledgments

Initial acknowledgment must go to Waleah Turner for bringing me a story that launched me on a fascinating journey. Thank you to Cecil Shipp, whose aid, patience, and perseverance made it possible for me to take on this project. To Jimmy Thompson and Amon Baker for sharing their funny, sad, and poignant memories of a remarkable man, a hero they loved and revered. To Sequoyah teacher Don Franklin for gifting me with valuable information and history on Sequoyah and the Cherokee Nation. To Marion Hagerstrand, who freely shared stories and anecdotes about her extraordinary father, Jack Brown. To Principal Chief Chad Smith and his staff for their enthusiasm and assistance. To Forman Ross, Oleta Pritchett, Dolly Raper, and Anna Huckaby for their translation skills with the Cherokee syllabary and to Beth Herrington for her genealogical talents.

On the writing front, thank you to fellow authors Elizabeth Lyon, Marcia Preston, and Mary Langer Smith, all of whom have experienced the peaks and valleys of writing and either pushed or pulled me when I needed it. To freelance copyeditor Sally Bennett, whose considerable talent and skills helped to make a good story even better. And heartfelt thanks to my husband, David, whose encouragement, patience, and unwavering faith made this incredible journey possible.

To "the boys of Sequoyah" (and to their wives, who encouraged them), thank you for sharing your stories and for answering my thousands of questions with enthusiasm, humor, and grace. My gratitude includes the men and women in this story who have passed away but whose participation makes them forever a part of the long, proud history of Sequoyah, symbol of the vision and progress of the Cherokee Nation.

Index

Abuse, 11, 73
Academic emphasis, Sequoyah, 1940–50s, 74
Alcohol: Thompson family history of abuse of, 7, 17, 35, 152; Tommy's struggle with, 29, 41, 44, 48, 50, 65, 152–53, 154 155, 247–48, 257, 260
Anderson, John, 136, 148, 151–52, 151, 166, 247; and baseball, 151; and basketball, 150, 188, 227, 229; and football, 170, 172, 176, 179, 180–85, 203, 207, 209, 214, 218, 221–23, 225, 229, 265

Bacone College, Muskogee, Okla., 217, 218, 220, 229, 265
Baker, Amon, 140–42, 143–45, 146, 152, 260, 263, 265, 271
Baker, Bill, 112, 118, 152, 154, 191, 199, 203, 205, 206; and football, 211–12, 214, 225, 229, 234, 241, 245, 252, 265
Baker, Jean Thompson (daughter), 43, 46, 49, 51, 64, 66, 103–104, 119, 124–26, 129, 140–41, 145, 146, 229, 240, 248, 259, 263, 265
Bald Hill, 100, 213, 214
Baseball, 151, 205, 237, 238
Basketball: Tommy's participation in, 13, 32, 129; Tommy's coaching career, 46, 48, 150, 151, 154, 188, 189, 196, 226, 229; Tommy's refereeing of, 78, 82, 141, 143
Batson, Thomas, 218, 263, 266; and baseball, 237, 238
Bell, Henry, 227, 229
Bible, D. X., 130
Board of Education, 136, 138, 205, 210–12, 214, 215, 229, 231. *See also* Punishment
Boots (school dog), 98–99, 100, 101, 121, 191–93, 194–96, 197–99, 200, 260, 262
Boxing team, 32, 136
Briartown, Okla., 36, 38, 39, 40, 42, 51
Bronze Star, recipients of, 167, 179, 237, 261, 269
Brown, Jack, 71; and football, 170, 235; and Sequoyah Vocational School, 128, 195, 199, 201, 204, 219, 220, 225, 235, 236, 239, 240, 248; Superintendent, Cherokee Orphan Training School and Sequoyah Orphan Training School, (1925–45), 70, 73, 74, 77, 78, 101, 106; on Tommy's drinking, 248, 257, 259, 261

INDEX

Bureau of Indian Affairs (BIA), 10, 27, 47, 51, 52, 53, 55, 64, 72, 87, 95, 103, 123–25, 126–28, 139, 263, 265, 267, 269, 271, 272; on economic self-sufficiency, 75–77

Cameron, Bill, 53–56, 57–59, 61, 101, 113, 115, 120, 147, 178, 216, 241, 242, 263, 266; and football, 121–23, 133
Cameron, George, 61, 81, 82, 85, 98, 100, 102, 113, 115, 116, 152, 196, 200, 202, 214, 217, 222, 224, 263, 266; and football, 139, 148, 166, 176, 178, 181, 186, 232, 236, 240
Camp Gruber, 85, 86, 87, 120
Carlisle Indian School, 16, 122, 220
Cascia Hall High School, Tulsa, Okla., 173, 174, 236
Checotah High School, Checotah, Okla., 132, 175, 176, 227, 234, 235
Cherokee Clans, 159, 161. *See also* Stomp Dance
Cherokee Female Seminary, 13, 31
Cherokee Male Seminary, 71
Cherokee Nation, 10, 53, 72, 75, 161, 262, 269, 275
Cherokee Orphan Training School (COTS), 5, 8, 10, 11–13, 14–16, 20, 21, 34, 63, 69, 70, 72, 260; name changes of school, 72
Chilocco Indian School, Chilocco, Okla., 52, 139, 273
Christmas, 7, 11, 12, 14, 20, 29, 57, 77, 84, 110, 113, 115, 116, 140, 141. *See also* Holidays
Church services, 77, 81, 82
Collier, John, 45, 46, 47

Company M, 279th Infantry 45th Division, Tahlequah, Okla., 216, 217, 221. *See also* National Guard unit
Coweta High School, Coweta, Okla., 236
Crackerjack (Sequoyah school bus), 168, 169, 175, 176, 178, 180, 195, 196, 199
Creek Nation, 103
Cully, Harris, 123, 148, 196, 203, 205, 206, 225; and basketball, 150, 227, 229; and football, 168, 254, 255, 267
Curriculum (Sequoyah), 74, 75, 262

Dairy barn duty, 117; as recruiting technique, 131, 132, 135
Dawes Act, 47
Department of Interior, 10, 63, 72, 102. *See also* Bureau of Indian Affairs
Dewar High School, Dewar, Okla., 148, 174, 177
Dropouts, 115
Dust Bowl, 43

Education Field Agent, Tommy's career as, 63, 103, 125
English language, 9, 12, 19, 31, 46, 56, 59, 61, 71, 72, 74, 86, 123, 164
Enid, Okla., state championship game, 3, 177, 178, 180–82, 186
Euchee Indian Boarding School, Sapulpa, Okla., 112, 123, 134

Fish, Elmer, 231, 267; and basketball, 150, 188, 227, 229; and football, 255

278

INDEX

Five Civilized Tribes, 51, 63, 149
Football, 108–10; Tommy's participation in, 14, 15, 19, 20, 31, 32, 34, 41; and Tommy's coaching career, 43, 128–31, 135, 139–40, 148–51, 153, 154, 165, 176 178, 182, 183, 188, 216, 217, 221, 224, 231, 236–37, 240–41, 243, 251, 254–56, 48, 132, 135, 136, 143, 147, 155, 176, 178, 182; and practice sessions, 133, 136, 166, 168, 232; and psychology, 3, 4, 170; and scheduling, 133, 169, 172, 202, 209, 234, 250; Sequoyah game, 235. *See also* individual players
Fudge, Dorothy Jean. *See* Thompson, Dorothy Jean Fudge (wife)

Gable Field, 148, 149, 174, 251. *See also* Northeastern State Teachers College
Gouge, Thompson, 138–39, 153, 196, 212, 225, 226, 263
Great bull market, 42–43
Great Depression, 43, 44, 52; legislation about, 44, 47

Haskell Indian School, Lawrence, Kans.: Tommy's attendance, 7, 15, 16, 17, 18, 21; and his being AWOL, 23, 25, 26, 27, 28; and football, 16, 19, 20, 26
Haskell Indian School Outings Program, Tommy's participation in, 19, 20
Holidays, 20, 47, 113, 115–17, 133, 175

Illinois River, 16, 65, 192, 204
Indian education, 73, 259, 261

Jones Academy, 125, 126, 127, 137

Korean conflict, 201, 207, 216, 224, 225, 236, 237, 241, 242, 244, 268, 272. *See also* Company M, 279th Infantry 45th Division

Lancaster, Burt, 219, 220, 221
Life Magazine, 236
Literature (Sequoyah), 74

McCrary, Jody Thompson (daughter), 119, 124, 126, 140, 146, 163–64, 186, 204, 245, 247–48, 259, 263
Medford High School, Medford, Okla. (state championship game), 177, 181–83, 184–86, 202
Medicine man, 54, 55, 94, 172, 163, 228, 229
Military (model), 74
Mouse, Andrew ("Rat"), 135, 136, 214, 224, 268; and basketball, 150, 188, 227, 229; and football, 150, 166, 170, 173, 182, 184, 186, 243–45, 253, 255
Movietone newsreels, 80, 102, 107
Music, 74, 77, 115–17, 262
Muskogee, Okla., 23, 27; affected by war, 84, 85, 86, 87. *See also* Camp Gruber

National Guard unit, 20, 22, 27, 29, 31, 65, 148, 180, 207, 209–10, 219, 222, 226, 227
Nave, Everett, 59, 60–62, 81–83, 86, 99, 108, 113, 115, 166, 196, 200, 202, 203, 205, 207, 214, 229, 268; and basketball, 150, 188, 227, 229; and football, 231, 253–254, 255

INDEX

Nighthawk Keetoowah. *See* Stomp dance

Northeastern Preparatory High School, Tahlequah, Okla., 28, 29, 30

Northeastern State Redmen football, Tommy's participation in, 30, 31, 33, 34, 35, 41

Northeastern State Teachers College, Tahlequah, Okla., 121, 125, 127, 129, 132, 140, 146, 148, 149, 174–75, 216, 226, 229, 230, 259, 263, 265, 267, 269, 270, 271, 272

Oklahoma A & M, Stillwater, Okla., 16, 226, 252, 253

Oklahoma Athletic Association (OAA), 148, 150, 173, 177, 251; high school classifications, 169

Oklahoma Statehood, 10

Oklahoma University, Norman, Okla., 15, 122, 226, 268

Okmulgee, Okla., 43, 102, 103, 119, 120, 124, 125, 126

Pawnee Indian Boarding School, Pawnee, Okla., 186

Peairs, H. B., 20–22, 25, 27

Pearl Harbor, 82–85, 102, 107, 216, 232

Pierre Indian School, Pierre, S.Dak., 45–47, 48, 50

POWs (prisoners of war), 86, 120. *See also* Camp Gruber

Public schools, 5, 15, 16, 44, 45, 46, 52, 112, 139, 152, 174; and football games, 154, 176, 177, 182, 183, 241, 242, 253

Punishment, 210, 215, 227. *See also* Board of Education

Riverside Indian School, Anadarko, Okla., 149, 172, 226, 267

Roosevelt, Franklin Delano, 44, 47, 81, 87, 107, 110

Ross, Forman, 3, 178, 184, 218–19, 221, 268–69, 276; and football, 173, 174, 233, 263

Rules: Tommy's enforcement of, 136, 166, 197, 211, 213; Tommy's philosophy about, 210

School uniforms, 6, 11, 23, 34, 58, 106, 108, 113, 120

Seneca Indian Boarding School, Wyandotte, Okla., 109, 110, 230, 272

Sequoyah Orphan Training School, Tahlequah, Okla., 53, 60, 72–75, 76–78, 84–86, 92, 94, 95, 98, 100, 102. *See also* Sequoyah Vocational School

Sequoyah Vocational School, 72, 106–108, 112, 115, 118, 120; and football, 128, 131, 133, 134, 136, 139, 140, 148, 149, 157, 165, 170, 176, 178, 182, 188, 216, 217, 221, 224, 231–32, 236, 240–41, 251, 253–56, 261, 263; holidays, 114, 115, 116, 117, 118

Shipp, Cecil ("Nip"), 73, 89, 94, 115, 117, 152, 155, 191–93, 197–98, 203, 207–208, 210–15, 222, 223, 228, 229, 245, 261, 269, 271, 275; and basketball, 150, 188, 227, 229; and football, 148, 219, 225, 232, 252, 253, 255

Shipp, Rudell, 89, 95, 96, 97, 108, 222, 223, 270; and basketball, 150, 188, 227, 229; and

INDEX

football, 148, 166, 203, 206, 207, 217, 253, 255

Skiatook High School, Skiatook, Okla., 250, 251, 252

Smith, Fields, 92, 93, 94, 99, 113–15, 157, 163, 196, 214, 215, 225, 228, 229; and basketball, 150, 188, 227, 229; and football, 166, 172, 203, 206, 207, 217, 225, 253, 254, 255

Smith, Redbird (Keetoowah leader), 163, 165. *See also* Stomp dance

Sooners. *See* Oklahoma University

Speaks family, 111, 112, 196, 261, 269; and football (Sterling), 250, 253

Spending money, working for, 19, 20, 106, 107, 202. *See also* Haskell Indian School Outings Program; Wisconsin pea harvest

Sports, 13, 14, 15, 18, 31–32, 34–35, 41, 46–48, 67, 69, 70, 75, 78, 120, 136, 151, 155, 175, 243, 249, 257, 261; Tommy's philosophy about, 144. *See also* individual sports

Stilwell, Okla., 51, 63–65; and basketball, 141, 142, 150, 222, 226, 227, 228

Stomp dance, 156, 163; arbors as components of, 159; Nighthawk Keetoowah history with, 157; preparation for, 158, 159, 160; sacred fire's place in, 159; Stick Ball importance of, 159; 161, 162; traditional foods at, 159, 160, 161

Stroud High School, Stroud, Okla., 250, 251

Tahlequah, Okla., 6, 7, 11, 13–14, 16–17, 21, 22, 25, 28, 29, 35–36, 38, 42, 43, 51, 53, 63, 64, 71, 72, 76, 78–79, 106, 145, 149, 227, 228, 229, 257, 259, 263, 266–67, 269, 271, 272; affected by war, 84, 86, 87, 101, 107, 121. *See also* Camp Gruber

Teachers, 14, 21, 73–75, 76–77, 97, 109, 116, 121, 151, 194, 219

Thompson, Dorothy Jean Fudge (wife), 36–40, 42, 44, 46, 48, 51, 63, 79, 103, 105, 125, 127, 129, 256, 259; as surrogate mother, 140, 147, 201, 203, 243, 246, 247, 270; on Tommy's drinking, 43, 49, 64, 68, 159, 238, 255, 256, 264, 265, 266

Thompson, Eloise (sister), 7, 16, 19–20, 21–22, 23, 26, 29, 66

Thompson, Ida (sister), 7, 16, 20, 21–22, 23, 26, 29, 66

Thompson, Jean (daughter). *See* Baker, Jean Thompson (daughter)

Thompson, Jimmy ("Boozy") (cousin), 16, 17, 22–25, 26, 28–29, 87

Thompson, Jimmy (son), 48–49, 51, 64, 66–67, 78, 80, 103, 104, 124, 126, 128–29, 140, 146, 150, 164, 186–87, 203, 207, 208, 220, 225–26, 246–47, 256, 259, 260, 275

Thompson, Jody (daughter). *See* McCrary, Jody Thompson

Thompson, Dr. Joe (uncle), 13, 16, 27, 28

Thompson, Robert (father), 5, 6, 8, 13–15, 16, 50, 67, 68

281

INDEX

Thompson, Rose Gritts (mother), 3, 4, 5, 6, 13, 31, 67, 260

Thompson, Sammie (sister), 5, 7, 8, 9, 15, 16

Thompson, Susie (sister), 5, 7–9, 13, 14, 16, 20–23, 25–27, 28, 29, 30

Thompson, Tommy: and BIA, work for, 45, 46, 48–51, 52, 63–65, 87, 102–104, 124, 127–28; Cherokee Orphan Training School, student at, 3–7, 10, 11, 15, 16; Haskell Indian School, student at, 17, 19, 22, 25; Northeastern Preparatory High School, student at, 28–30; Northeastern State Teachers College, student at, 30, 31, 41; and public schools, employed at, 42, 44. *See also* Northeastern State Redmen football

Thorpe, Jim, 32, 122, 220

Tonkawa High School, Tonkawa, Okla., 114, 252, 253, 254, 255

Truman, Harry S., 105, 106, 113, 146, 149, 207

University of Oklahoma. *See* Oklahoma University

USO (Tahlequah, Okla.), 84, 87, 107

Vocational training, 8, 15, 31, 74, 106, 113, 126, 132, 151, 152, 216, 262, 267

Wadley, Doc (best friend), 32, 34, 272

Wahpeton Indian School, Wahpeton, N.Dak., 28, 49, 227

War fever, 87

Warner, Glen ("Pop"), 32, 130

Westville High School, Westville, Okla., 109, 141–43, 151, 171, 227, 244

Wheatley, Warren, 250, 252, 255

Whitecrow, Jay, 137, 238, 196, 212, 229, 263, 271; and basketball, 150, 188, 227, 229; and football, 231, 253, 255

Whitekiller, Danny, 109, 110, 111, 115, 217, 220, 272; and basketball, 150, 188, 227, 229; and football, 133, 148, 153, 166 171, 178, 185, 186, 218, 29, 224

Wisconsin pea harvest, 203, 204, 205–207, 208

World War I, 10, 14, 66

World War II, 86, 140; Japanese surrender, 107. *See also* Pearl Harbor

Yellowhead, Milo, 134, 201–202, 210, 216, 237, 272; and basketball, 150, 188, 227, 229; and football, 166, 168, 174, 178, 179, 186, 201, 219, 114, 238

www.ingramcontent.com/pod-product-compliance
Lightning Source LLC
Chambersburg PA
CBHW020831160426
43192CB00007B/604